Notes for a War Story

Gipi

Notes for a War Story

Gipi

TRANSLATED BY SPECTRUM

:01

First Second

NEW YORK & LONDON

1

From the Hills to the City

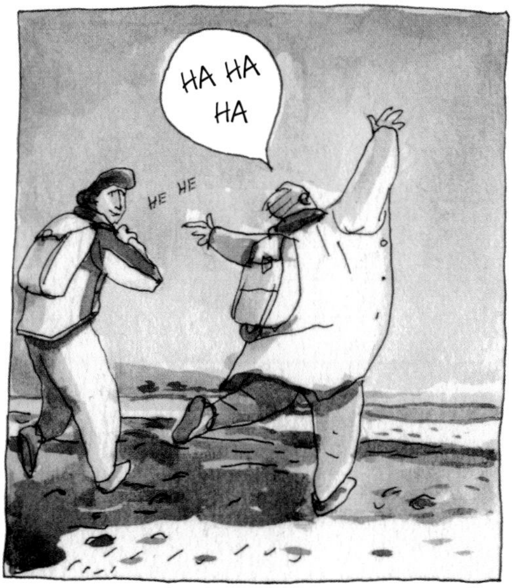
HA HA HA
HE HE

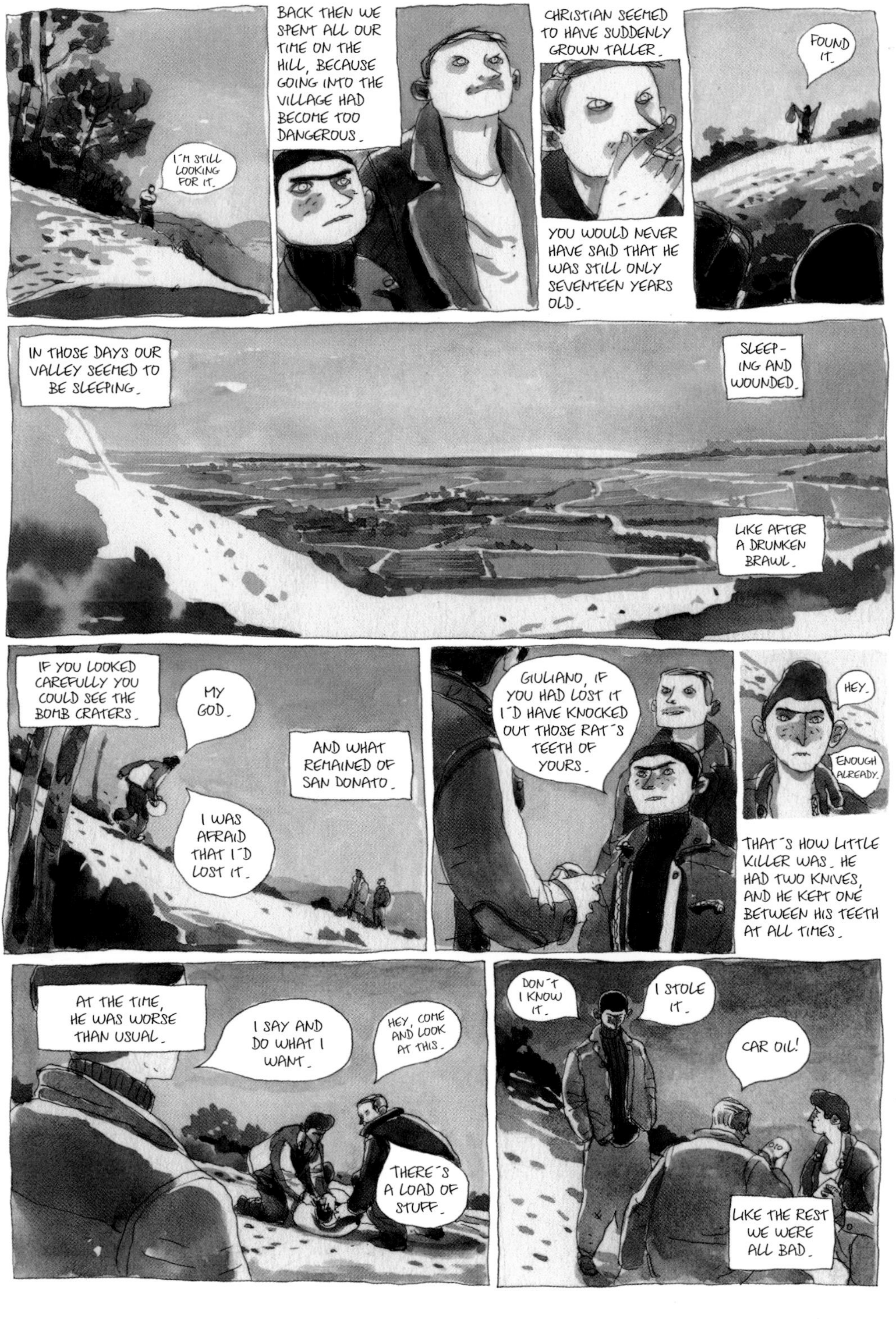
I'M STILL LOOKING FOR IT.
BACK THEN WE SPENT ALL OUR TIME ON THE HILL, BECAUSE GOING INTO THE VILLAGE HAD BECOME TOO DANGEROUS.
CHRISTIAN SEEMED TO HAVE SUDDENLY GROWN TALLER.
YOU WOULD NEVER HAVE SAID THAT HE WAS STILL ONLY SEVENTEEN YEARS OLD.
FOUND IT.
IN THOSE DAYS OUR VALLEY SEEMED TO BE SLEEPING.
SLEEPING AND WOUNDED.
LIKE AFTER A DRUNKEN BRAWL.
IF YOU LOOKED CAREFULLY YOU COULD SEE THE BOMB CRATERS.
MY GOD.
AND WHAT REMAINED OF SAN DONATO.
I WAS AFRAID THAT I'D LOST IT.
GIULIANO, IF YOU HAD LOST IT I'D HAVE KNOCKED OUT THOSE RAT'S TEETH OF YOURS.
HEY.
ENOUGH ALREADY.
THAT'S HOW LITTLE KILLER WAS. HE HAD TWO KNIVES, AND HE KEPT ONE BETWEEN HIS TEETH AT ALL TIMES.
AT THE TIME, HE WAS WORSE THAN USUAL.
I SAY AND DO WHAT I WANT.
HEY, COME AND LOOK AT THIS.
THERE'S A LOAD OF STUFF.
DON'T I KNOW IT.
I STOLE IT.
CAR OIL!
LIKE THE REST WE WERE ALL BAD.

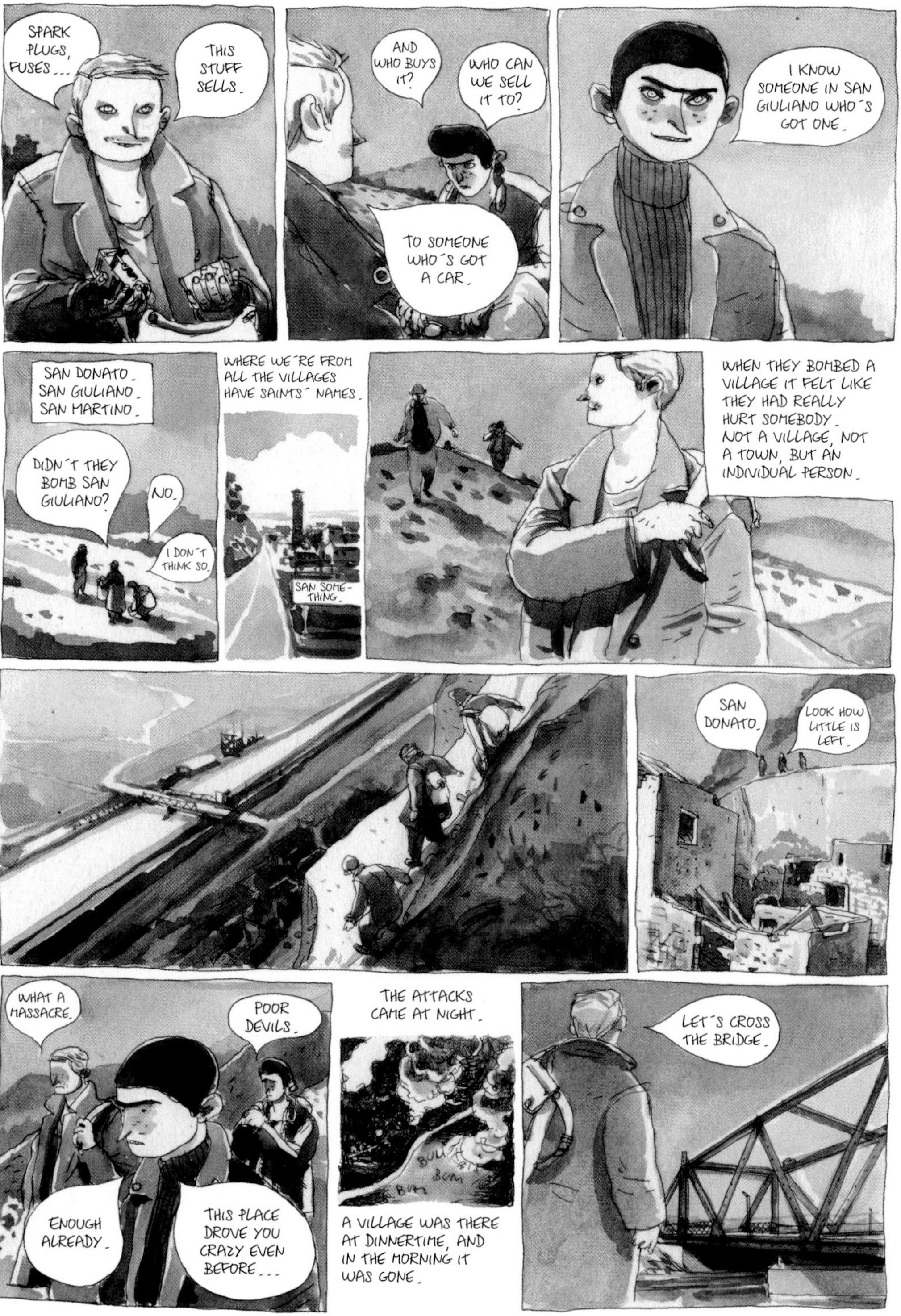
SPARK PLUGS, FUSES...
THIS STUFF SELLS.
AND WHO BUYS IT?
WHO CAN WE SELL IT TO?
TO SOMEONE WHO'S GOT A CAR.
I KNOW SOMEONE IN SAN GIULIANO WHO'S GOT ONE.
SAN DONATO. SAN GIULIANO. SAN MARTINO.
DIDN'T THEY BOMB SAN GIULIANO?
NO.
I DON'T THINK SO.
WHERE WE'RE FROM ALL THE VILLAGES HAVE SAINTS' NAMES.
SAN SOME-THING.
WHEN THEY BOMBED A VILLAGE IT FELT LIKE THEY HAD REALLY HURT SOMEBODY. NOT A VILLAGE, NOT A TOWN, BUT AN INDIVIDUAL PERSON.
SAN DONATO.
LOOK HOW LITTLE IS LEFT.
WHAT A MASSACRE.
POOR DEVILS.
ENOUGH ALREADY.
THIS PLACE DROVE YOU CRAZY EVEN BEFORE...
THE ATTACKS CAME AT NIGHT.
BUM
BUM
BUM
A VILLAGE WAS THERE AT DINNERTIME, AND IN THE MORNING IT WAS GONE.
LET'S CROSS THE BRIDGE.

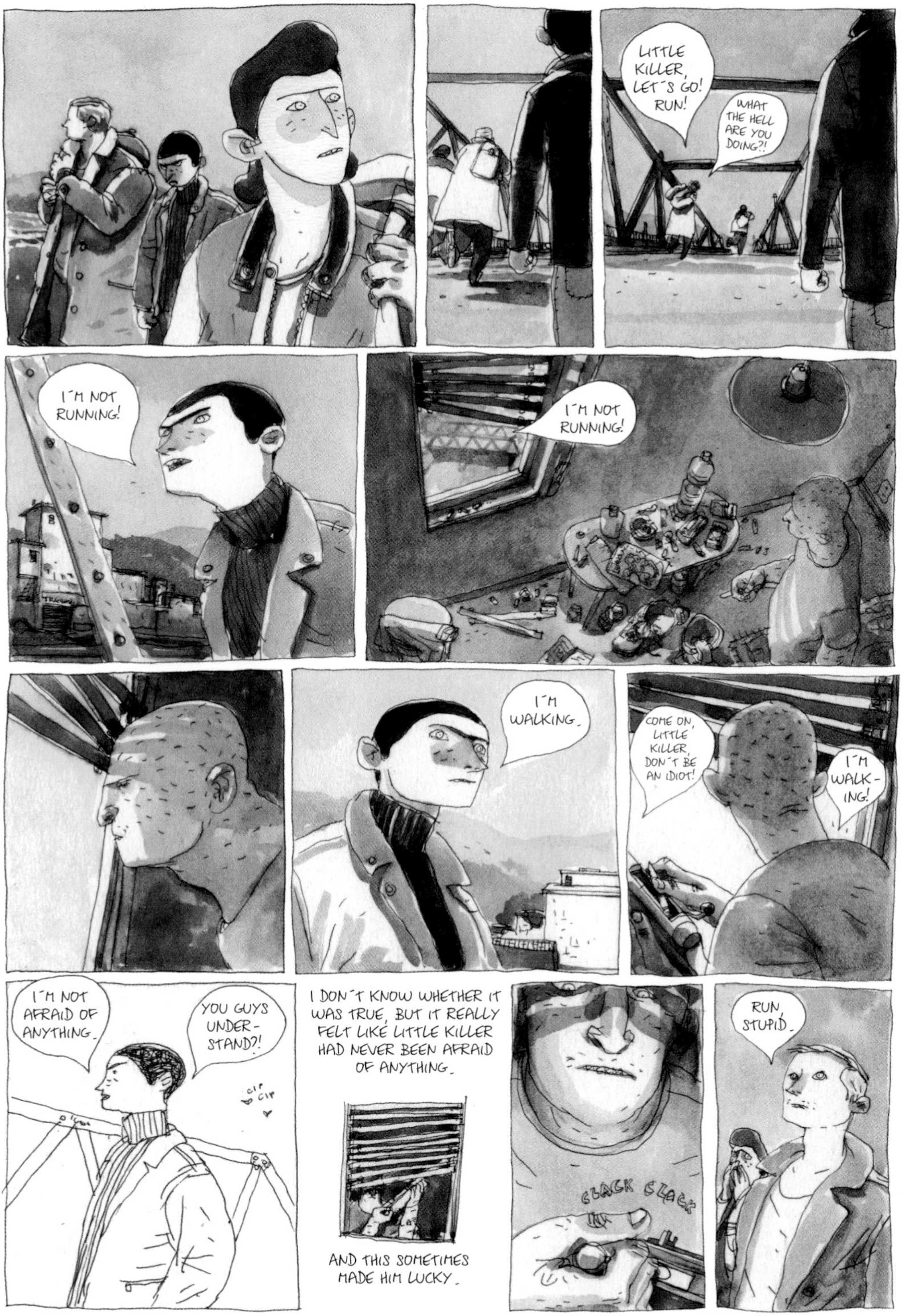
LITTLE KILLER, LET´S GO! RUN!
WHAT THE HELL ARE YOU DOING?!
I´M NOT RUNNING!
I´M NOT RUNNING!
I´M WALKING.
COME ON, LITTLE KILLER, DON´T BE AN IDIOT!
I´M WALK-ING!
I´M NOT AFRAID OF ANYTHING.
YOU GUYS UNDER-STAND?!
I DON´T KNOW WHETHER IT WAS TRUE, BUT IT REALLY FELT LIKE LITTLE KILLER HAD NEVER BEEN AFRAID OF ANYTHING.
AND THIS SOMETIMES MADE HIM LUCKY.
CLACK CLACK
RUN, STUPID.

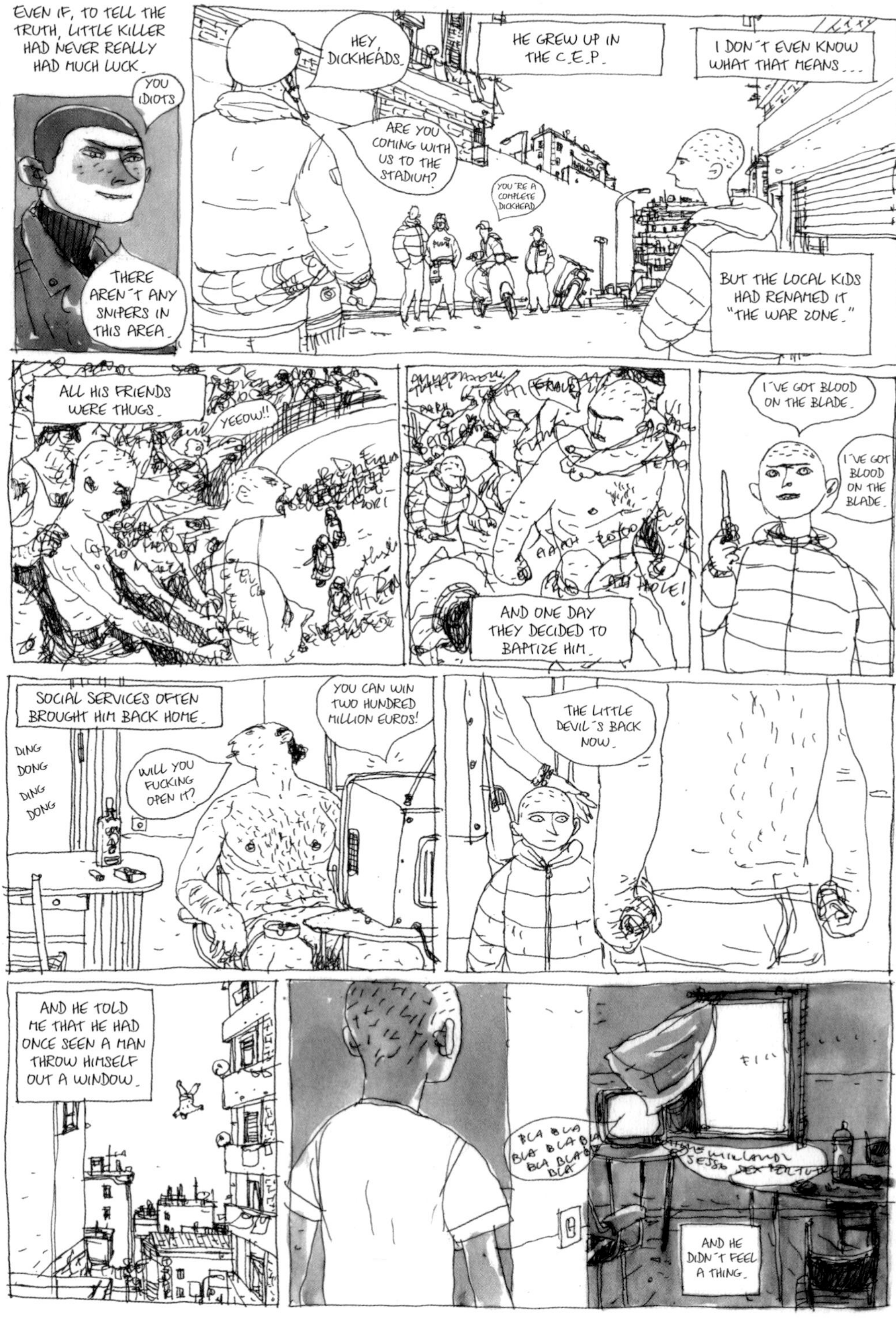
EVEN IF, TO TELL THE TRUTH, LITTLE KILLER HAD NEVER REALLY HAD MUCH LUCK.
YOU IDIOTS.
THERE AREN'T ANY SNIPERS IN THIS AREA.
HEY, DICKHEADS.
ARE YOU COMING WITH US TO THE STADIUM?
YOU'RE A COMPLETE DICKHEAD.
HE GREW UP IN THE C.E.P.
I DON'T EVEN KNOW WHAT THAT MEANS...
BUT THE LOCAL KIDS HAD RENAMED IT "THE WAR ZONE."
ALL HIS FRIENDS WERE THUGS.
YEEOW!!
AND ONE DAY THEY DECIDED TO BAPTIZE HIM.
I'VE GOT BLOOD ON THE BLADE.
I'VE GOT BLOOD ON THE BLADE.
SOCIAL SERVICES OFTEN BROUGHT HIM BACK HOME.
DING DONG DING DONG
WILL YOU FUCKING OPEN IT?
YOU CAN WIN TWO HUNDRED MILLION EUROS!
THE LITTLE DEVIL'S BACK NOW.
AND HE TOLD ME THAT HE HAD ONCE SEEN A MAN THROW HIMSELF OUT A WINDOW.
BLA BLA BLA BLA BLA BLA BLA
AND HE DIDN'T FEEL A THING.

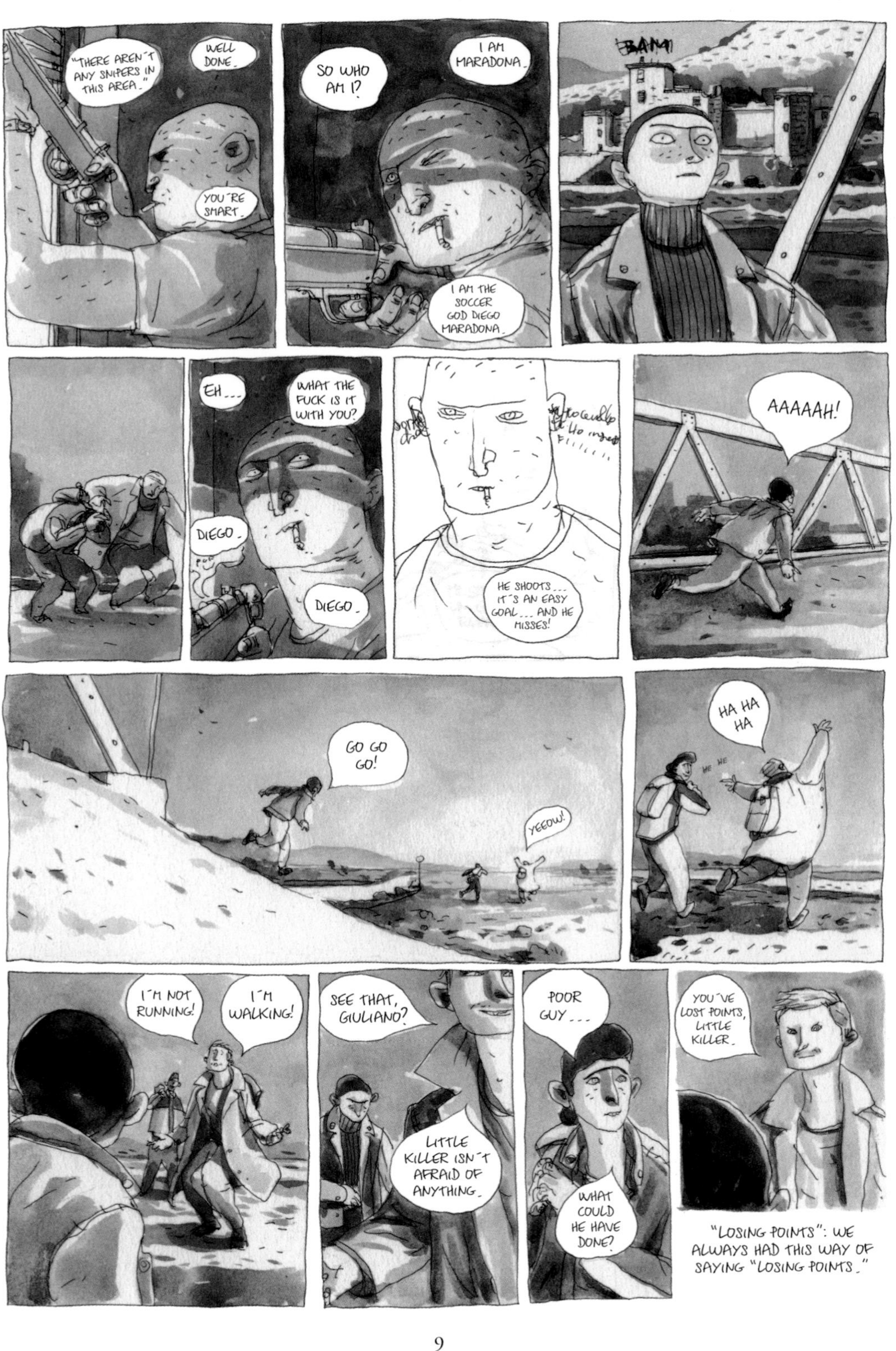
"THERE AREN'T ANY SNIPERS IN THIS AREA."
WELL DONE.
YOU'RE SMART.
SO WHO AM I?
I AM MARADONA.
I AM THE SOCCER GOD DIEGO MARADONA.
EH...
WHAT THE FUCK IS IT WITH YOU?
DIEGO.
DIEGO.
HE SHOOTS... IT'S AN EASY GOAL... AND HE MISSES!
AAAAAH!
GO GO GO!
YEEOW!
HA HA HA
HE HE
I'M NOT RUNNING!
I'M WALKING!
SEE THAT, GIULIANO?
LITTLE KILLER ISN'T AFRAID OF ANYTHING.
POOR GUY...
WHAT COULD HE HAVE DONE?
YOU'VE LOST POINTS, LITTLE KILLER.
"LOSING POINTS": WE ALWAYS HAD THIS WAY OF SAYING "LOSING POINTS."

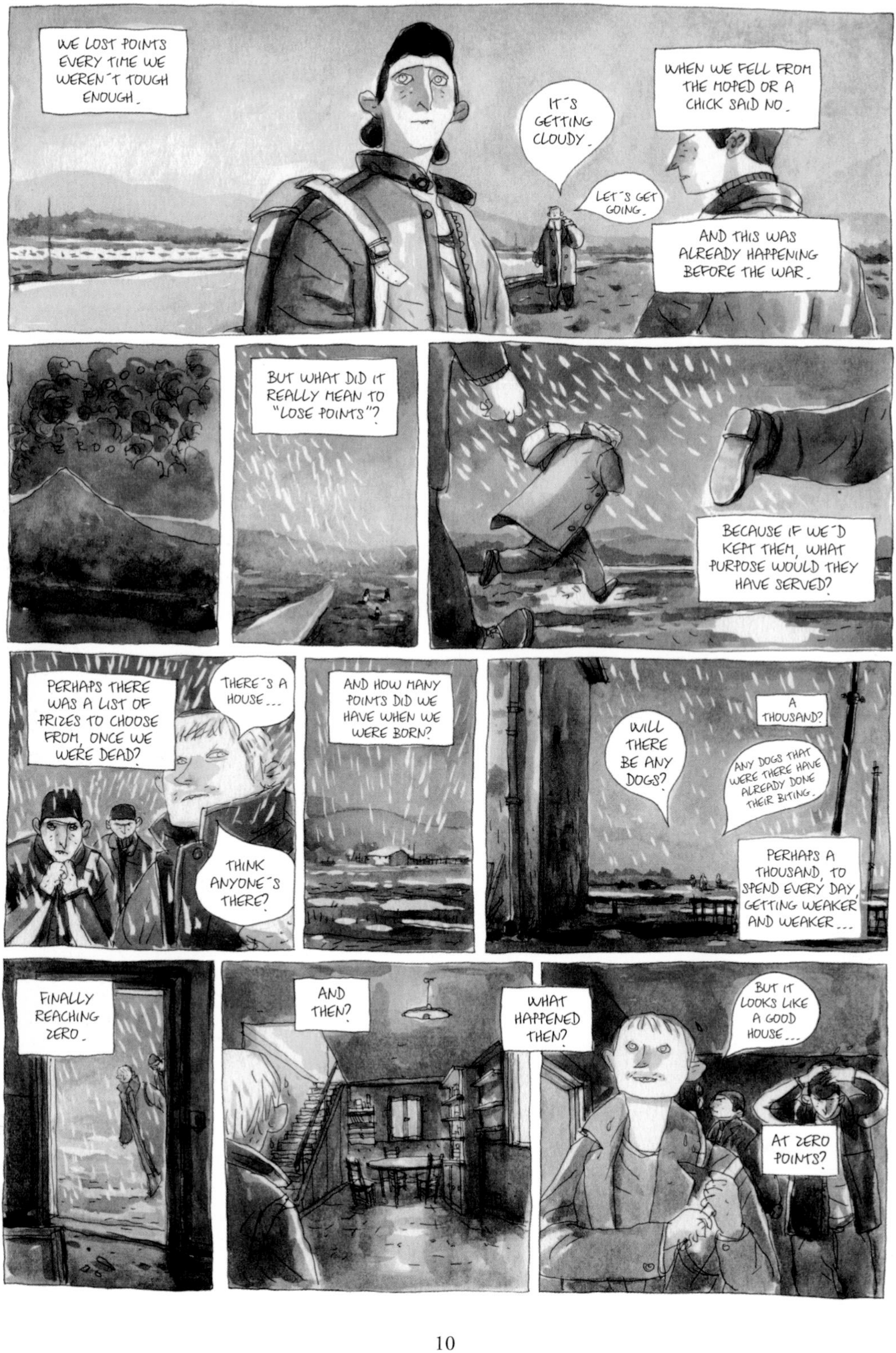

WE LOST POINTS EVERY TIME WE WEREN'T TOUGH ENOUGH.
IT'S GETTING CLOUDY.
LET'S GET GOING.
WHEN WE FELL FROM THE MOPED OR A CHICK SAID NO.
AND THIS WAS ALREADY HAPPENING BEFORE THE WAR.
BUT WHAT DID IT REALLY MEAN TO "LOSE POINTS"?
BECAUSE IF WE'D KEPT THEM, WHAT PURPOSE WOULD THEY HAVE SERVED?
PERHAPS THERE WAS A LIST OF PRIZES TO CHOOSE FROM, ONCE WE WERE DEAD?
THERE'S A HOUSE...
THINK ANYONE'S THERE?
AND HOW MANY POINTS DID WE HAVE WHEN WE WERE BORN?
WILL THERE BE ANY DOGS?
A THOUSAND?
ANY DOGS THAT WERE THERE HAVE ALREADY DONE THEIR BITING.
PERHAPS A THOUSAND, TO SPEND EVERY DAY, GETTING WEAKER AND WEAKER...
FINALLY REACHING ZERO.
AND THEN?
WHAT HAPPENED THEN?
BUT IT LOOKS LIKE A GOOD HOUSE...
AT ZERO POINTS?

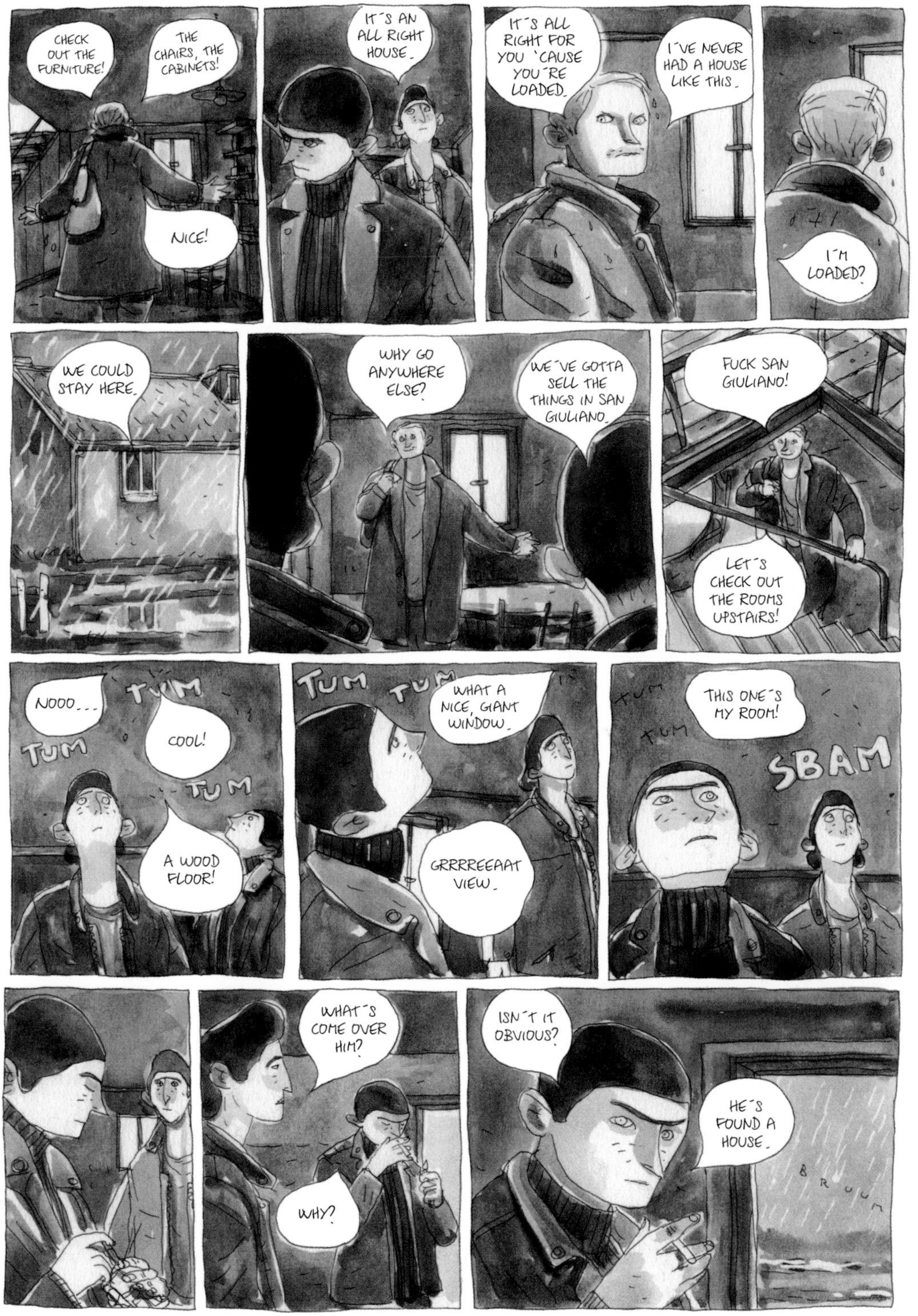
CHECK OUT THE FURNITURE!
THE CHAIRS, THE CABINETS!
NICE!
IT'S AN ALL RIGHT HOUSE.
IT'S ALL RIGHT FOR YOU 'CAUSE YOU'RE LOADED.
I'VE NEVER HAD A HOUSE LIKE THIS.
I'M LOADED?
WE COULD STAY HERE.
WHY GO ANYWHERE ELSE?
WE'VE GOTTA SELL THE THINGS IN SAN GIULIANO.
FUCK SAN GIULIANO!
LET'S CHECK OUT THE ROOMS UPSTAIRS!
NOOO...
TUM
TUM
COOL!
TUM
A WOOD FLOOR!
TUM
TUM
WHAT A NICE, GIANT WINDOW.
GRRRREEAAT VIEW.
TUM
TUM
THIS ONE'S MY ROOM!
SBAM
WHAT'S COME OVER HIM?
WHY?
ISN'T IT OBVIOUS?
HE'S FOUND A HOUSE.
BRUUM

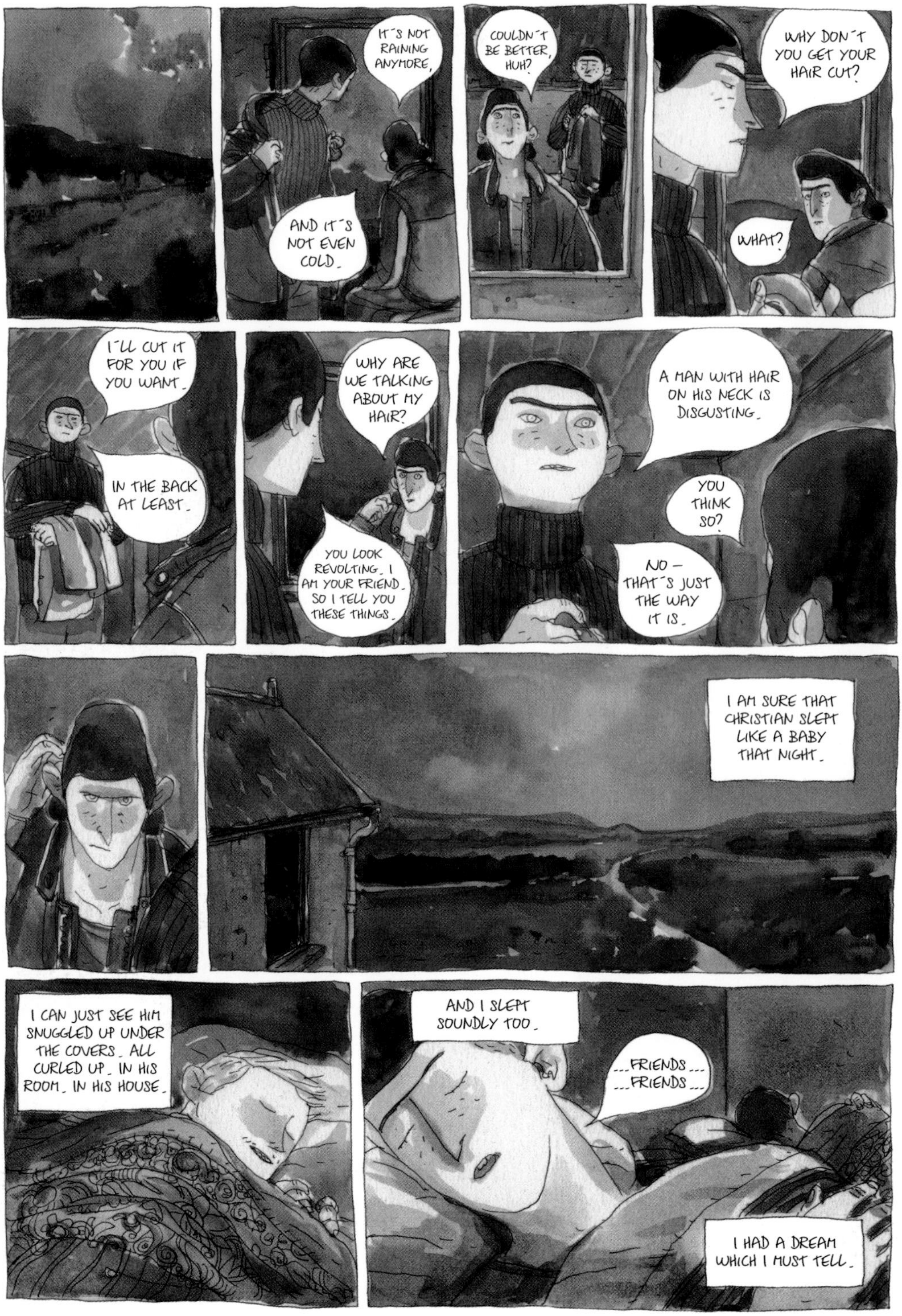
IT'S NOT RAINING ANYMORE.
AND IT'S NOT EVEN COLD.
COULDN'T BE BETTER, HUH?
WHY DON'T YOU GET YOUR HAIR CUT?
WHAT?
I'LL CUT IT FOR YOU IF YOU WANT.
IN THE BACK AT LEAST.
WHY ARE WE TALKING ABOUT MY HAIR?
YOU LOOK REVOLTING. I AM YOUR FRIEND. SO I TELL YOU THESE THINGS.
A MAN WITH HAIR ON HIS NECK IS DISGUSTING.
YOU THINK SO?
NO — THAT'S JUST THE WAY IT IS.
I AM SURE THAT CHRISTIAN SLEPT LIKE A BABY THAT NIGHT.
I CAN JUST SEE HIM SNUGGLED UP UNDER THE COVERS. ALL CURLED UP. IN HIS ROOM. IN HIS HOUSE.
AND I SLEPT SOUNDLY TOO.
...FRIENDS...
...FRIENDS...
I HAD A DREAM WHICH I MUST TELL.

I WAS IN A DESERTED PARKING LOT.

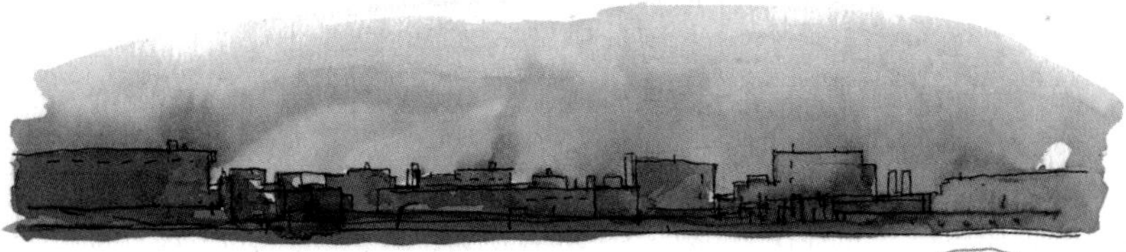

G I U L I A N O !

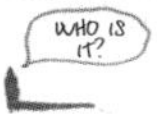
WHO IS IT?

I HEARD MYSELF SHOUTING.

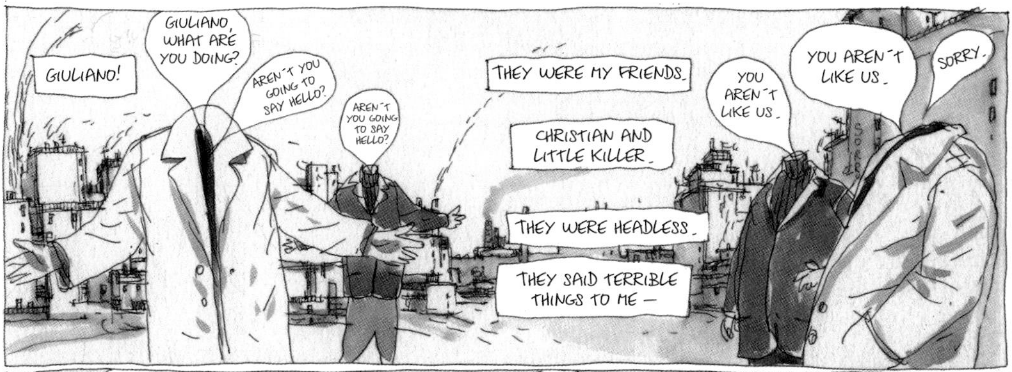
GIULIANO!
GIULIANO, WHAT ARE YOU DOING?
AREN'T YOU GOING TO SAY HELLO?
AREN'T YOU GOING TO SAY HELLO?
THEY WERE MY FRIENDS.
CHRISTIAN AND LITTLE KILLER.
THEY WERE HEADLESS.
THEY SAID TERRIBLE THINGS TO ME —
YOU AREN'T LIKE US.
YOU AREN'T LIKE US.
SORRY.

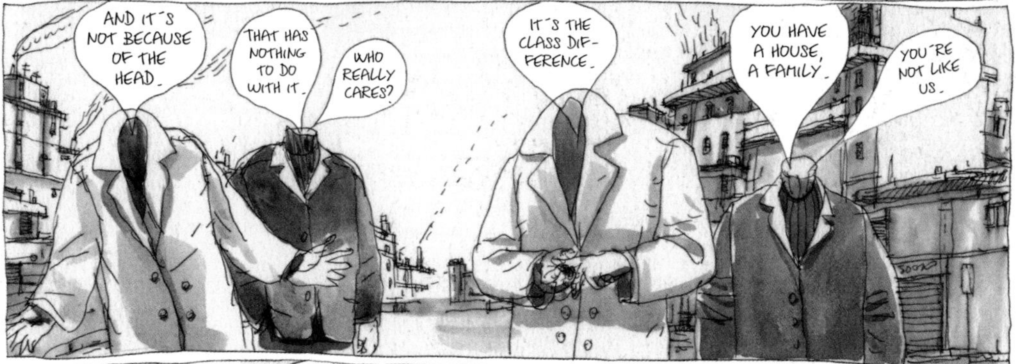
AND IT'S NOT BECAUSE OF THE HEAD.
THAT HAS NOTHING TO DO WITH IT.
WHO REALLY CARES?
IT'S THE CLASS DIFFERENCE.
YOU HAVE A HOUSE, A FAMILY.
YOU'RE NOT LIKE US.

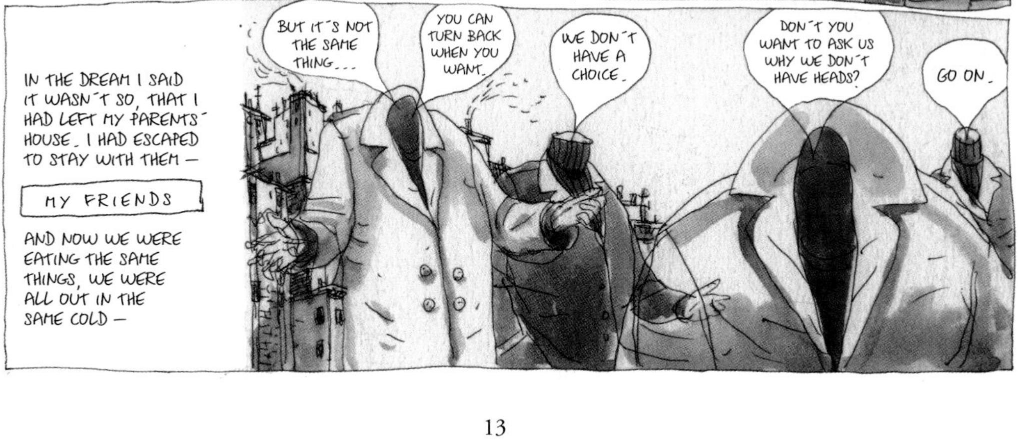
IN THE DREAM I SAID IT WASN'T SO, THAT I HAD LEFT MY PARENTS' HOUSE. I HAD ESCAPED TO STAY WITH THEM —
MY FRIENDS
AND NOW WE WERE EATING THE SAME THINGS, WE WERE ALL OUT IN THE SAME COLD —
BUT IT'S NOT THE SAME THING...
YOU CAN TURN BACK WHEN YOU WANT.
WE DON'T HAVE A CHOICE.
DON'T YOU WANT TO ASK US WHY WE DON'T HAVE HEADS?
GO ON.

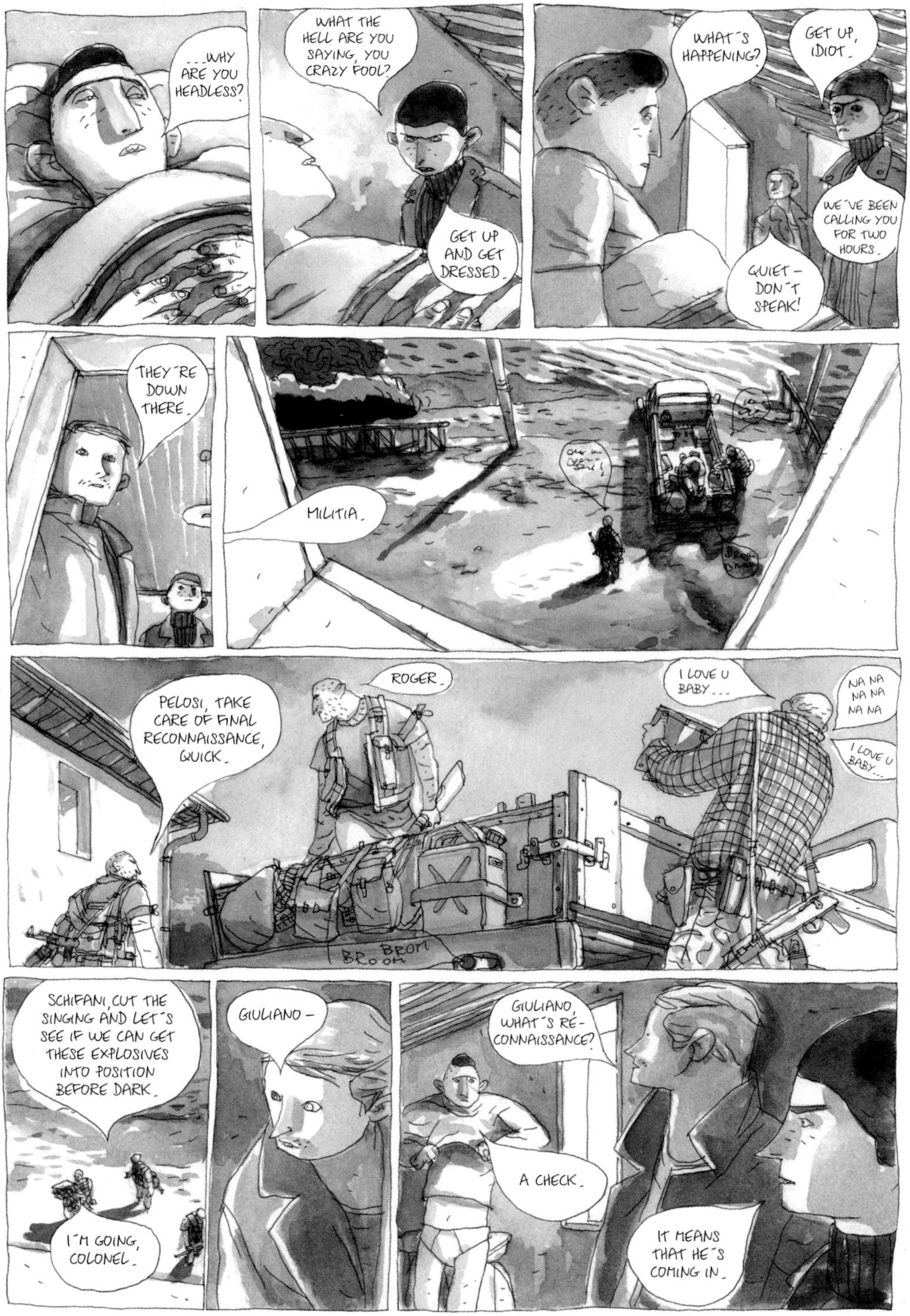
...WHY ARE YOU HEADLESS?
WHAT THE HELL ARE YOU SAYING, YOU CRAZY FOOL?
GET UP AND GET DRESSED.
WHAT'S HAPPENING?
GET UP, IDIOT.
WE'VE BEEN CALLING YOU FOR TWO HOURS.
QUIET – DON'T SPEAK!
THEY'RE DOWN THERE.
MILITIA.
PELOSI, TAKE CARE OF FINAL RECONNAISSANCE, QUICK.
ROGER.
I LOVE U BABY...
NA NA NA NA NA NA
I LOVE U BABY...
BROOM BROM
SCHIFANI, CUT THE SINGING AND LET'S SEE IF WE CAN GET THESE EXPLOSIVES INTO POSITION BEFORE DARK.
I'M GOING, COLONEL.
GIULIANO –
GIULIANO, WHAT'S RE-CONNAISSANCE?
A CHECK.
IT MEANS THAT HE'S COMING IN.

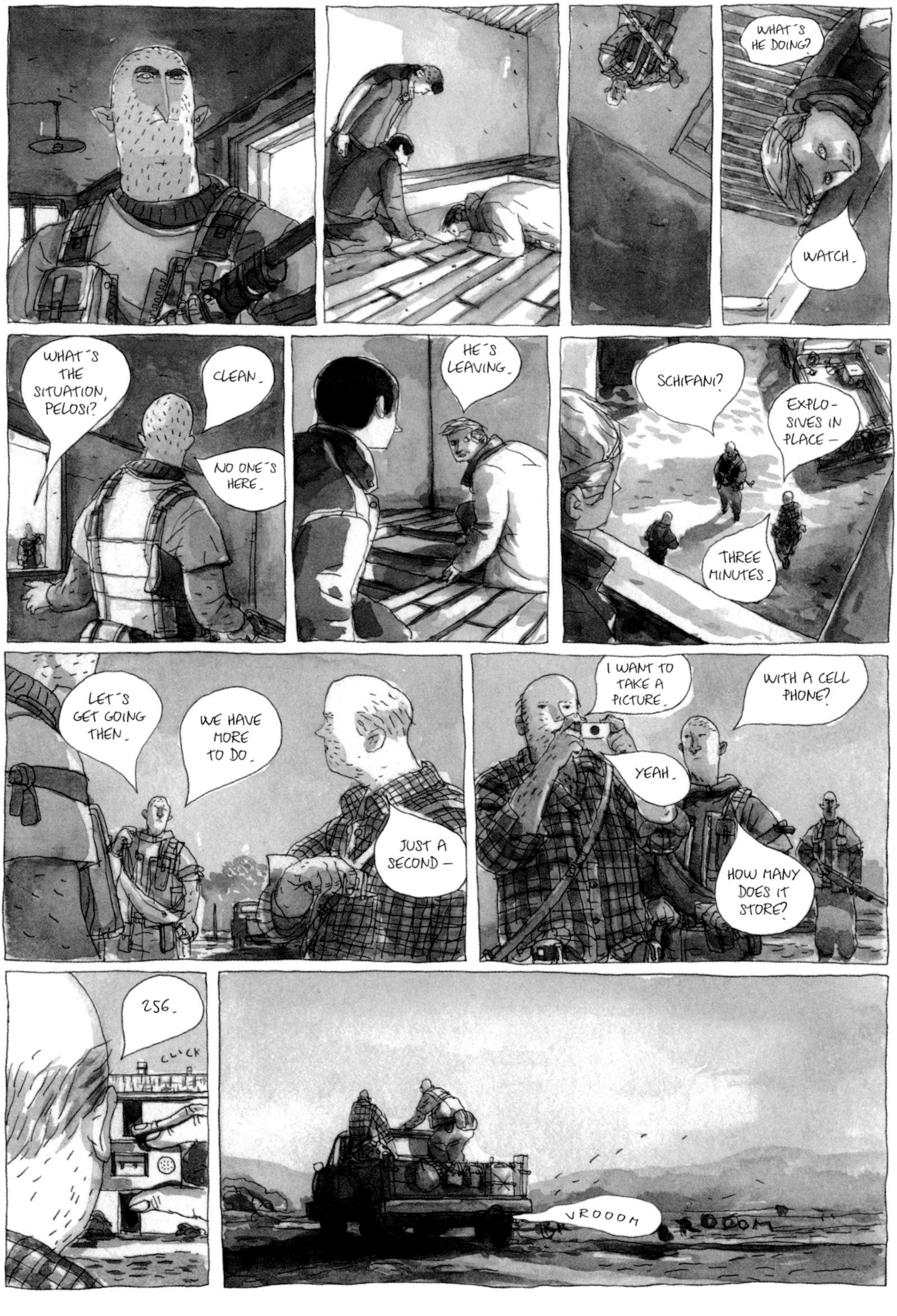
WHAT'S HE DOING?
WATCH_
WHAT'S THE SITUATION, PELOSI?
CLEAN_
NO ONE'S HERE_
HE'S LEAVING_
SCHIFANI?
EXPLO-SIVES IN PLACE —
THREE MINUTES_
LET'S GET GOING THEN_
WE HAVE MORE TO DO_
JUST A SECOND —
I WANT TO TAKE A PICTURE_
WITH A CELL PHONE?
YEAH_
HOW MANY DOES IT STORE?
256_
CLICK
VROOOM
BROOOM

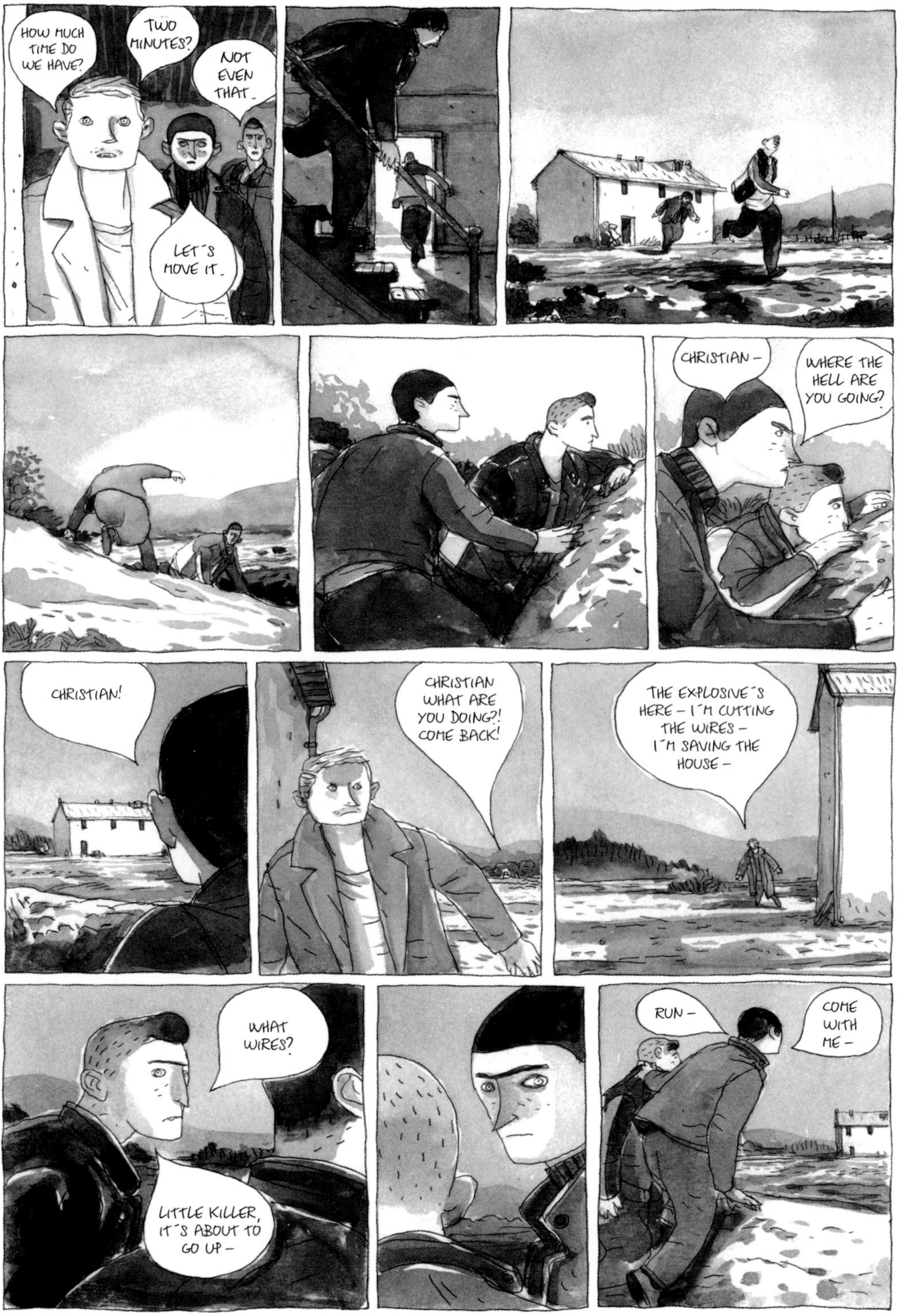
HOW MUCH TIME DO WE HAVE?
TWO MINUTES?
NOT EVEN THAT_
LET'S MOVE IT_
CHRISTIAN –
WHERE THE HELL ARE YOU GOING?
CHRISTIAN!
CHRISTIAN WHAT ARE YOU DOING?! COME BACK!
THE EXPLOSIVE'S HERE – I'M CUTTING THE WIRES – I'M SAVING THE HOUSE –
WHAT WIRES?
LITTLE KILLER, IT'S ABOUT TO GO UP –
RUN –
COME WITH ME –

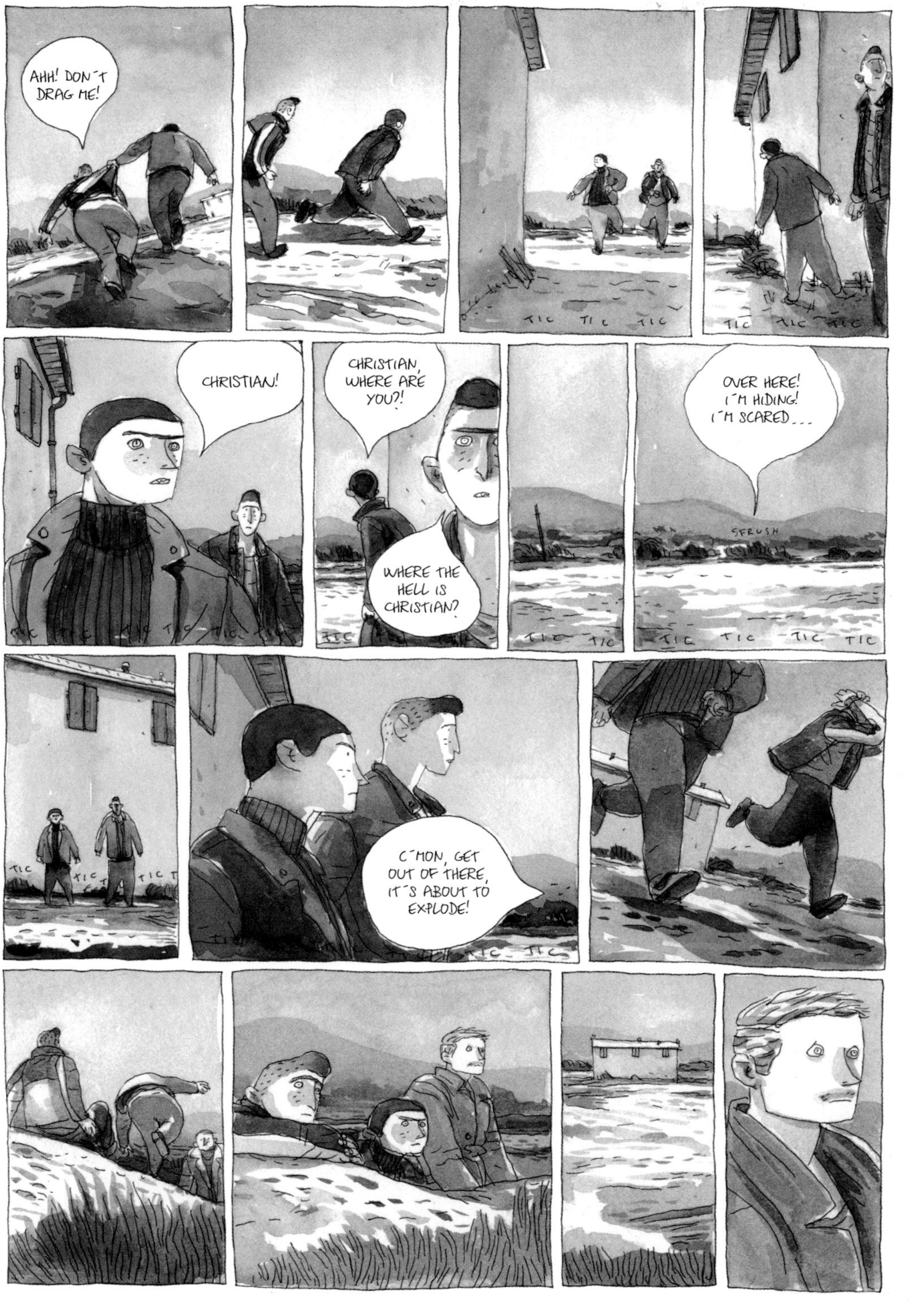
AHH! DON'T DRAG ME!
TIC TIC TIC
TIC TIC TIC
CHRISTIAN!
TIC TIC TIC TIC
CHRISTIAN, WHERE ARE YOU?!
WHERE THE HELL IS CHRISTIAN?
TIC
TIC TIC
OVER HERE! I'M HIDING! I'M SCARED...
SFRUSH
TIC TIC TIC TIC
TIC TIC TIC
C'MON, GET OUT OF THERE, IT'S ABOUT TO EXPLODE!
TIC TIC

A RUSTIC COTTAGE WITH TWO FLOORS.

THE GROUND FLOOR COMPRISES A SPACIOUS LIVING ROOM WITH A CORNER KITCHEN, WELL-LIT, FIREPLACE NEEDS SOME WORK. ON THE UPPER FLOOR THERE ARE THREE BEDROOMS AND A SMALL BATHROOM WITH SPACE FOR AN EXTENSION, FOR A TOTAL OF 1,200 SQUARE FEET.

DON'T MISS THIS OPPORTUNITY.

MY MOTHER WAS A REAL ESTATE AGENT, SHE BOUGHT AND SOLD HOUSES. LITTLE KILLER'S MOTHER DIED WHEN HE WAS YOUNG. CHRISTIAN'S WAS A SIGNATURE ON AN ABANDONED CHILDREN'S LIST AT A CONVENT.

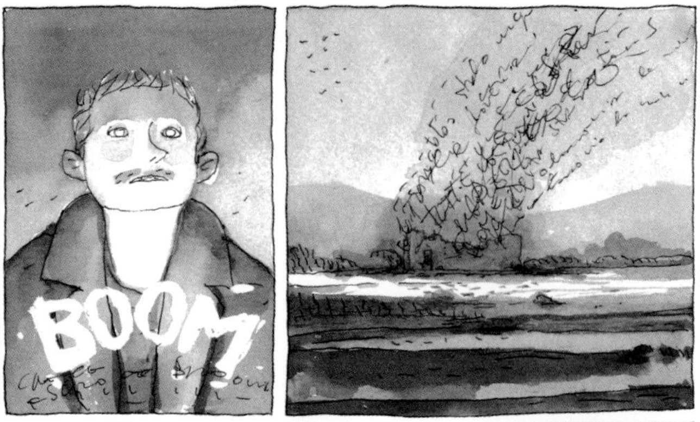
BOOM

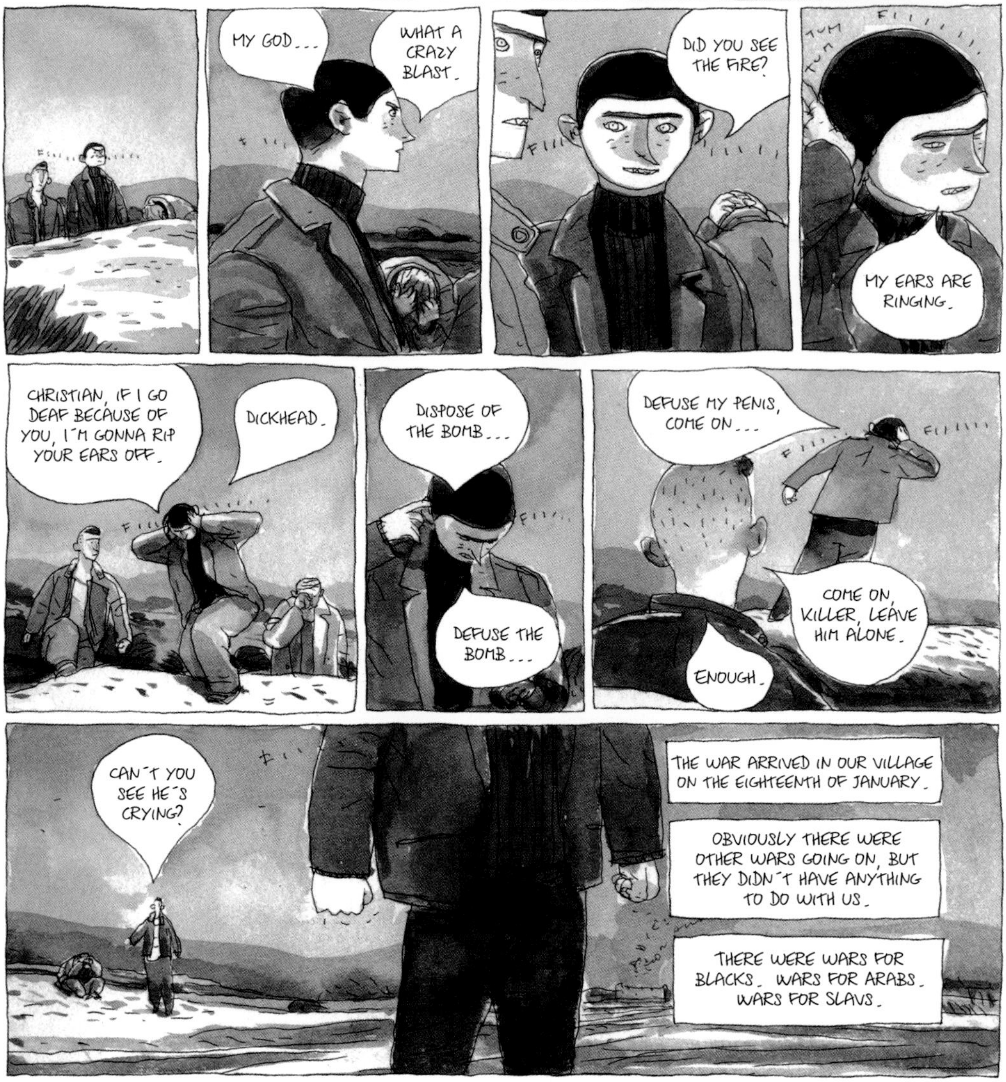
MY GOD...
WHAT A CRAZY BLAST.
DID YOU SEE THE FIRE?
MY EARS ARE RINGING.
CHRISTIAN, IF I GO DEAF BECAUSE OF YOU, I'M GONNA RIP YOUR EARS OFF.
DICKHEAD.
DISPOSE OF THE BOMB...
DEFUSE THE BOMB...
DEFUSE MY PENIS, COME ON...
COME ON, KILLER, LEAVE HIM ALONE.
ENOUGH.
CAN'T YOU SEE HE'S CRYING?
THE WAR ARRIVED IN OUR VILLAGE ON THE EIGHTEENTH OF JANUARY.
OBVIOUSLY THERE WERE OTHER WARS GOING ON, BUT THEY DIDN'T HAVE ANYTHING TO DO WITH US.
THERE WERE WARS FOR BLACKS. WARS FOR ARABS. WARS FOR SLAVS.

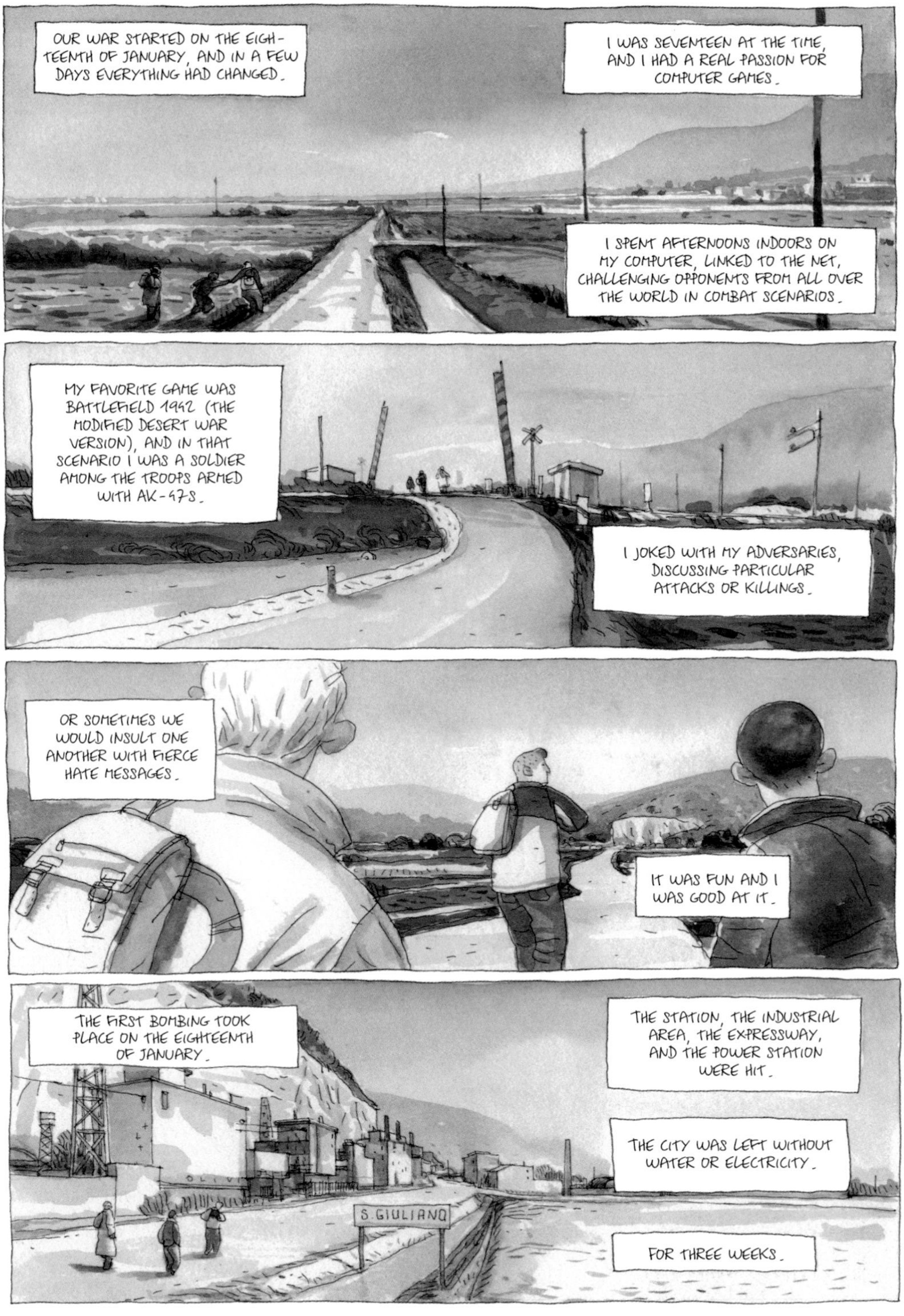
OUR WAR STARTED ON THE EIGHTEENTH OF JANUARY, AND IN A FEW DAYS EVERYTHING HAD CHANGED.
I WAS SEVENTEEN AT THE TIME, AND I HAD A REAL PASSION FOR COMPUTER GAMES.
I SPENT AFTERNOONS INDOORS ON MY COMPUTER, LINKED TO THE NET, CHALLENGING OPPONENTS FROM ALL OVER THE WORLD IN COMBAT SCENARIOS.
MY FAVORITE GAME WAS BATTLEFIELD 1942 (THE MODIFIED DESERT WAR VERSION), AND IN THAT SCENARIO I WAS A SOLDIER AMONG THE TROOPS ARMED WITH AK-47S.
I JOKED WITH MY ADVERSARIES, DISCUSSING PARTICULAR ATTACKS OR KILLINGS.
OR SOMETIMES WE WOULD INSULT ONE ANOTHER WITH FIERCE HATE MESSAGES.
IT WAS FUN AND I WAS GOOD AT IT.
THE FIRST BOMBING TOOK PLACE ON THE EIGHTEENTH OF JANUARY.
THE STATION, THE INDUSTRIAL AREA, THE EXPRESSWAY, AND THE POWER STATION WERE HIT.
THE CITY WAS LEFT WITHOUT WATER OR ELECTRICITY.
FOR THREE WEEKS.
S. GIULIANO

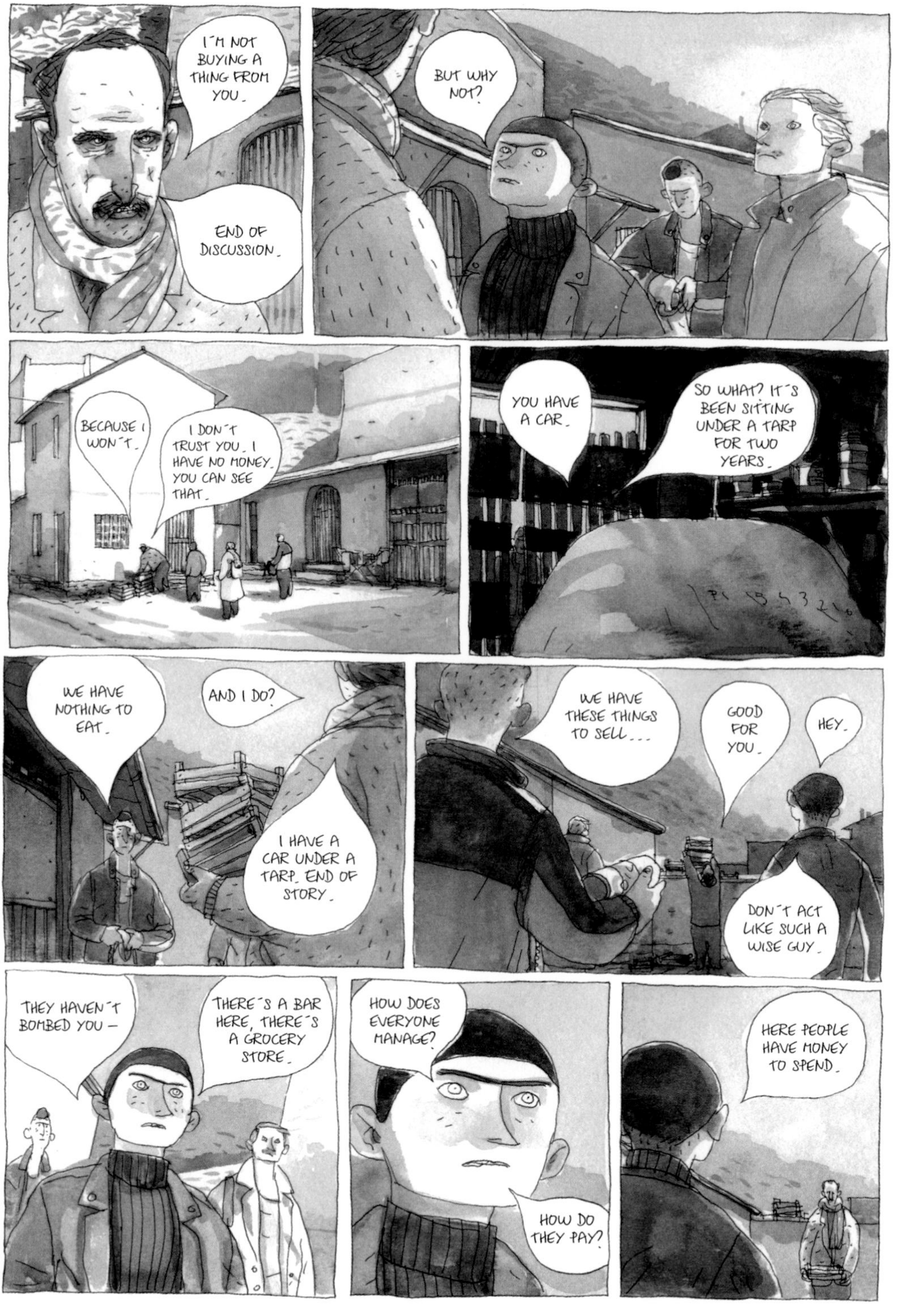

I'M NOT BUYING A THING FROM YOU.
END OF DISCUSSION.
BUT WHY NOT?
BECAUSE I WON'T.
I DON'T TRUST YOU. I HAVE NO MONEY. YOU CAN SEE THAT.
YOU HAVE A CAR.
SO WHAT? IT'S BEEN SITTING UNDER A TARP FOR TWO YEARS.
WE HAVE NOTHING TO EAT.
AND I DO?
I HAVE A CAR UNDER A TARP. END OF STORY.
WE HAVE THESE THINGS TO SELL...
GOOD FOR YOU.
HEY.
DON'T ACT LIKE SUCH A WISE GUY.
THEY HAVEN'T BOMBED YOU –
THERE'S A BAR HERE, THERE'S A GROCERY STORE.
HOW DOES EVERYONE MANAGE?
HOW DO THEY PAY?
HERE PEOPLE HAVE MONEY TO SPEND.

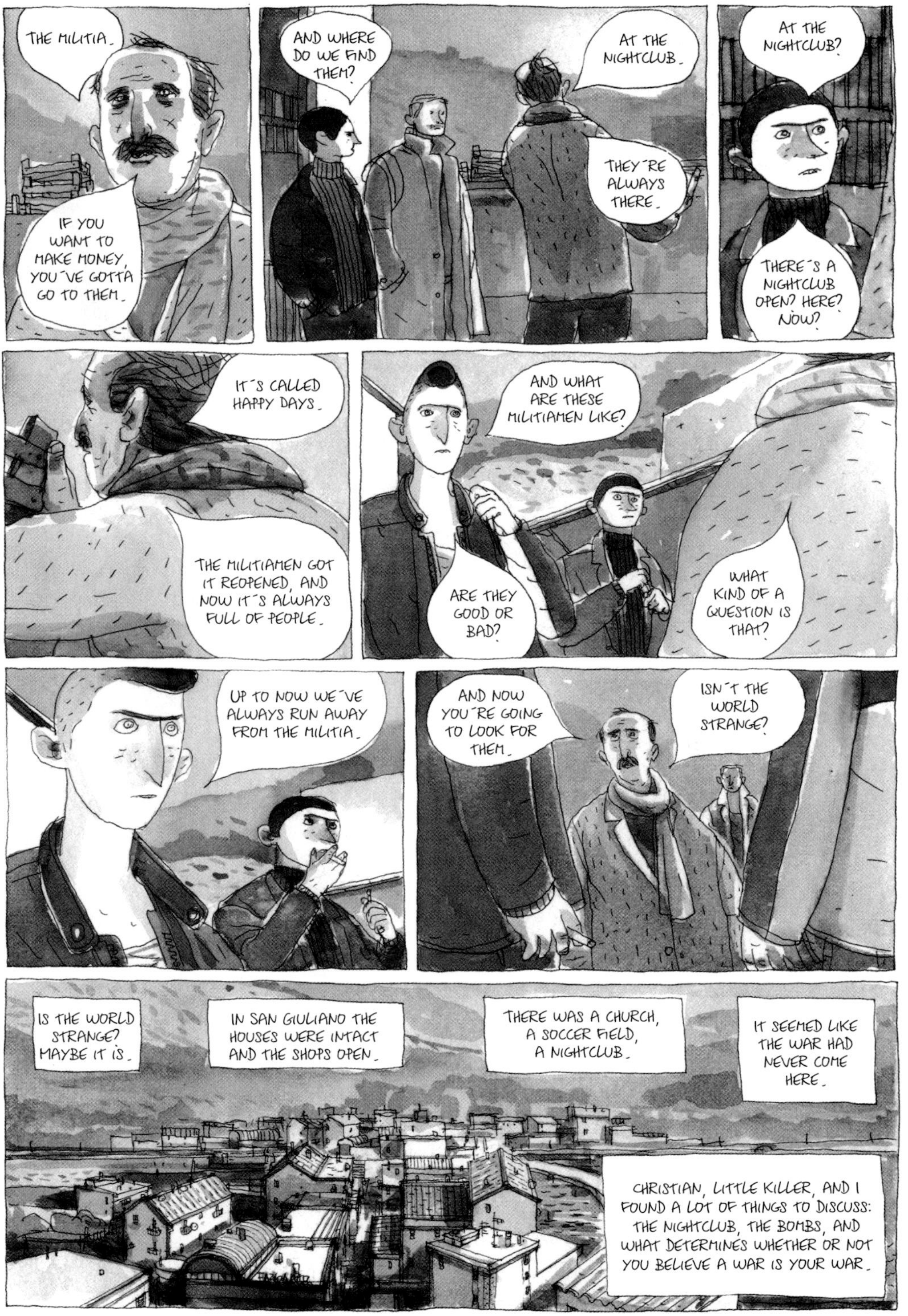
THE MILITIA.
IF YOU WANT TO MAKE MONEY, YOU'VE GOTTA GO TO THEM.
AND WHERE DO WE FIND THEM?
AT THE NIGHTCLUB.
THEY'RE ALWAYS THERE.
AT THE NIGHTCLUB?
THERE'S A NIGHTCLUB OPEN? HERE? NOW?
IT'S CALLED HAPPY DAYS.
THE MILITIAMEN GOT IT REOPENED, AND NOW IT'S ALWAYS FULL OF PEOPLE.
AND WHAT ARE THESE MILITIAMEN LIKE?
ARE THEY GOOD OR BAD?
WHAT KIND OF A QUESTION IS THAT?
UP TO NOW WE'VE ALWAYS RUN AWAY FROM THE MILITIA.
AND NOW YOU'RE GOING TO LOOK FOR THEM.
ISN'T THE WORLD STRANGE?
IS THE WORLD STRANGE? MAYBE IT IS.
IN SAN GIULIANO THE HOUSES WERE INTACT AND THE SHOPS OPEN.
THERE WAS A CHURCH, A SOCCER FIELD, A NIGHTCLUB.
IT SEEMED LIKE THE WAR HAD NEVER COME HERE.
CHRISTIAN, LITTLE KILLER, AND I FOUND A LOT OF THINGS TO DISCUSS: THE NIGHTCLUB, THE BOMBS, AND WHAT DETERMINES WHETHER OR NOT YOU BELIEVE A WAR IS YOUR WAR.

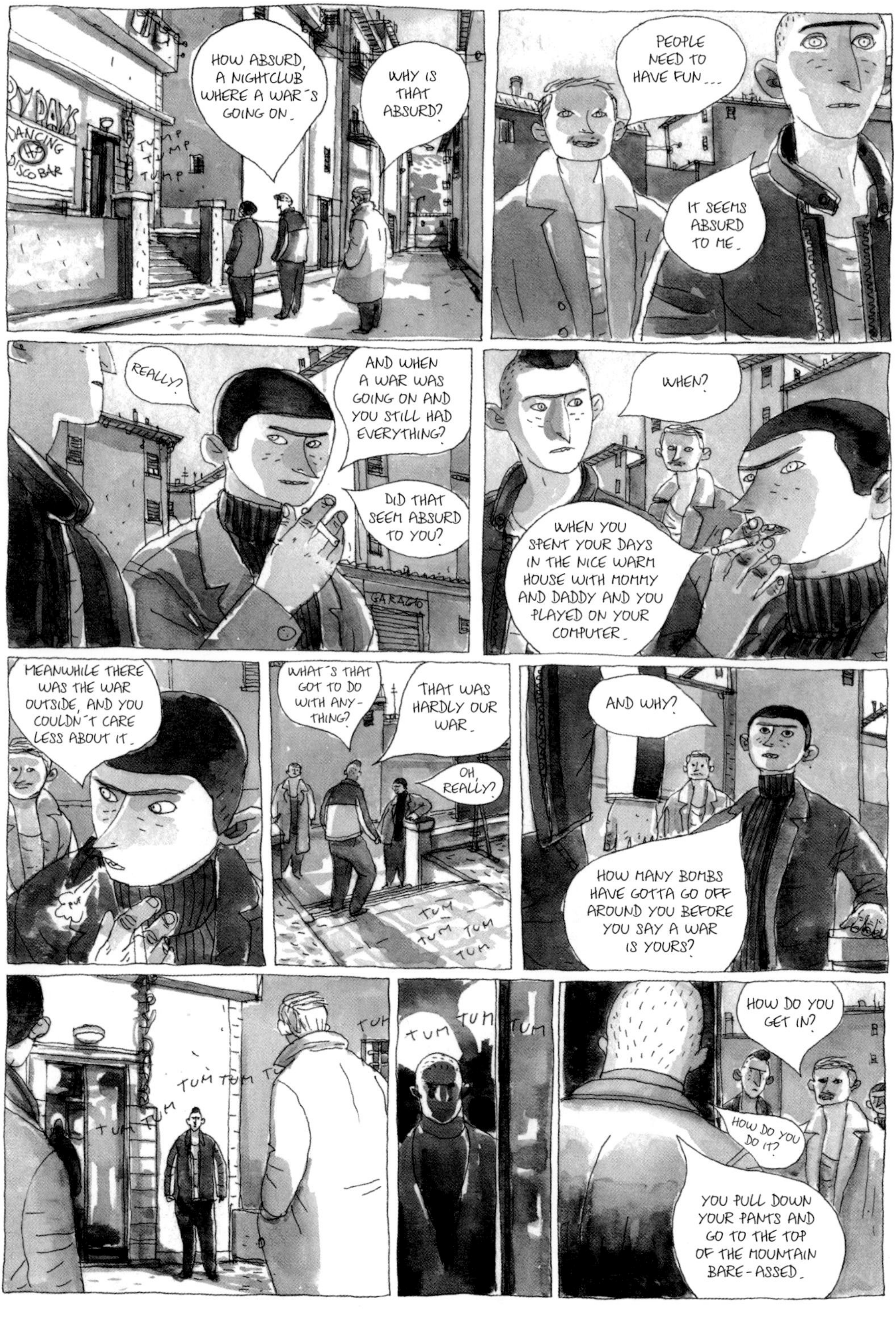

DANCING
DISCO BAR
TUMP TUMP TUMP
HOW ABSURD, A NIGHTCLUB WHERE A WAR'S GOING ON.
WHY IS THAT ABSURD?
PEOPLE NEED TO HAVE FUN...
IT SEEMS ABSURD TO ME.
REALLY?
AND WHEN A WAR WAS GOING ON AND YOU STILL HAD EVERYTHING?
DID THAT SEEM ABSURD TO YOU?
GARAGE
WHEN?
WHEN YOU SPENT YOUR DAYS IN THE NICE WARM HOUSE WITH MOMMY AND DADDY AND YOU PLAYED ON YOUR COMPUTER.
MEANWHILE THERE WAS THE WAR OUTSIDE, AND YOU COULDN'T CARE LESS ABOUT IT.
WHAT'S THAT GOT TO DO WITH ANYTHING?
THAT WAS HARDLY OUR WAR.
OH REALLY?
TUM TUM TUM TUM
AND WHY?
HOW MANY BOMBS HAVE GOTTA GO OFF AROUND YOU BEFORE YOU SAY A WAR IS YOURS?
TUM TUM TUM TUM TU
TUM TUM TUM TUM
HOW DO YOU GET IN?
HOW DO YOU DO IT?
YOU PULL DOWN YOUR PANTS AND GO TO THE TOP OF THE MOUNTAIN BARE-ASSED.

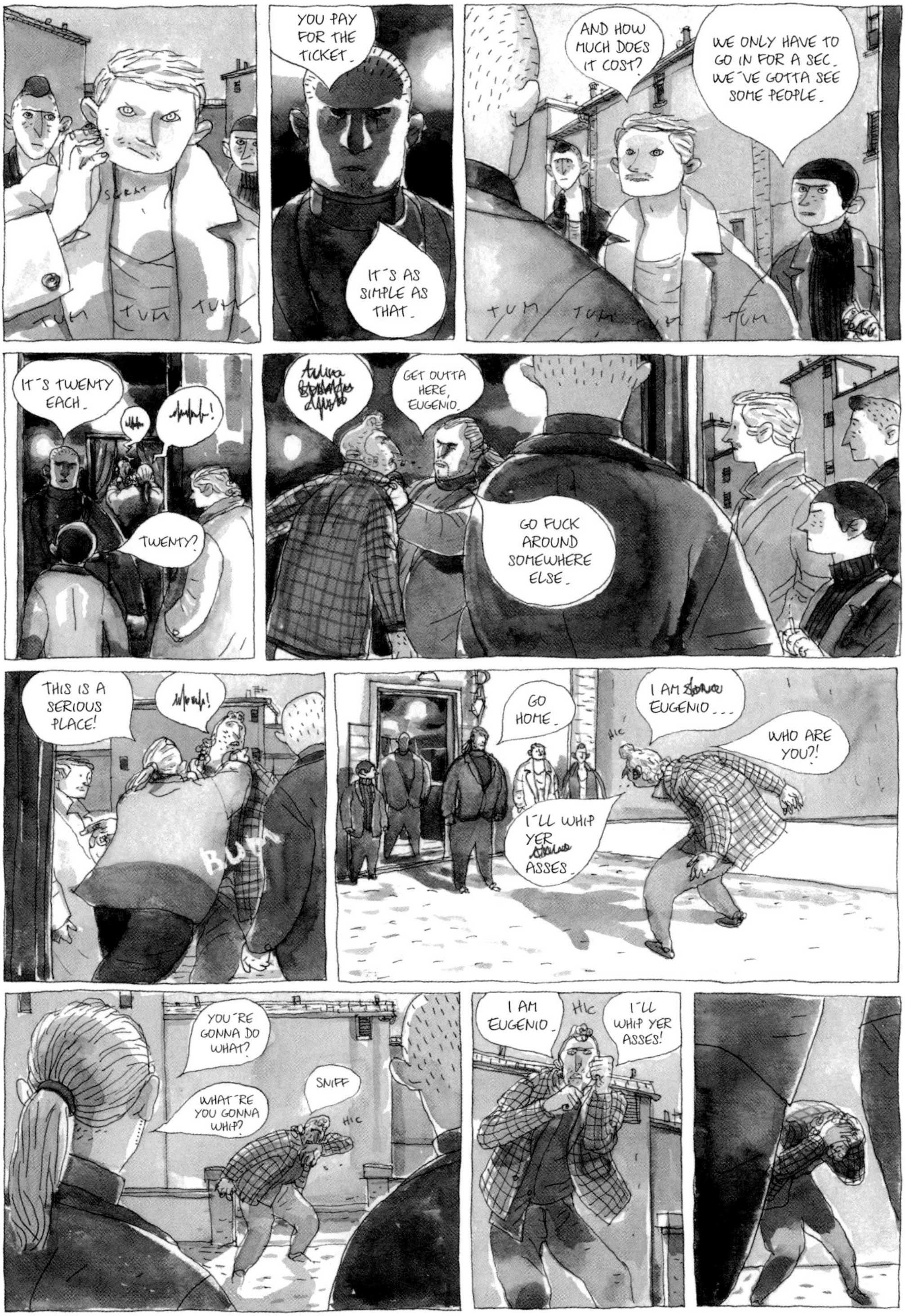

TUM TUM TUM
YOU PAY FOR THE TICKET.
IT'S AS SIMPLE AS THAT.
AND HOW MUCH DOES IT COST?
WE ONLY HAVE TO GO IN FOR A SEC. WE'VE GOTTA SEE SOME PEOPLE.
TUM TUM TUM
IT'S TWENTY EACH.
TWENTY?
GET OUTTA HERE, EUGENIO.
GO FUCK AROUND SOMEWHERE ELSE.
THIS IS A SERIOUS PLACE!
GO HOME.
I AM EUGENIO...
WHO ARE YOU?!
I'LL WHIP YER ASSES.
YOU'RE GONNA DO WHAT?
WHAT'RE YOU GONNA WHIP?
SNIFF
HIC
I AM EUGENIO.
HIC
I'LL WHIP YER ASSES!

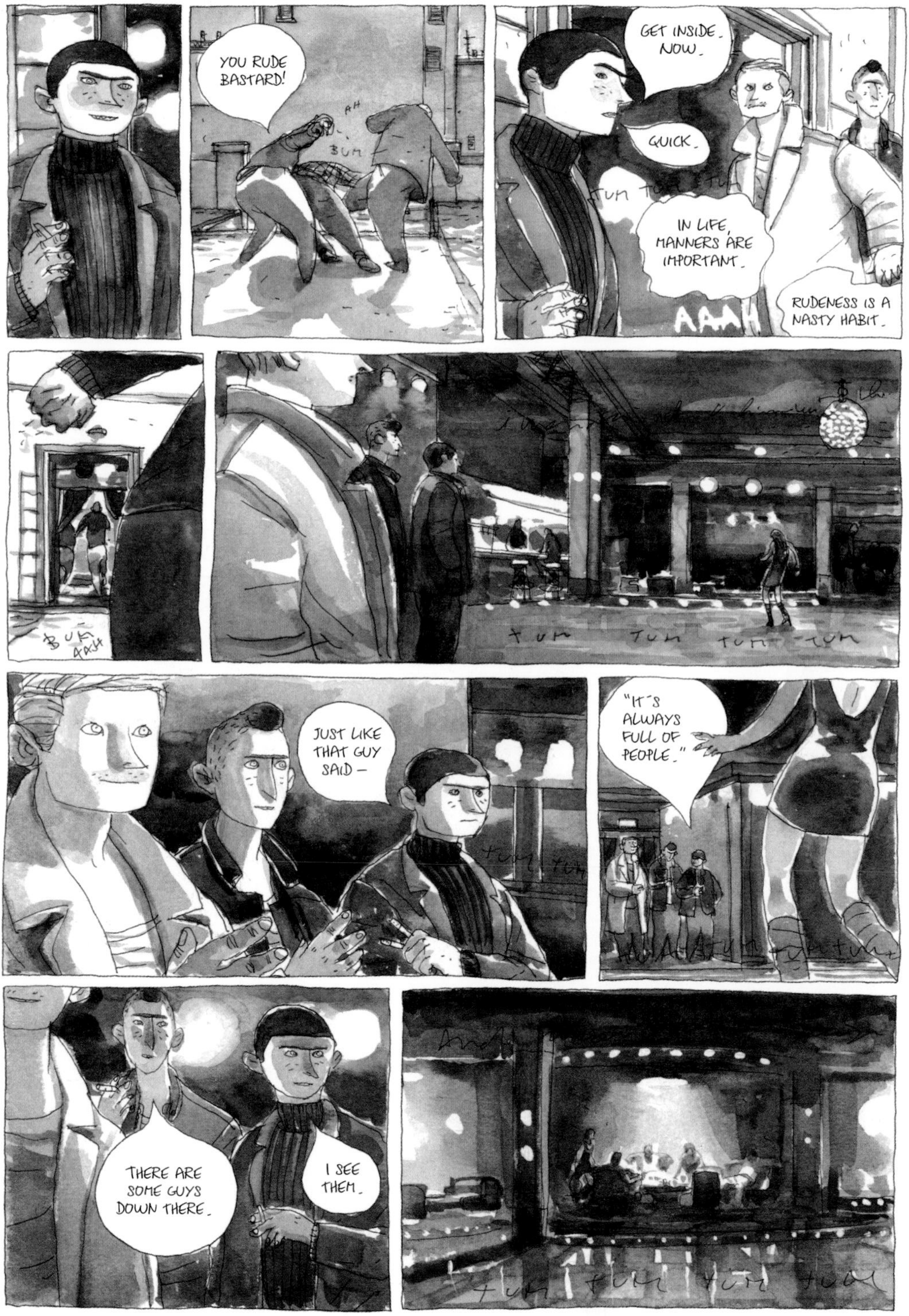
YOU RUDE BASTARD!
AH
BUM
GET INSIDE. NOW.
QUICK.
TUM TUM TUM
IN LIFE, MANNERS ARE IMPORTANT.
AAAH
RUDENESS IS A NASTY HABIT.
BUM AAH
TUM TUM TUM TUM
JUST LIKE THAT GUY SAID –
"IT'S ALWAYS FULL OF PEOPLE."
THERE ARE SOME GUYS DOWN THERE.
I SEE THEM.

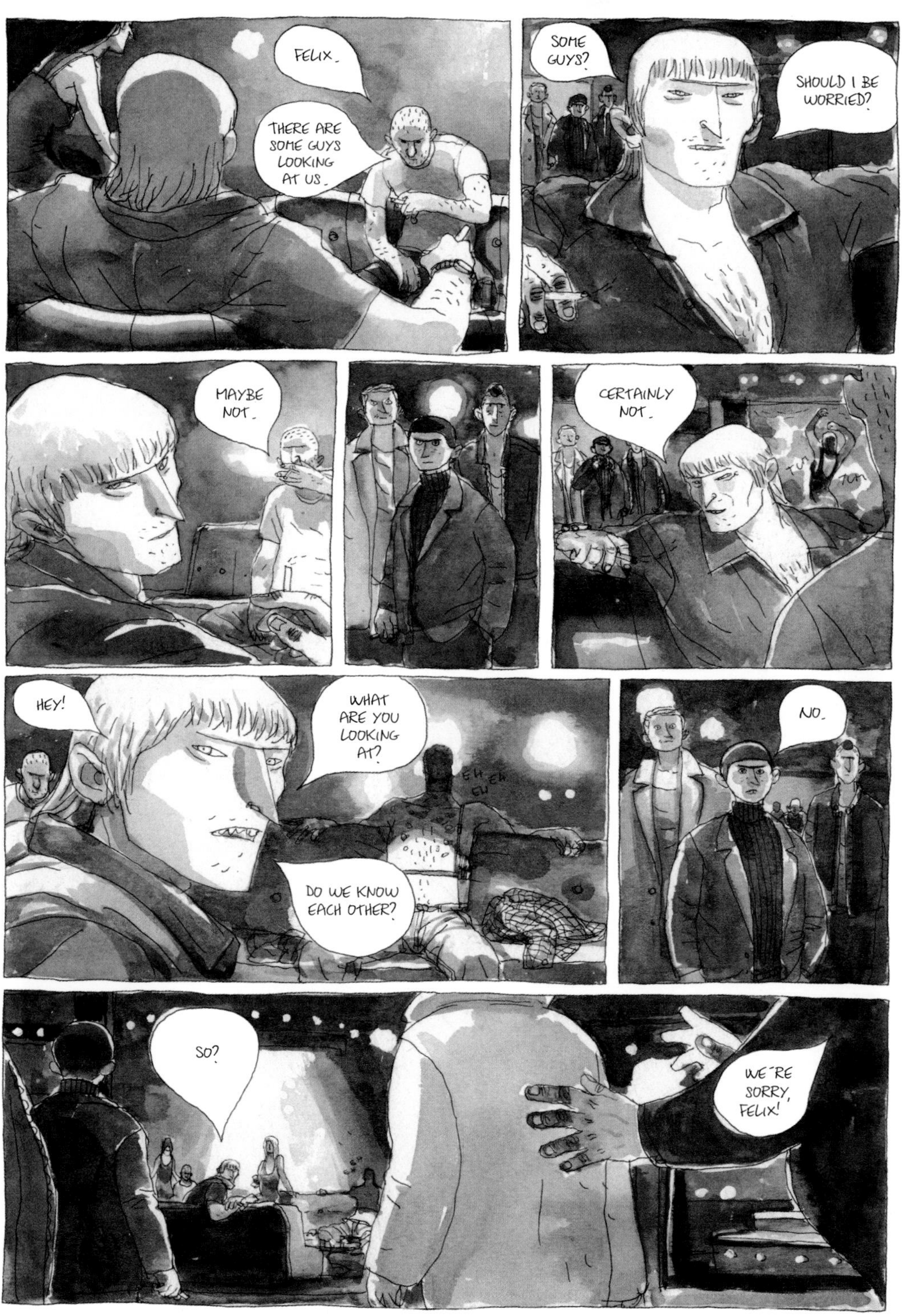
FELIX.
THERE ARE SOME GUYS LOOKING AT US.
SOME GUYS?
SHOULD I BE WORRIED?
MAYBE NOT.
CERTAINLY NOT.
HEY!
WHAT ARE YOU LOOKING AT?
DO WE KNOW EACH OTHER?
NO.
SO?
WE'RE SORRY, FELIX!

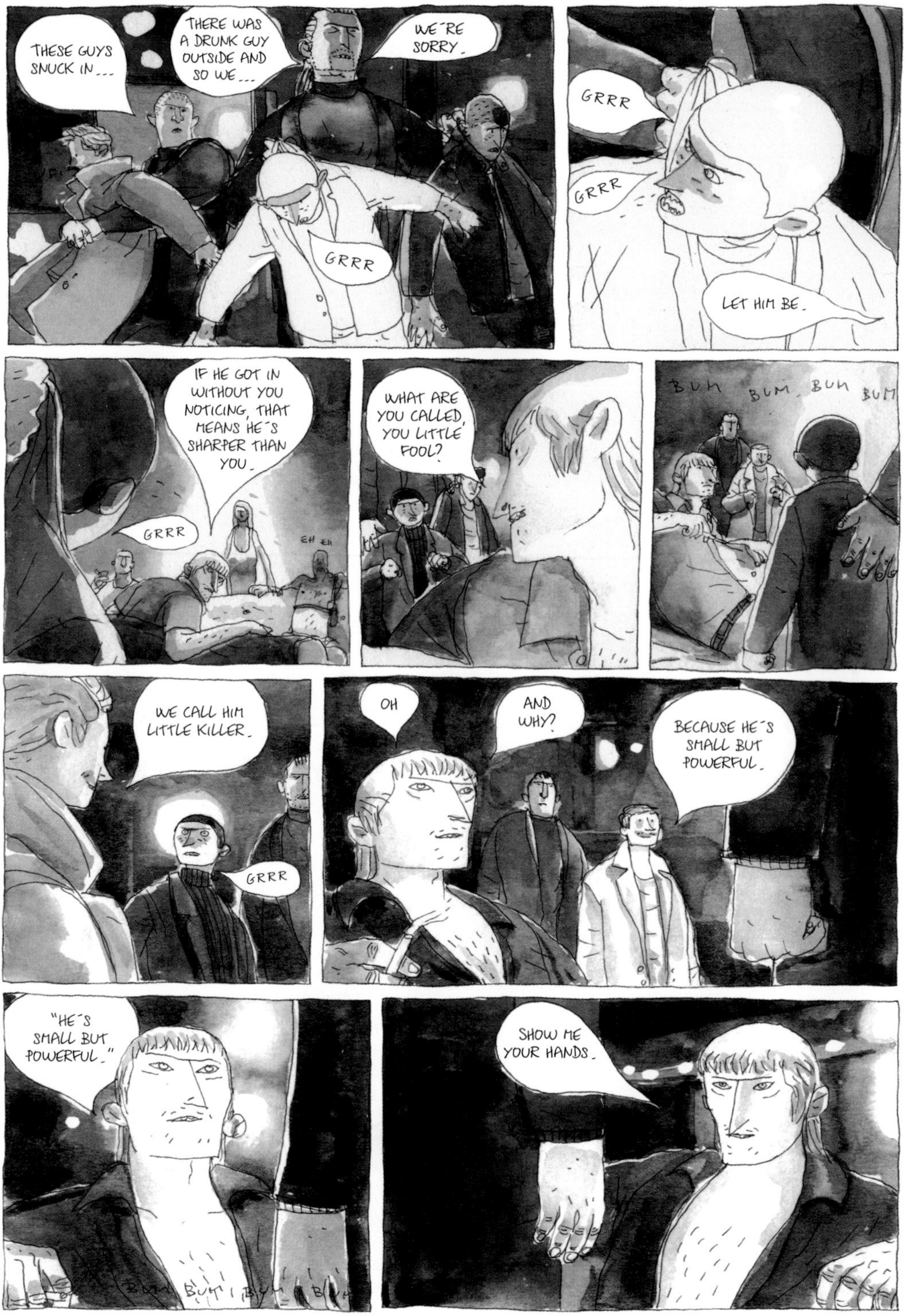
THESE GUYS SNUCK IN...
THERE WAS A DRUNK GUY OUTSIDE AND SO WE...
WE'RE SORRY.
GRRR
GRRR
GRRR
LET HIM BE.
IF HE GOT IN WITHOUT YOU NOTICING, THAT MEANS HE'S SHARPER THAN YOU.
GRRR
EH EH
WHAT ARE YOU CALLED, YOU LITTLE FOOL?
BUM BUM BUM BUM
WE CALL HIM LITTLE KILLER.
GRRR
OH
AND WHY?
BECAUSE HE'S SMALL BUT POWERFUL.
"HE'S SMALL BUT POWERFUL."
SHOW ME YOUR HANDS.

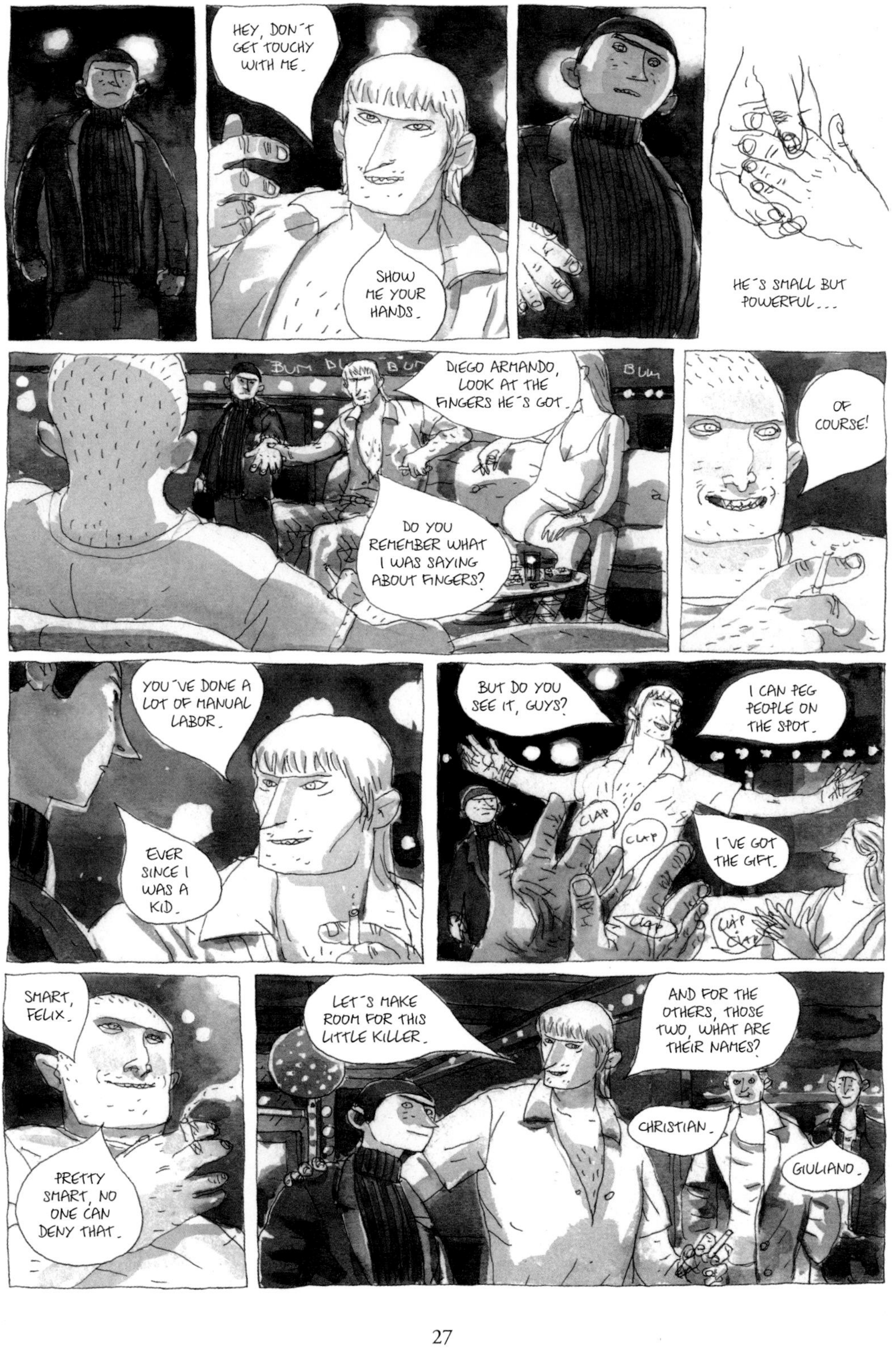
HEY, DON'T GET TOUCHY WITH ME.
SHOW ME YOUR HANDS.
HE'S SMALL BUT POWERFUL...
BUM BUM BUM
BUM
DIEGO ARMANDO, LOOK AT THE FINGERS HE'S GOT.
DO YOU REMEMBER WHAT I WAS SAYING ABOUT FINGERS?
OF COURSE!
YOU'VE DONE A LOT OF MANUAL LABOR.
EVER SINCE I WAS A KID.
BUT DO YOU SEE IT, GUYS?
I CAN PEG PEOPLE ON THE SPOT.
CLAP
CLAP
I'VE GOT THE GIFT.
CLAP
CLAP
SMART, FELIX.
PRETTY SMART, NO ONE CAN DENY THAT.
LET'S MAKE ROOM FOR THIS LITTLE KILLER.
AND FOR THE OTHERS, THOSE TWO, WHAT ARE THEIR NAMES?
CHRISTIAN.
GIULIANO.

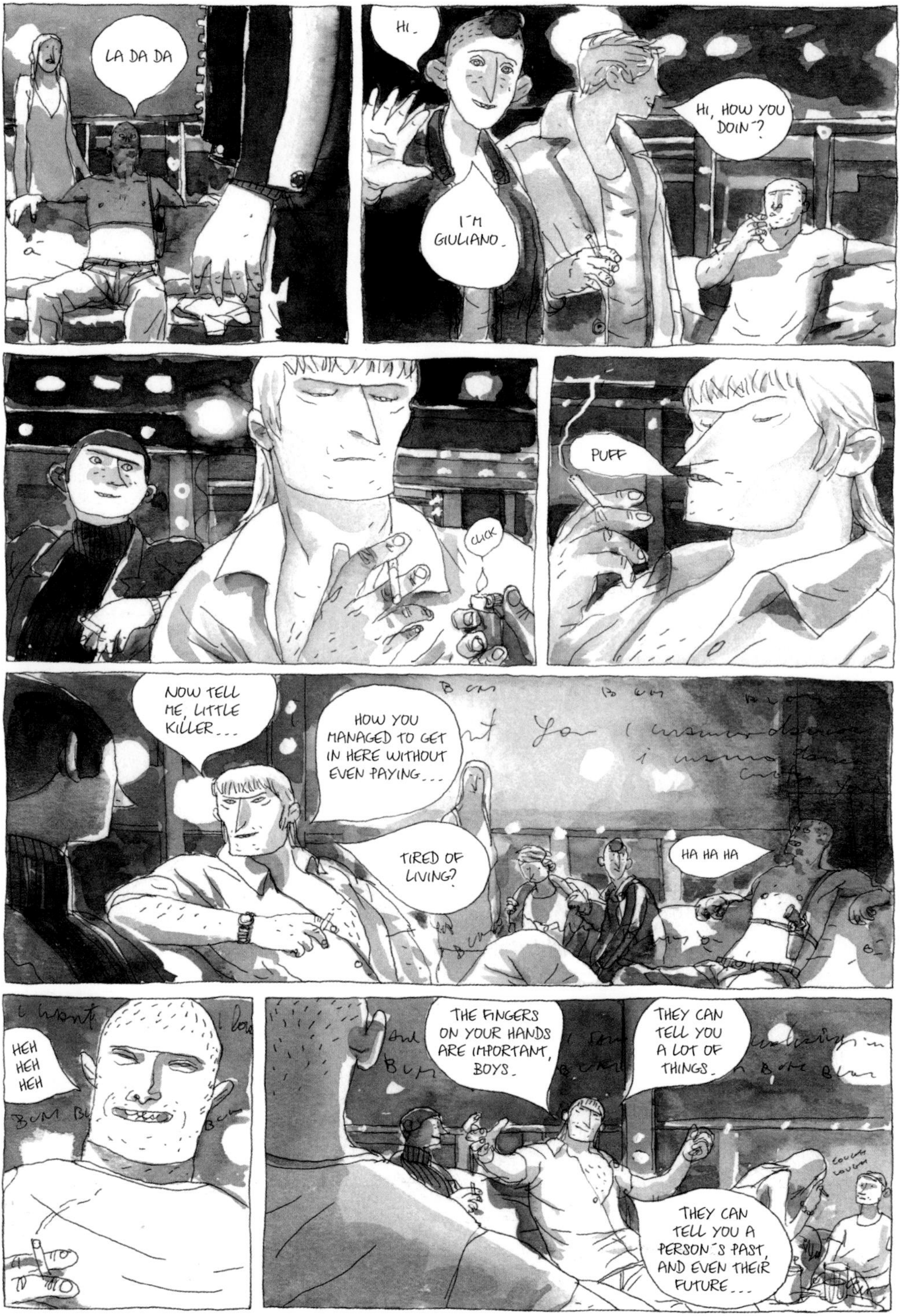
LA DA DA
HI_
HI, HOW YOU DOIN'?
I'M GIULIANO_
CLICK
PUFF
NOW TELL ME, LITTLE KILLER...
HOW YOU MANAGED TO GET IN HERE WITHOUT EVEN PAYING...
TIRED OF LIVING?
HA HA HA
HEH HEH HEH
THE FINGERS ON YOUR HANDS ARE IMPORTANT, BOYS_
THEY CAN TELL YOU A LOT OF THINGS_
THEY CAN TELL YOU A PERSON'S PAST, AND EVEN THEIR FUTURE...

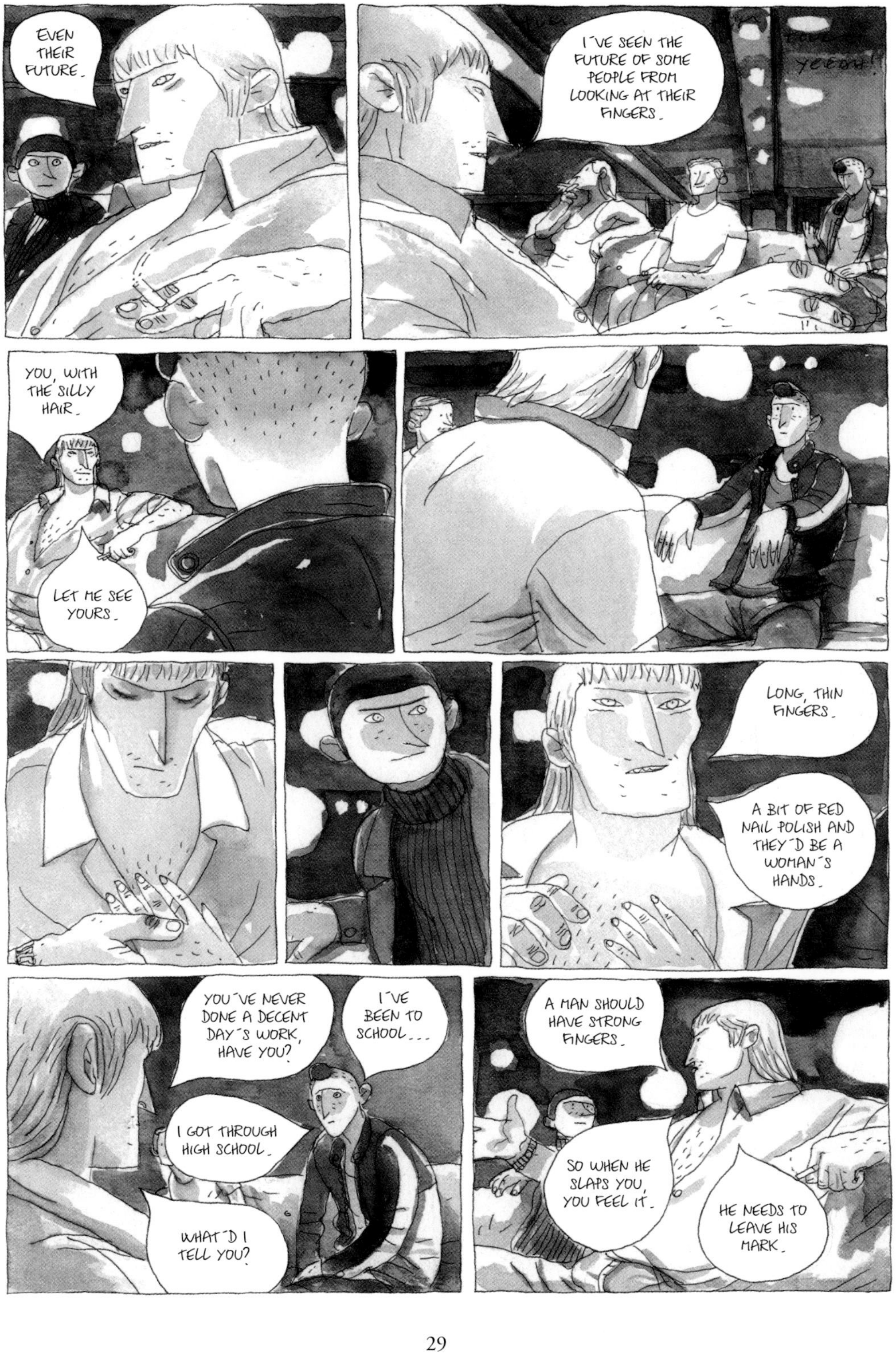
EVEN THEIR FUTURE.
I'VE SEEN THE FUTURE OF SOME PEOPLE FROM LOOKING AT THEIR FINGERS.
YOU, WITH THE SILLY HAIR.
LET ME SEE YOURS.
LONG, THIN FINGERS.
A BIT OF RED NAIL POLISH AND THEY'D BE A WOMAN'S HANDS.
YOU'VE NEVER DONE A DECENT DAY'S WORK, HAVE YOU?
I'VE BEEN TO SCHOOL...
I GOT THROUGH HIGH SCHOOL.
WHAT'D I TELL YOU?
A MAN SHOULD HAVE STRONG FINGERS.
SO WHEN HE SLAPS YOU, YOU FEEL IT.
HE NEEDS TO LEAVE HIS MARK.

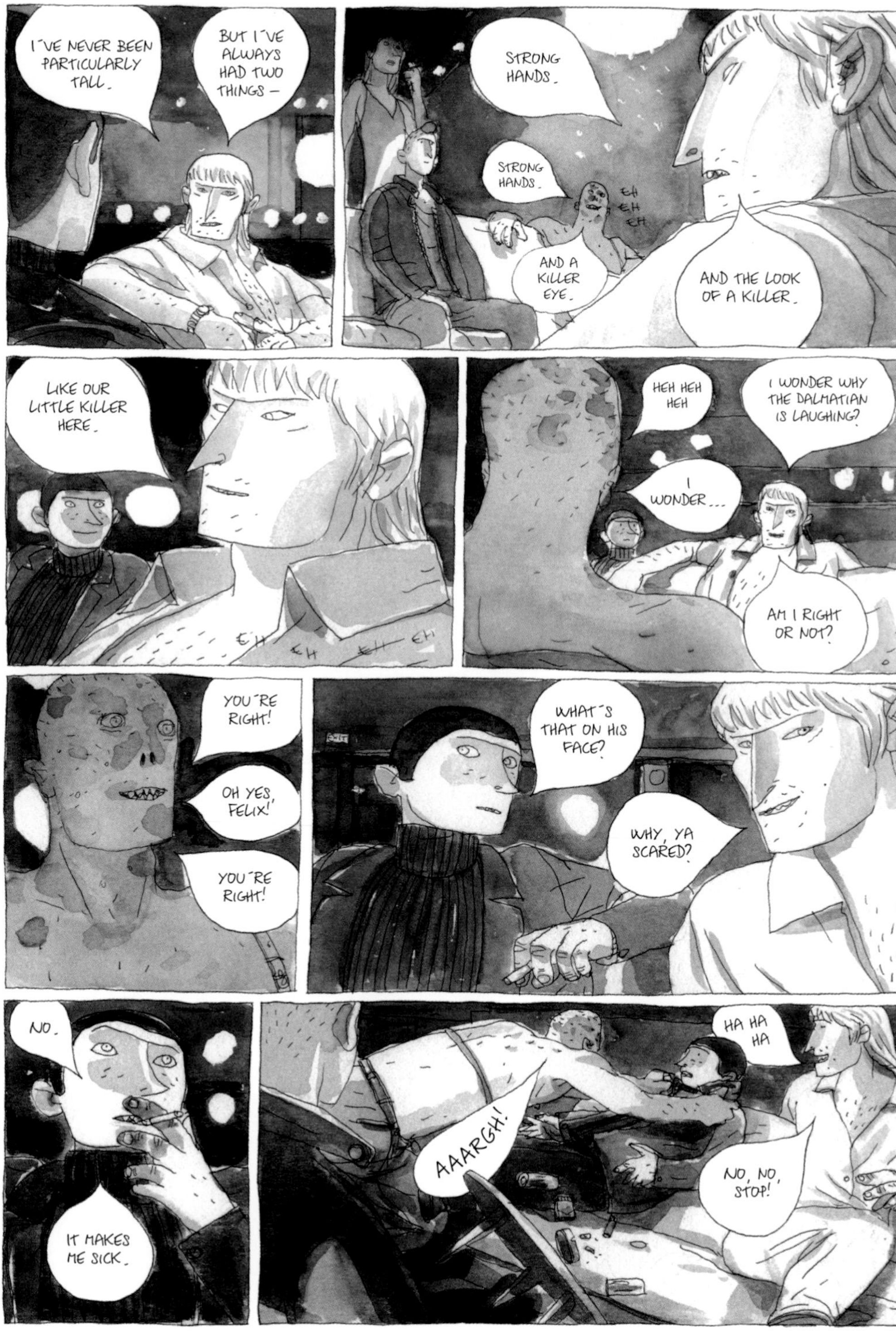
I´VE NEVER BEEN PARTICULARLY TALL.
BUT I´VE ALWAYS HAD TWO THINGS –
STRONG HANDS.
STRONG HANDS.
EH EH EH
AND A KILLER EYE.
AND THE LOOK OF A KILLER.
LIKE OUR LITTLE KILLER HERE.
EH EH EH EH
HEH HEH HEH
I WONDER WHY THE DALMATIAN IS LAUGHING?
I WONDER...
AM I RIGHT OR NOT?
YOU´RE RIGHT!
OH YES, FELIX!
YOU´RE RIGHT!
WHAT´S THAT ON HIS FACE?
WHY, YA SCARED?
NO.
IT MAKES ME SICK.
AAARGH!
HA HA HA
NO, NO, STOP!

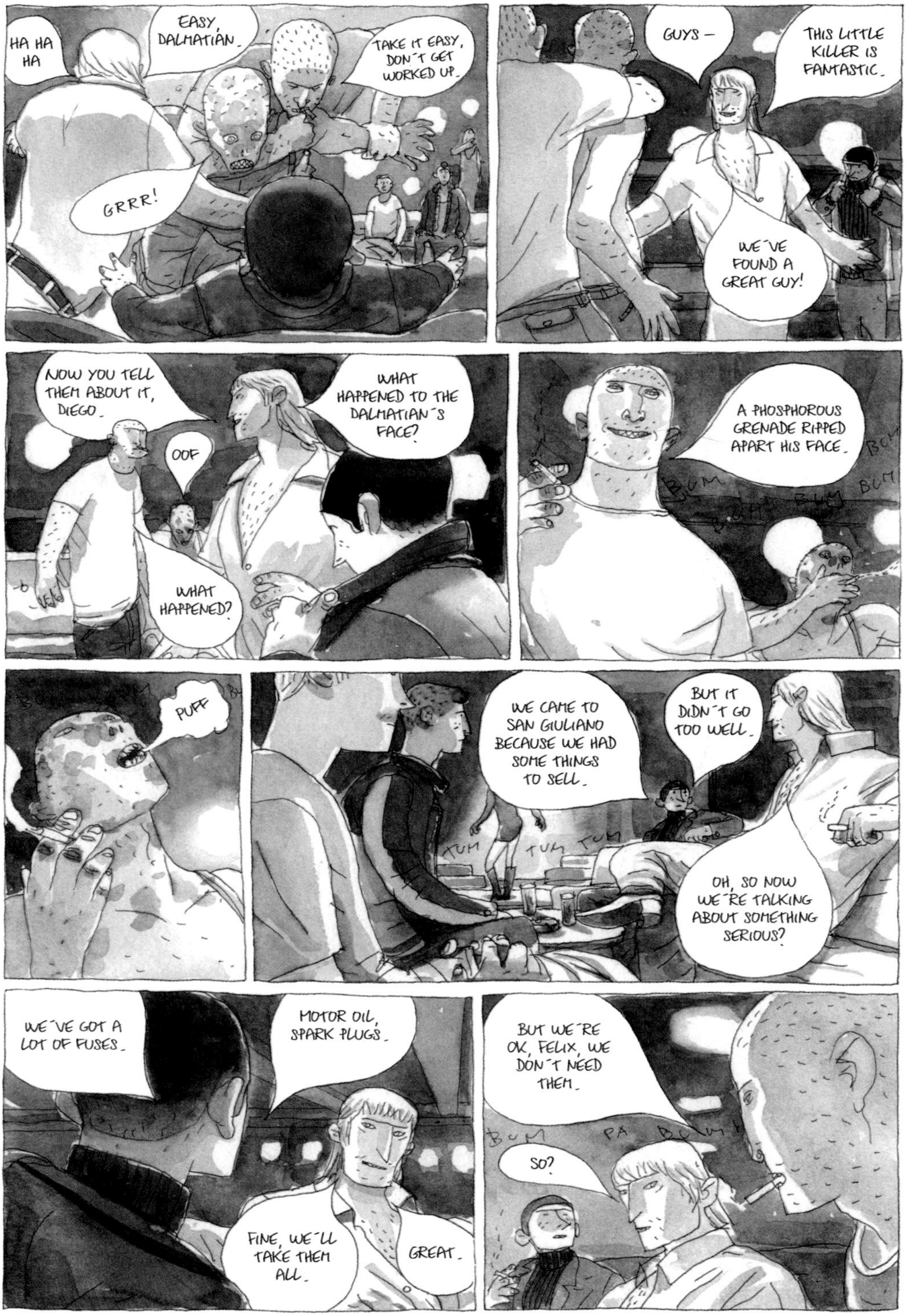
HA HA HA
EASY, DALMATIAN_
TAKE IT EASY, DON'T GET WORKED UP_
GRRR!
GUYS —
THIS LITTLE KILLER IS FANTASTIC_
WE'VE FOUND A GREAT GUY!
NOW YOU TELL THEM ABOUT IT, DIEGO_
WHAT HAPPENED TO THE DALMATIAN'S FACE?
OOF
WHAT HAPPENED?
A PHOSPHOROUS GRENADE RIPPED APART HIS FACE_
BUM BUM BUM BUM
PUFF
WE CAME TO SAN GIULIANO BECAUSE WE HAD SOME THINGS TO SELL_
BUT IT DIDN'T GO TOO WELL_
TUM TUM TUM
OH, SO NOW WE'RE TALKING ABOUT SOMETHING SERIOUS?
WE'VE GOT A LOT OF FUSES_
MOTOR OIL, SPARK PLUGS_
FINE, WE'LL TAKE THEM ALL_
GREAT_
BUT WE'RE OK, FELIX, WE DON'T NEED THEM_
BUM PA BUM
SO?

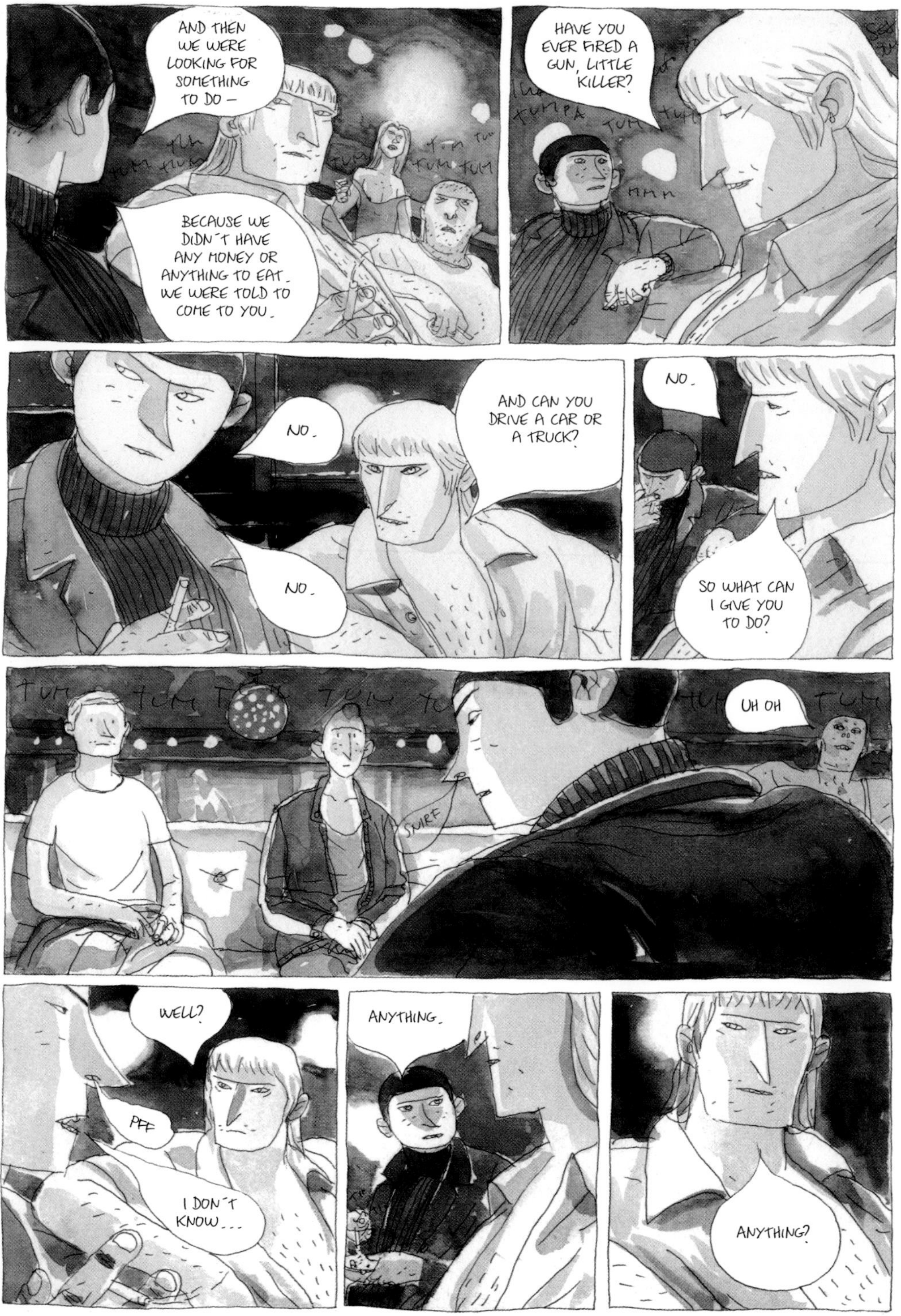
AND THEN WE WERE LOOKING FOR SOMETHING TO DO –
BECAUSE WE DIDN'T HAVE ANY MONEY OR ANYTHING TO EAT. WE WERE TOLD TO COME TO YOU.
HAVE YOU EVER FIRED A GUN, LITTLE KILLER?
NO.
AND CAN YOU DRIVE A CAR OR A TRUCK?
NO.
NO.
SO WHAT CAN I GIVE YOU TO DO?
UH OH
WELL?
PFF
I DON'T KNOW...
ANYTHING.
ANYTHING?

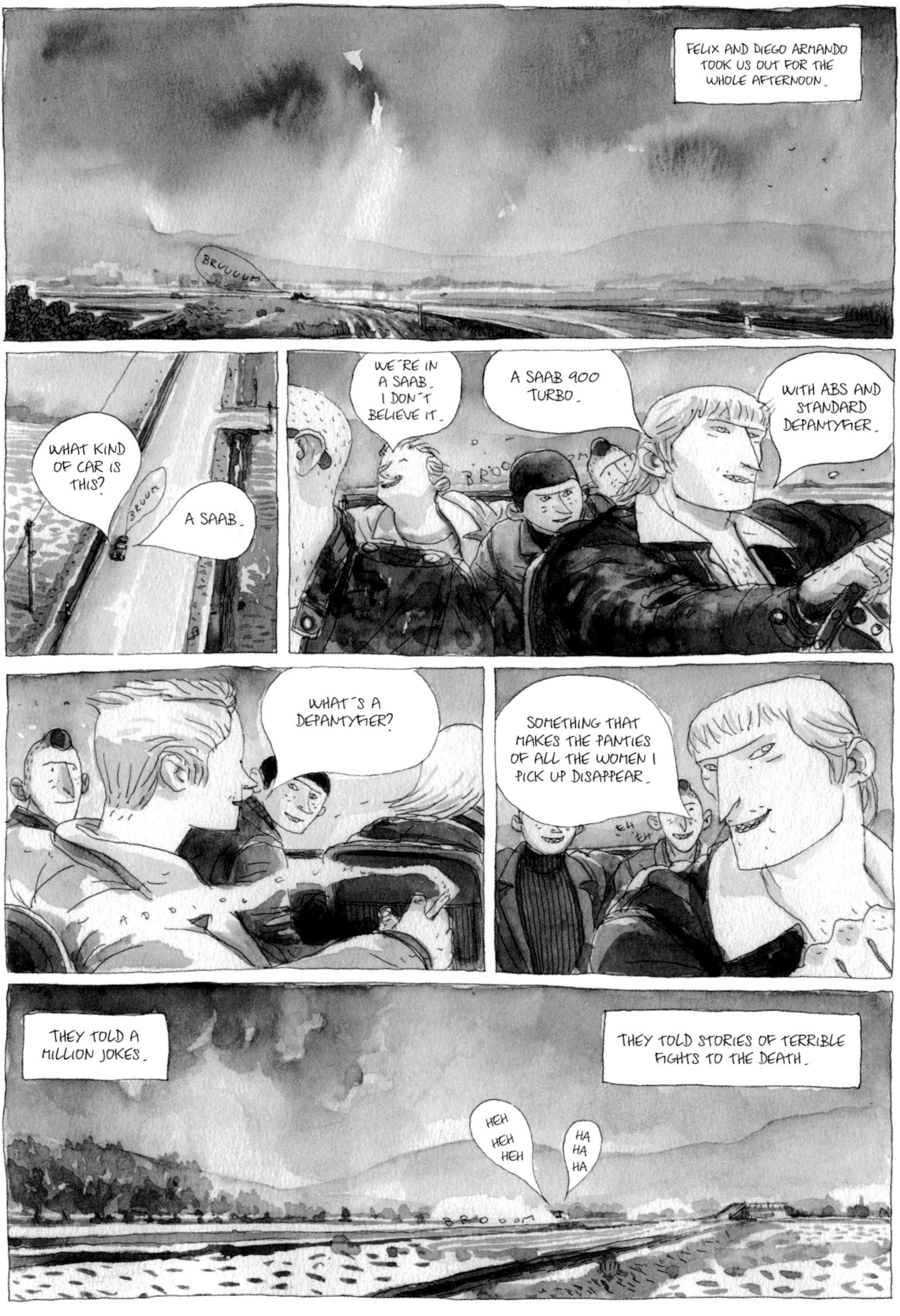
FELIX AND DIEGO ARMANDO TOOK US OUT FOR THE WHOLE AFTERNOON.
BRUUUUM
WHAT KIND OF CAR IS THIS?
BRUUM
A SAAB.
WE'RE IN A SAAB. I DON'T BELIEVE IT.
A SAAB 900 TURBO.
WITH ABS AND STANDARD DEPANTYFIER.
BROOOM
WHAT'S A DEPANTYFIER?
SOMETHING THAT MAKES THE PANTIES OF ALL THE WOMEN I PICK UP DISAPPEAR.
EH EH
THEY TOLD A MILLION JOKES.
THEY TOLD STORIES OF TERRIBLE FIGHTS TO THE DEATH.
HEH HEH HEH
HA HA HA
BROOOM

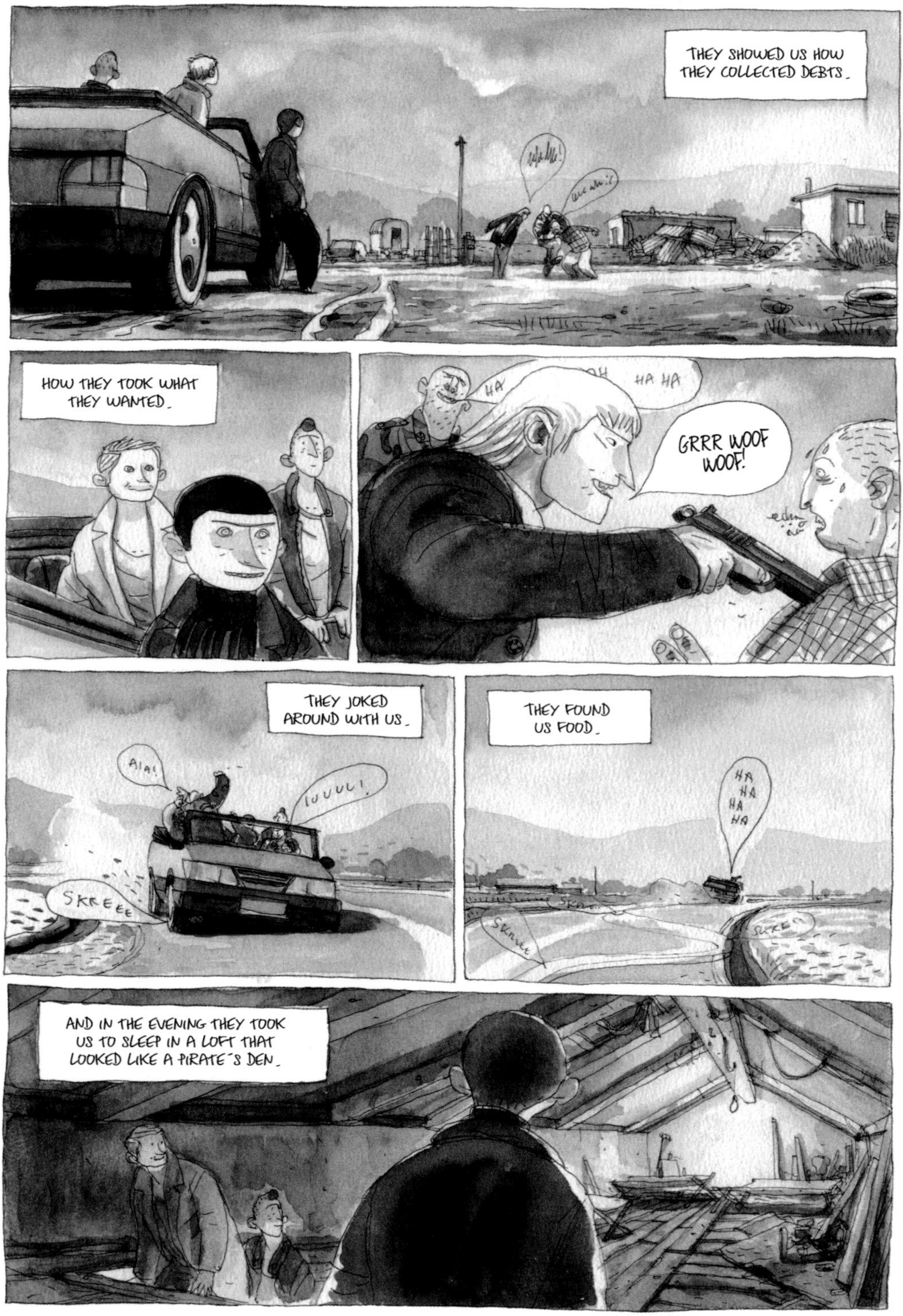
THEY SHOWED US HOW THEY COLLECTED DEBTS.
HOW THEY TOOK WHAT THEY WANTED.
HA
HA HA
GRRR WOOF WOOF!
THEY JOKED AROUND WITH US.
AIA!
IUUULI!
SKREEE
THEY FOUND US FOOD.
HA HA HA HA
AND IN THE EVENING THEY TOOK US TO SLEEP IN A LOFT THAT LOOKED LIKE A PIRATE'S DEN.

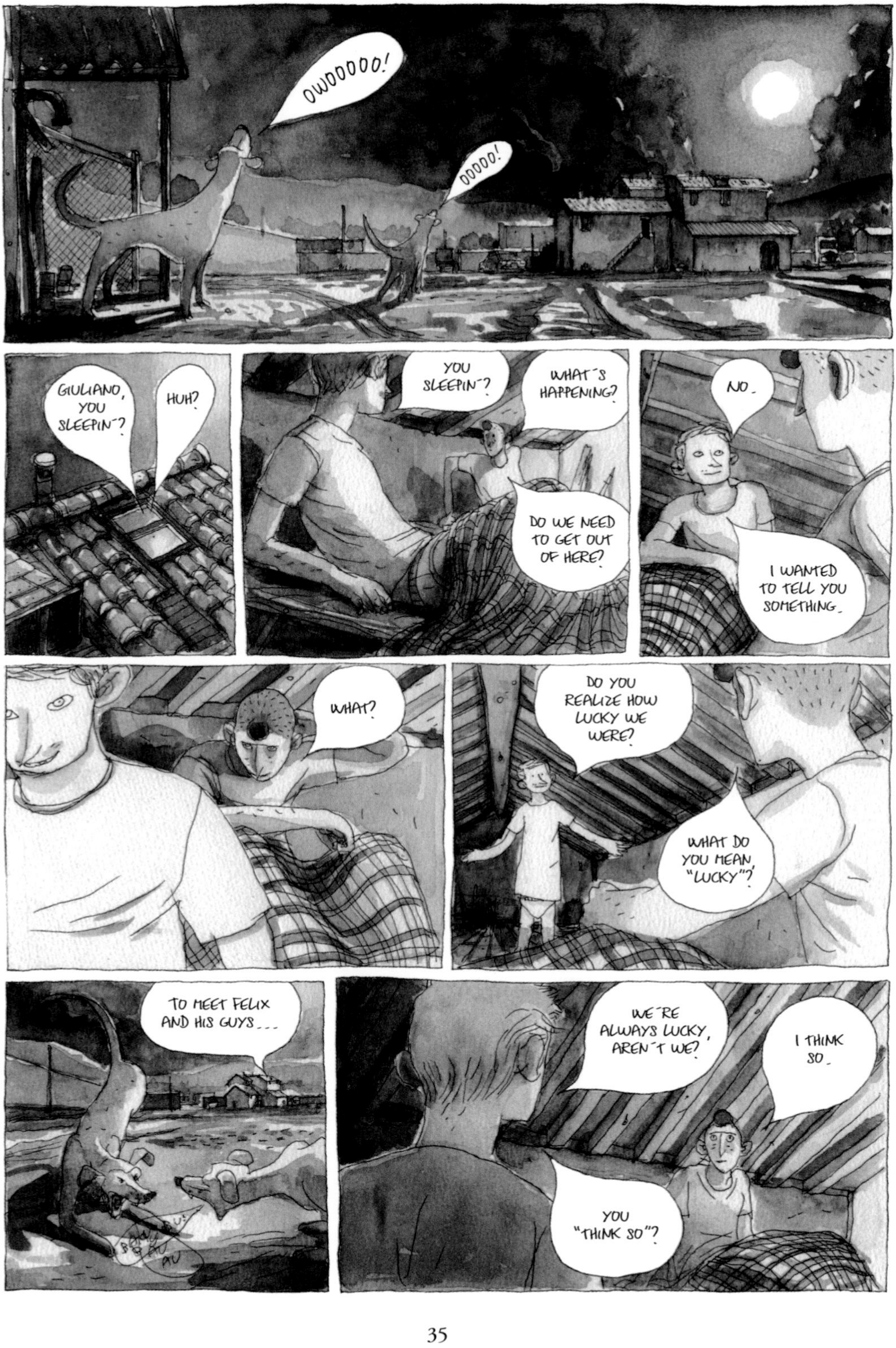
OWOOOOO!
OOOOO!
GIULIANO, YOU SLEEPIN'?
HUH?
YOU SLEEPIN'?
WHAT'S HAPPENING?
DO WE NEED TO GET OUT OF HERE?
NO.
I WANTED TO TELL YOU SOMETHING.
WHAT?
DO YOU REALIZE HOW LUCKY WE WERE?
WHAT DO YOU MEAN, "LUCKY"?
TO MEET FELIX AND HIS GUYS...
WE'RE ALWAYS LUCKY, AREN'T WE?
I THINK SO.
YOU "THINK SO"?

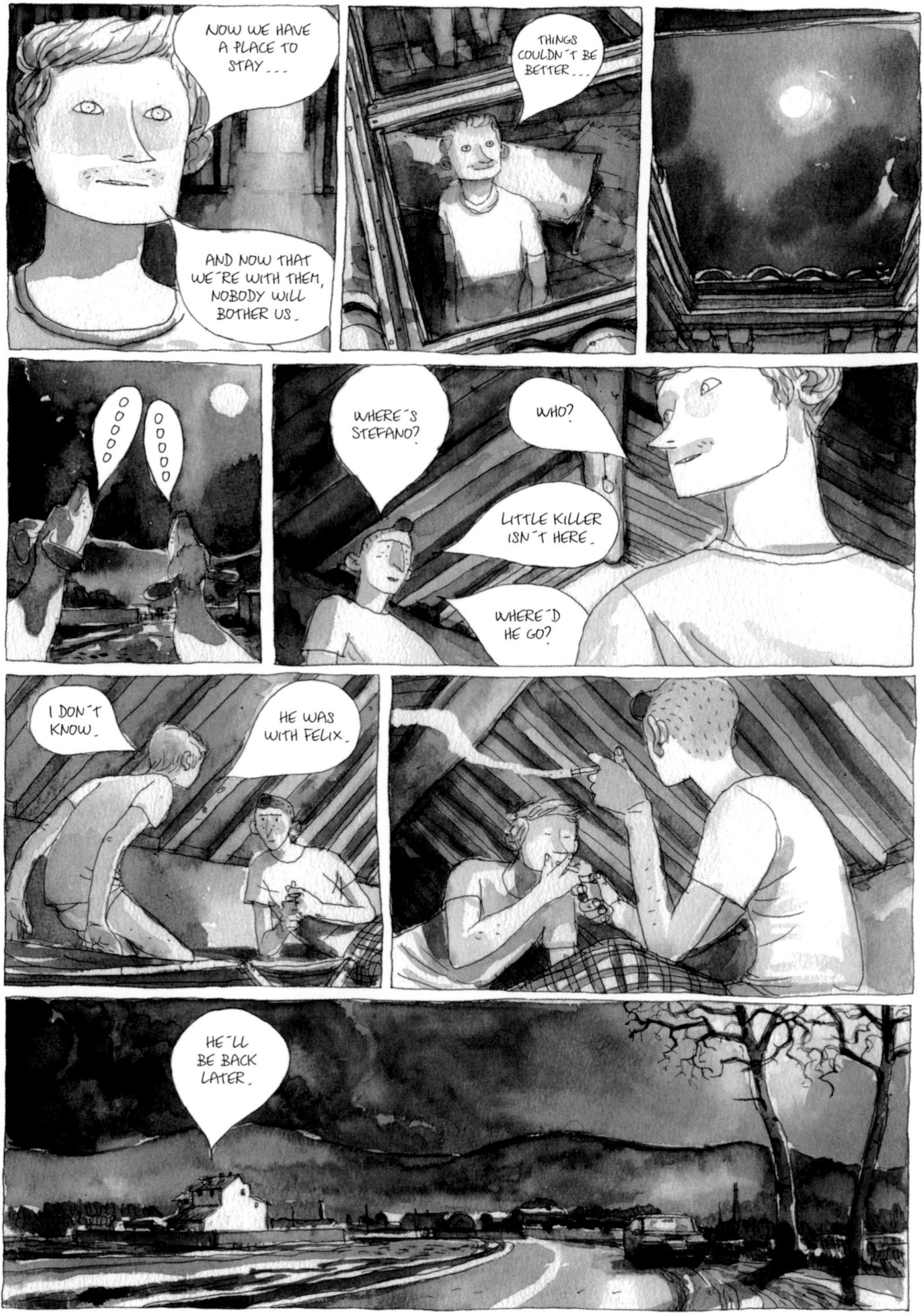
NOW WE HAVE A PLACE TO STAY...
AND NOW THAT WE'RE WITH THEM, NOBODY WILL BOTHER US.
THINGS COULDN'T BE BETTER...
OOOOO
OOOOO
WHERE'S STEFANO?
WHO?
LITTLE KILLER ISN'T HERE.
WHERE'D HE GO?
I DON'T KNOW.
HE WAS WITH FELIX.
HE'LL BE BACK LATER.

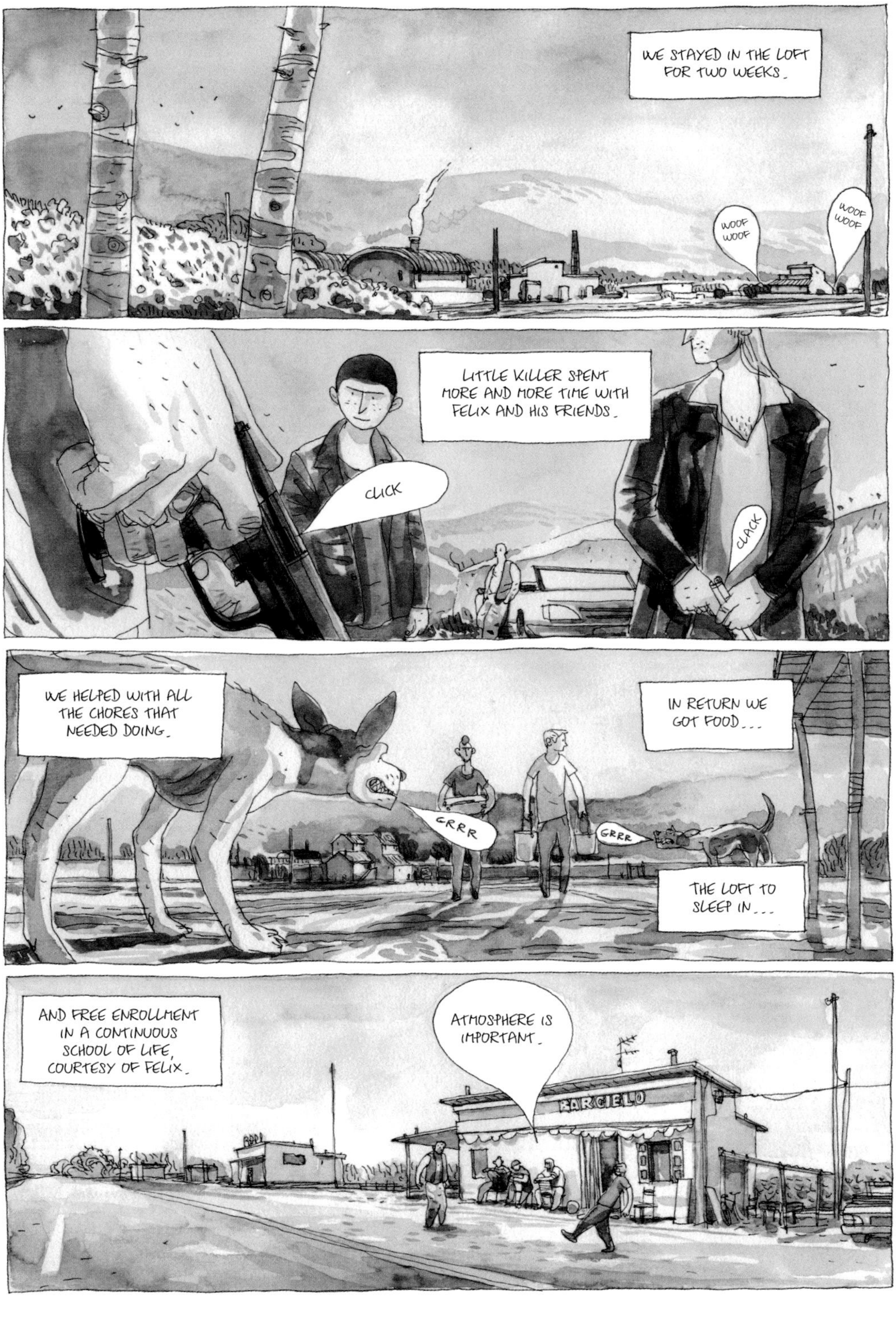
WE STAYED IN THE LOFT FOR TWO WEEKS.
WOOF WOOF
WOOF WOOF
LITTLE KILLER SPENT MORE AND MORE TIME WITH FELIX AND HIS FRIENDS.
CLICK
CLACK
WE HELPED WITH ALL THE CHORES THAT NEEDED DOING.
IN RETURN WE GOT FOOD...
GRRR
GRRR
THE LOFT TO SLEEP IN...
AND FREE ENROLLMENT IN A CONTINUOUS SCHOOL OF LIFE, COURTESY OF FELIX.
ATMOSPHERE IS IMPORTANT.
BARCIELO

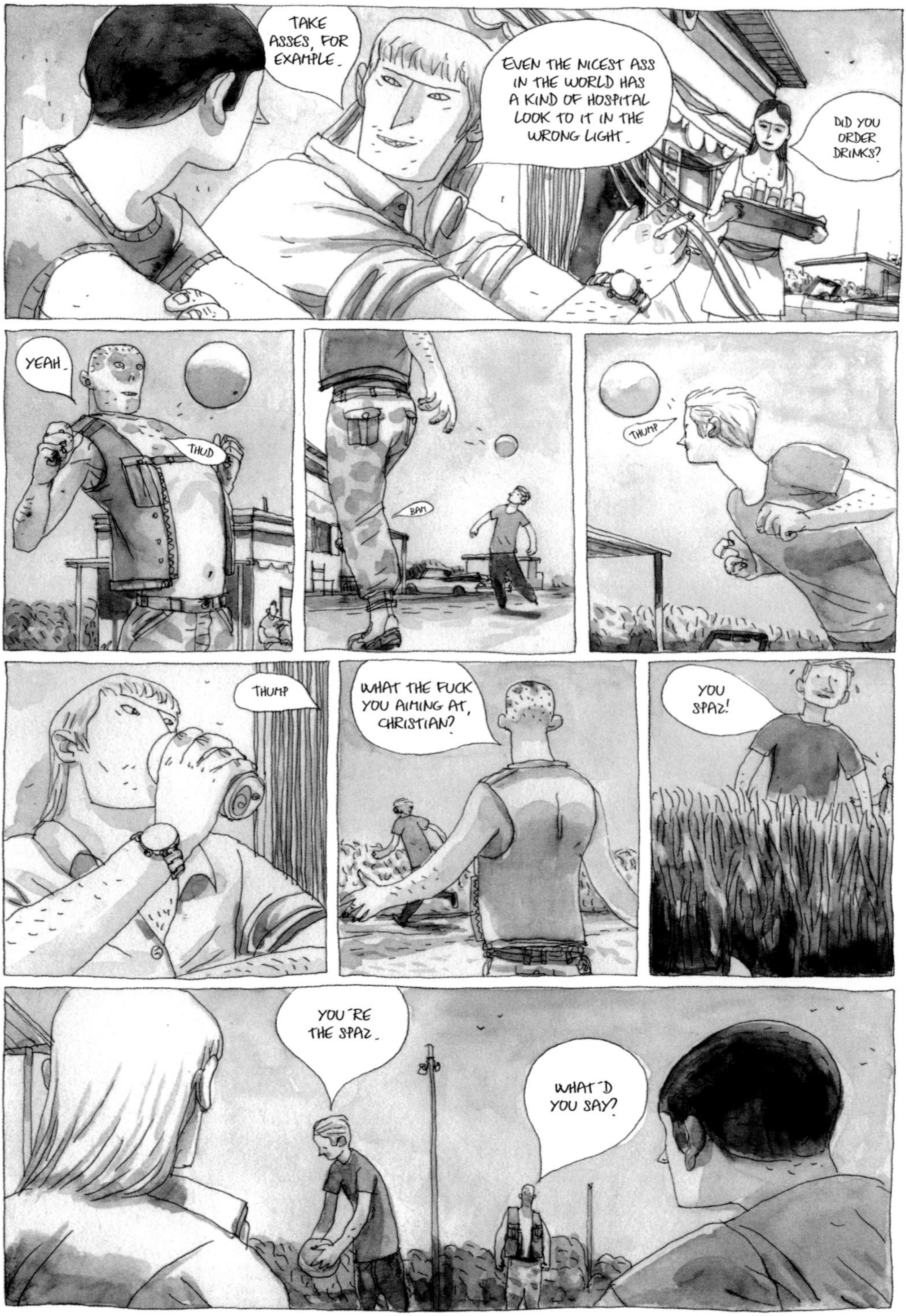
TAKE ASSES, FOR EXAMPLE.
EVEN THE NICEST ASS IN THE WORLD HAS A KIND OF HOSPITAL LOOK TO IT IN THE WRONG LIGHT.
DID YOU ORDER DRINKS?
YEAH.
THUD
BAM
THUMP
THUMP
WHAT THE FUCK YOU AIMING AT, CHRISTIAN?
YOU SPAZ!
YOU'RE THE SPAZ.
WHAT'D YOU SAY?

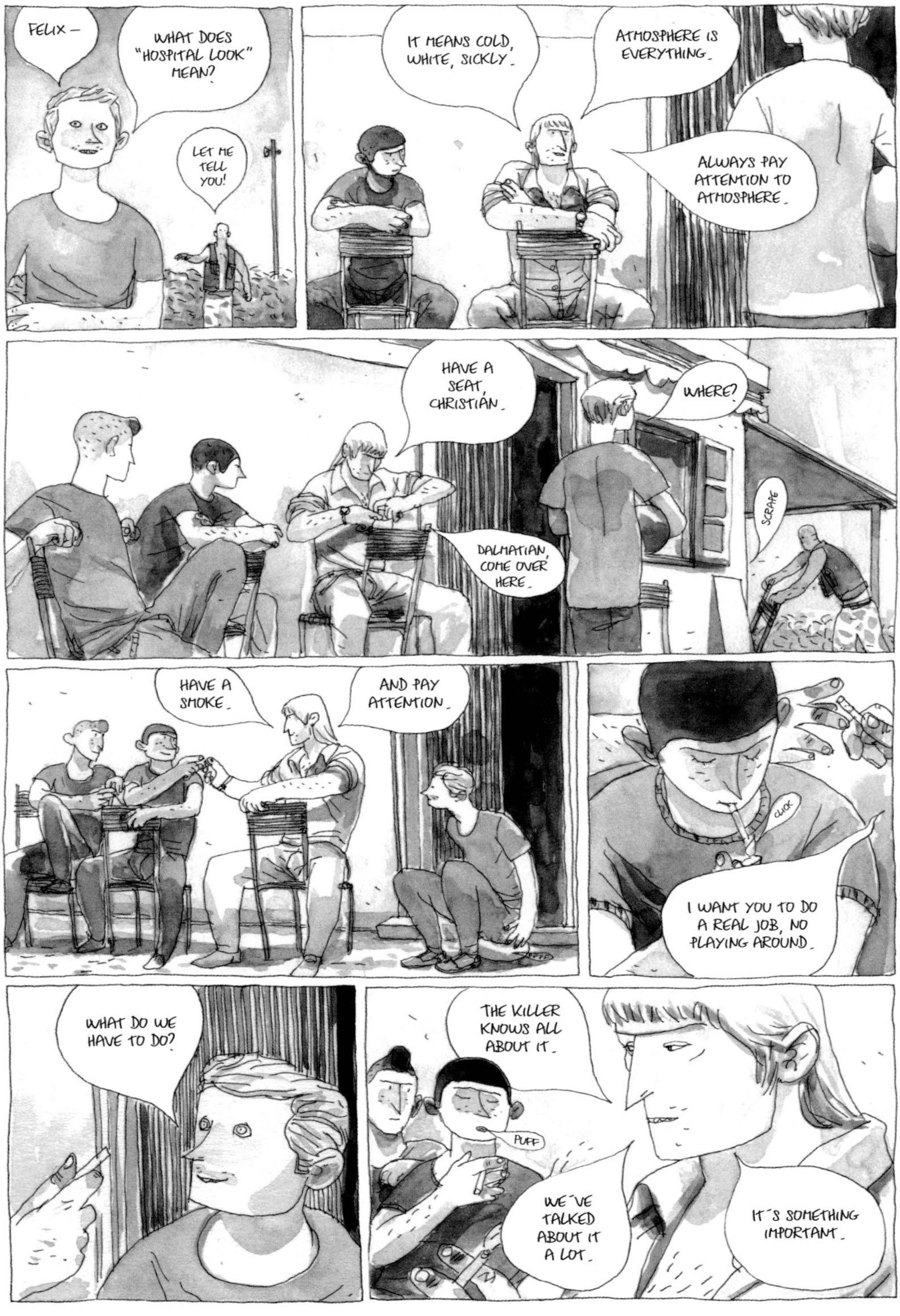

FELIX —
WHAT DOES "HOSPITAL LOOK" MEAN?
LET ME TELL YOU!
IT MEANS COLD, WHITE, SICKLY.
ATMOSPHERE IS EVERYTHING.
ALWAYS PAY ATTENTION TO ATMOSPHERE.
HAVE A SEAT, CHRISTIAN.
WHERE?
DALMATIAN, COME OVER HERE.
SCRAPE
HAVE A SMOKE.
AND PAY ATTENTION.
CLICK
I WANT YOU TO DO A REAL JOB, NO PLAYING AROUND.
WHAT DO WE HAVE TO DO?
THE KILLER KNOWS ALL ABOUT IT.
PUFF
WE'VE TALKED ABOUT IT A LOT.
IT'S SOMETHING IMPORTANT.

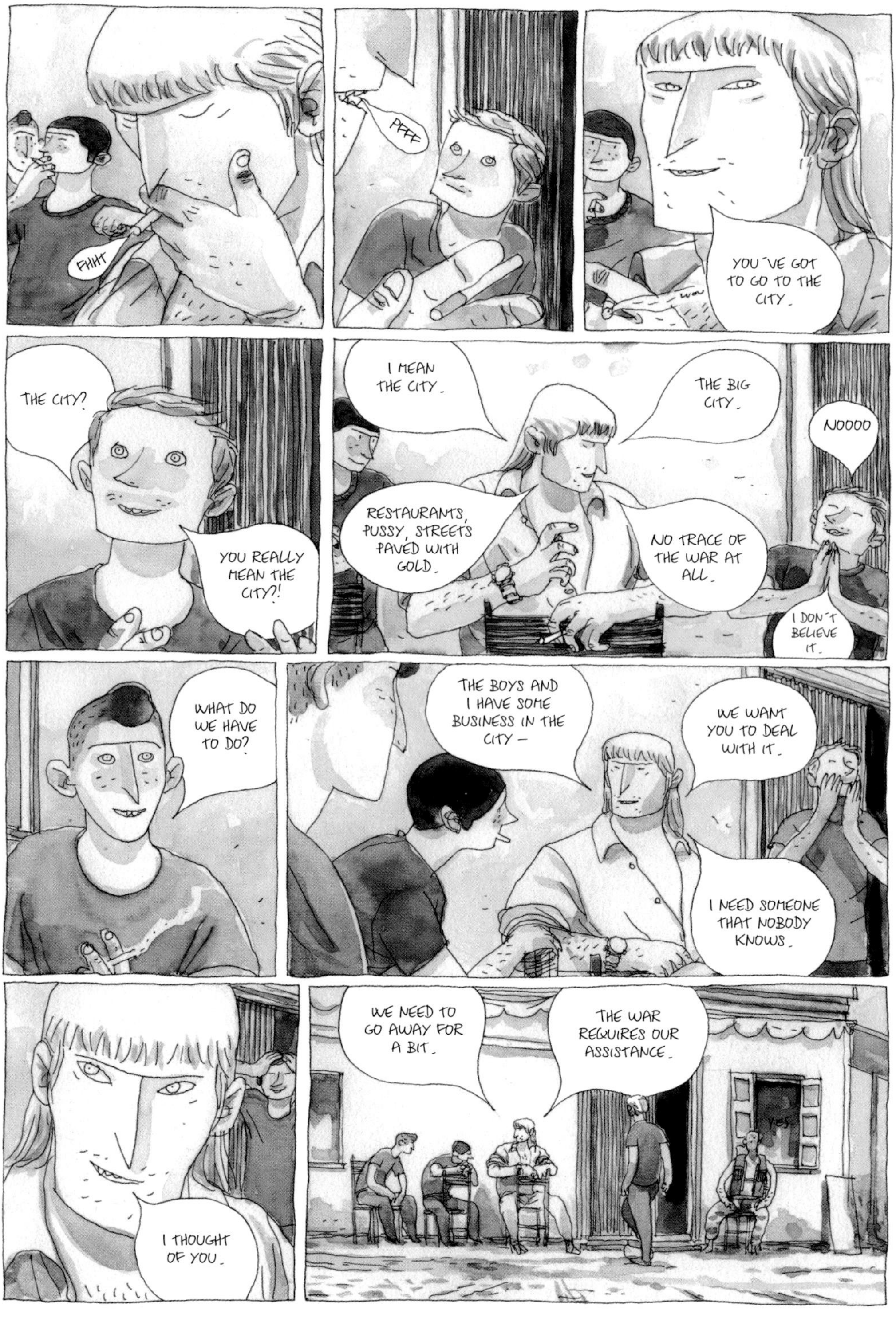
FHHT
PFFF
YOU´VE GOT TO GO TO THE CITY.
THE CITY?
YOU REALLY MEAN THE CITY?!
I MEAN THE CITY.
THE BIG CITY.
RESTAURANTS, PUSSY, STREETS PAVED WITH GOLD.
NO TRACE OF THE WAR AT ALL.
NOOOO
I DON´T BELIEVE IT.
WHAT DO WE HAVE TO DO?
THE BOYS AND I HAVE SOME BUSINESS IN THE CITY –
WE WANT YOU TO DEAL WITH IT.
I NEED SOMEONE THAT NOBODY KNOWS.
I THOUGHT OF YOU.
WE NEED TO GO AWAY FOR A BIT.
THE WAR REQUIRES OUR ASSISTANCE.

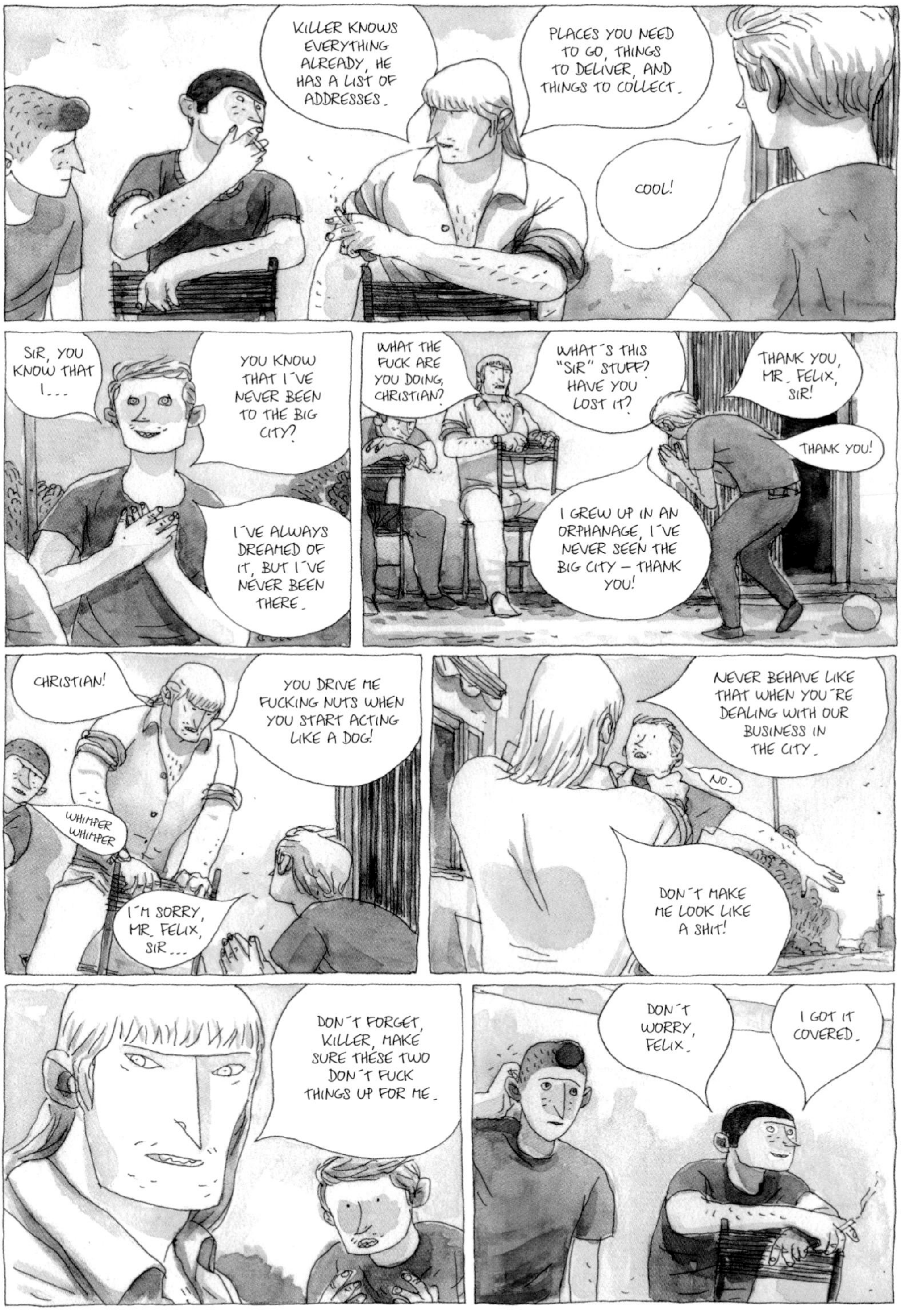

KILLER KNOWS EVERYTHING ALREADY, HE HAS A LIST OF ADDRESSES.
PLACES YOU NEED TO GO, THINGS TO DELIVER, AND THINGS TO COLLECT.
COOL!
SIR, YOU KNOW THAT I...
YOU KNOW THAT I'VE NEVER BEEN TO THE BIG CITY?
I'VE ALWAYS DREAMED OF IT, BUT I'VE NEVER BEEN THERE.
WHAT THE FUCK ARE YOU DOING, CHRISTIAN?
WHAT'S THIS "SIR" STUFF? HAVE YOU LOST IT?
THANK YOU, MR. FELIX, SIR!
THANK YOU!
I GREW UP IN AN ORPHANAGE, I'VE NEVER SEEN THE BIG CITY — THANK YOU!
CHRISTIAN!
YOU DRIVE ME FUCKING NUTS WHEN YOU START ACTING LIKE A DOG!
WHIMPER WHIMPER
I'M SORRY, MR. FELIX, SIR...
NEVER BEHAVE LIKE THAT WHEN YOU'RE DEALING WITH OUR BUSINESS IN THE CITY.
NO.
DON'T MAKE ME LOOK LIKE A SHIT!
DON'T FORGET, KILLER, MAKE SURE THESE TWO DON'T FUCK THINGS UP FOR ME.
DON'T WORRY, FELIX.
I GOT IT COVERED.

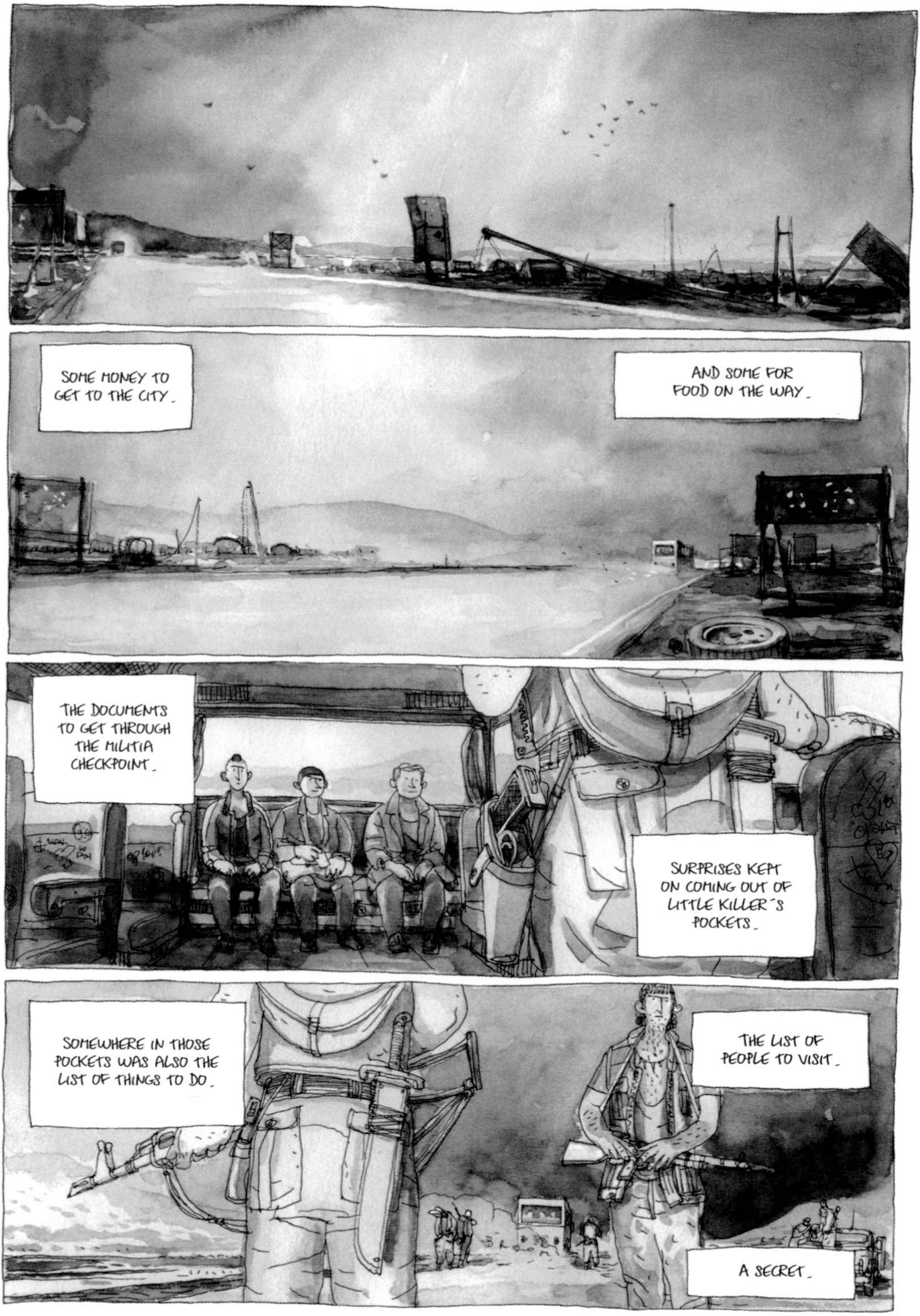
SOME MONEY TO GET TO THE CITY.
AND SOME FOR FOOD ON THE WAY.
THE DOCUMENTS TO GET THROUGH THE MILITIA CHECKPOINT.
SURPRISES KEPT ON COMING OUT OF LITTLE KILLER'S POCKETS.
SOMEWHERE IN THOSE POCKETS WAS ALSO THE LIST OF THINGS TO DO.
THE LIST OF PEOPLE TO VISIT.
A SECRET.

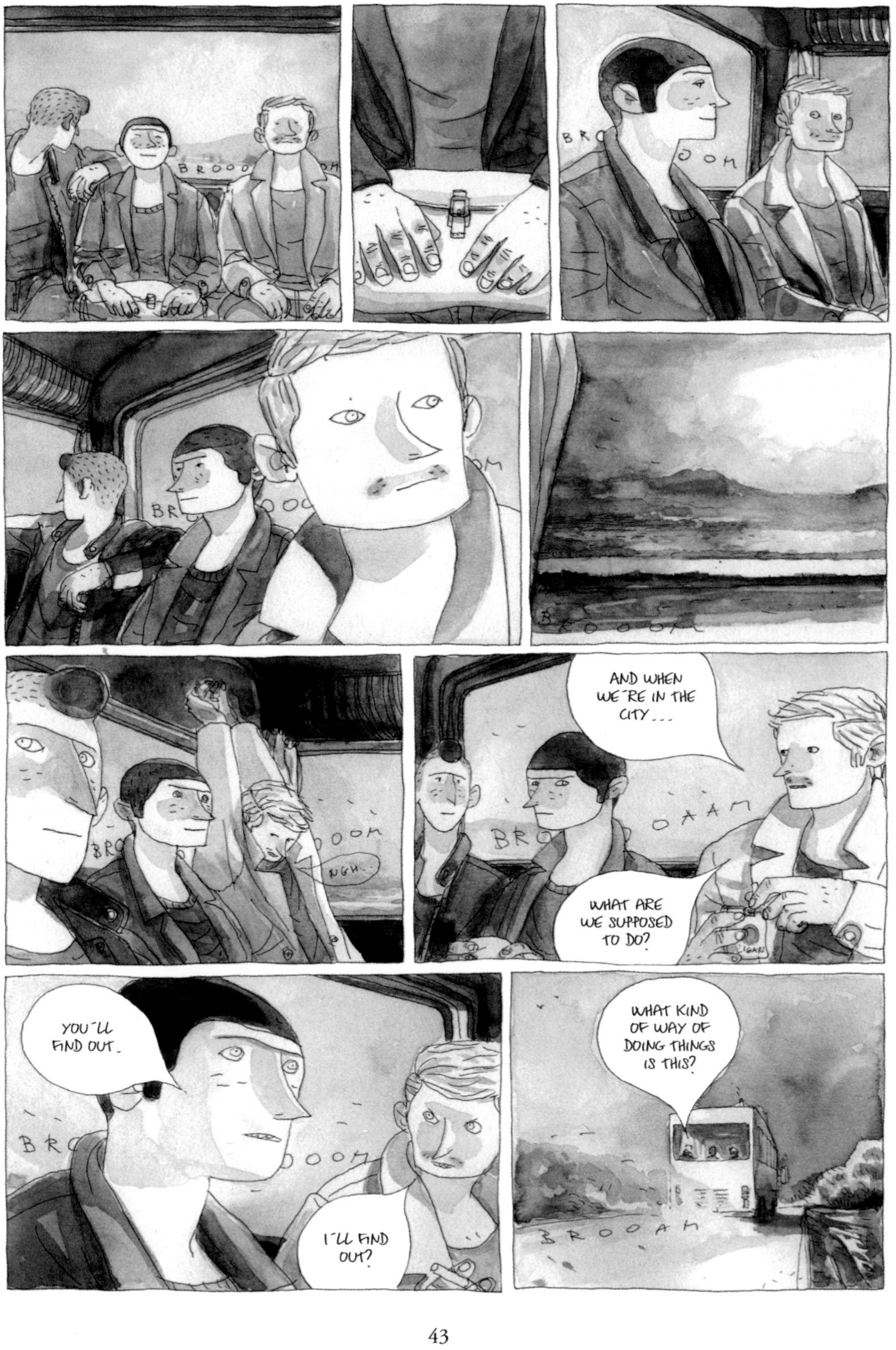
NGH...
AND WHEN WE'RE IN THE CITY...
WHAT ARE WE SUPPOSED TO DO?
YOU'LL FIND OUT.
I'LL FIND OUT?
WHAT KIND OF WAY OF DOING THINGS IS THIS?
BROOAM

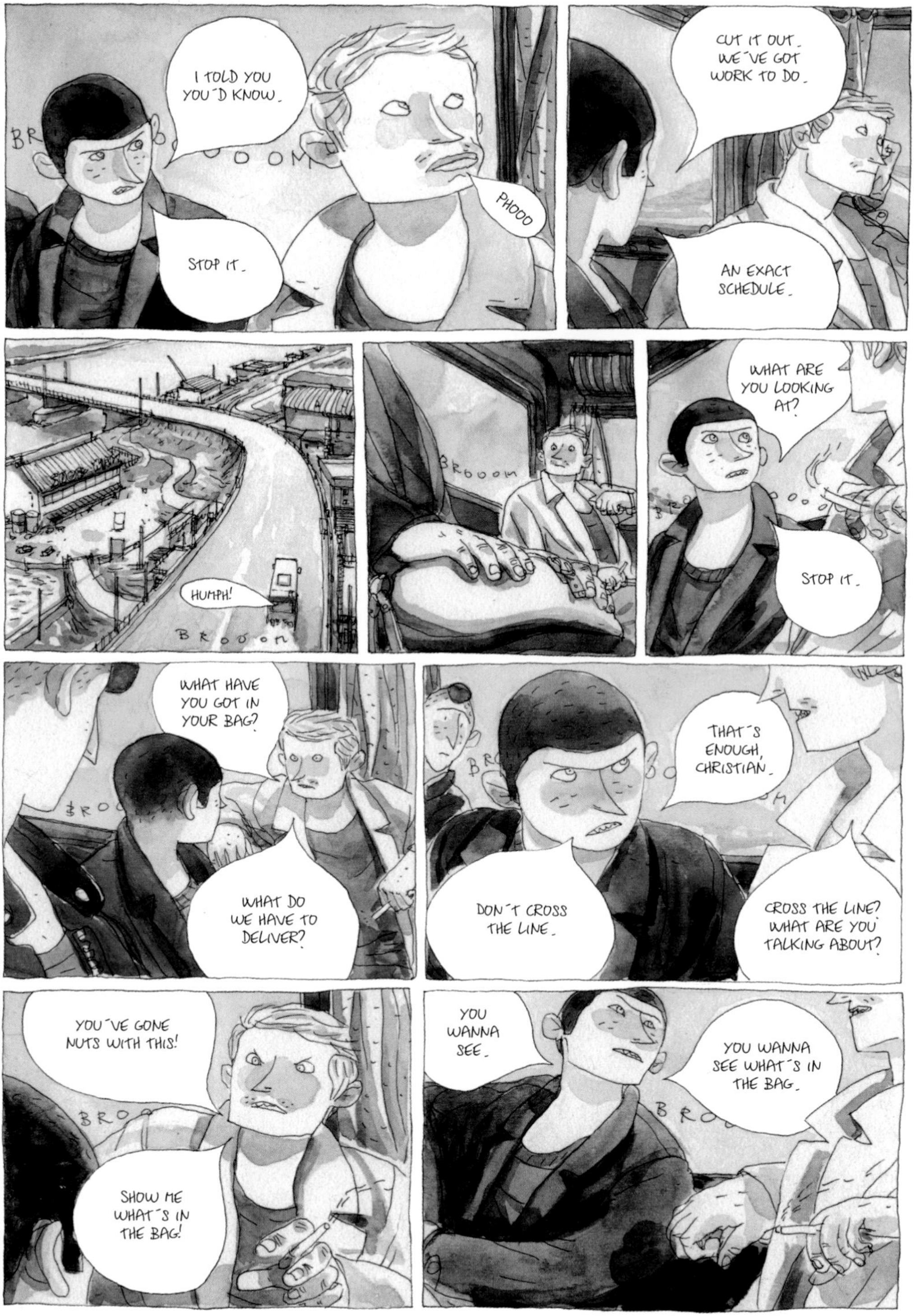
I TOLD YOU YOU'D KNOW.
BROOOOM
STOP IT.
PHOOO
CUT IT OUT. WE'VE GOT WORK TO DO.
AN EXACT SCHEDULE.
HUMPH!
BROOOM
BROOOM
WHAT ARE YOU LOOKING AT?
STOP IT.
WHAT HAVE YOU GOT IN YOUR BAG?
WHAT DO WE HAVE TO DELIVER?
THAT'S ENOUGH, CHRISTIAN.
DON'T CROSS THE LINE.
CROSS THE LINE? WHAT ARE YOU TALKING ABOUT?
YOU'VE GONE NUTS WITH THIS!
SHOW ME WHAT'S IN THE BAG!
YOU WANNA SEE.
YOU WANNA SEE WHAT'S IN THE BAG.

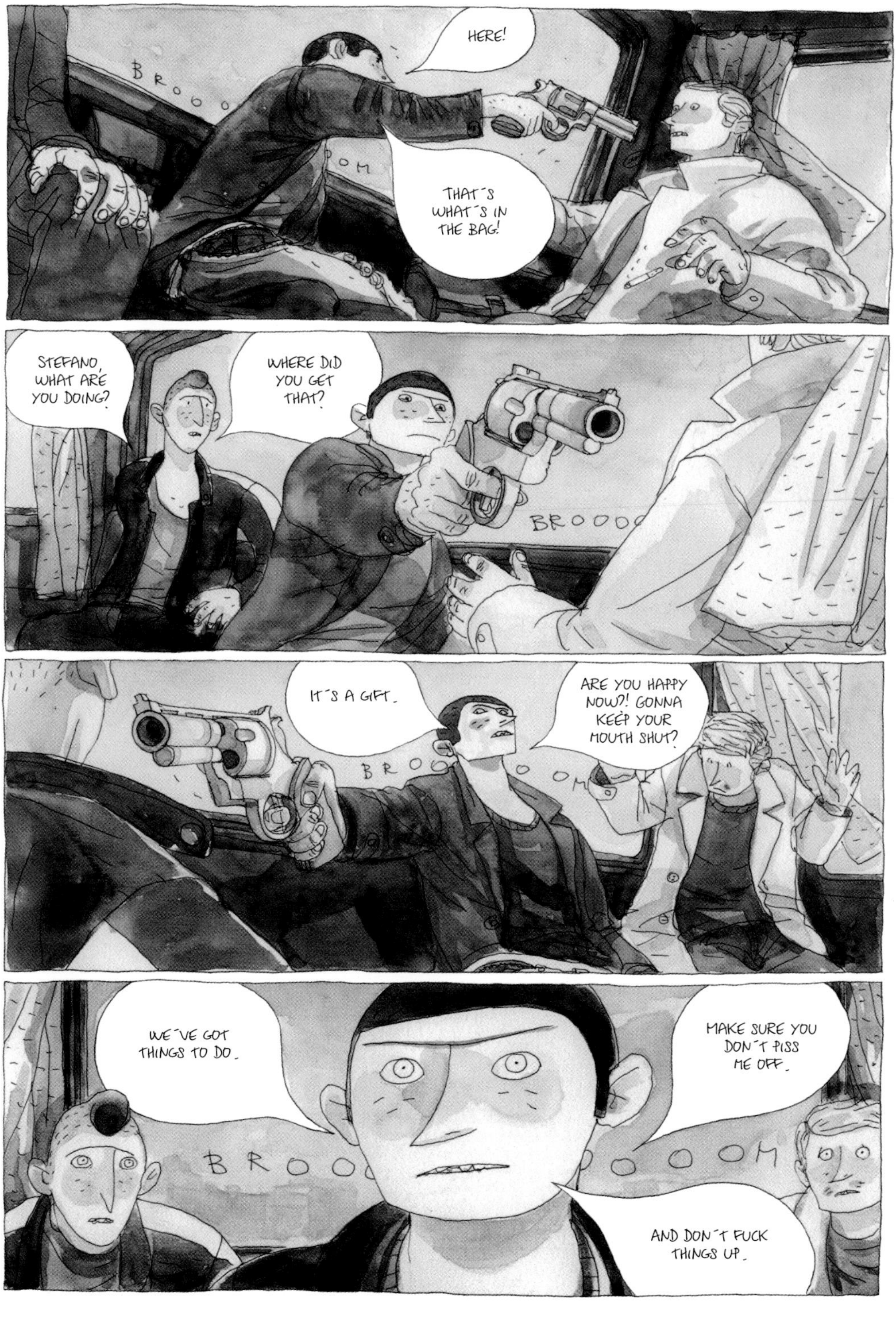
HERE!
THAT´S WHAT´S IN THE BAG!
BROOOOOM
STEFANO, WHAT ARE YOU DOING?
WHERE DID YOU GET THAT?
BROOOO
IT´S A GIFT.
ARE YOU HAPPY NOW?! GONNA KEEP YOUR MOUTH SHUT?
BROOOOOM
WE´VE GOT THINGS TO DO.
MAKE SURE YOU DON´T PISS ME OFF.
BROOOOOOOOM
AND DON´T FUCK THINGS UP.

2

In the Big City

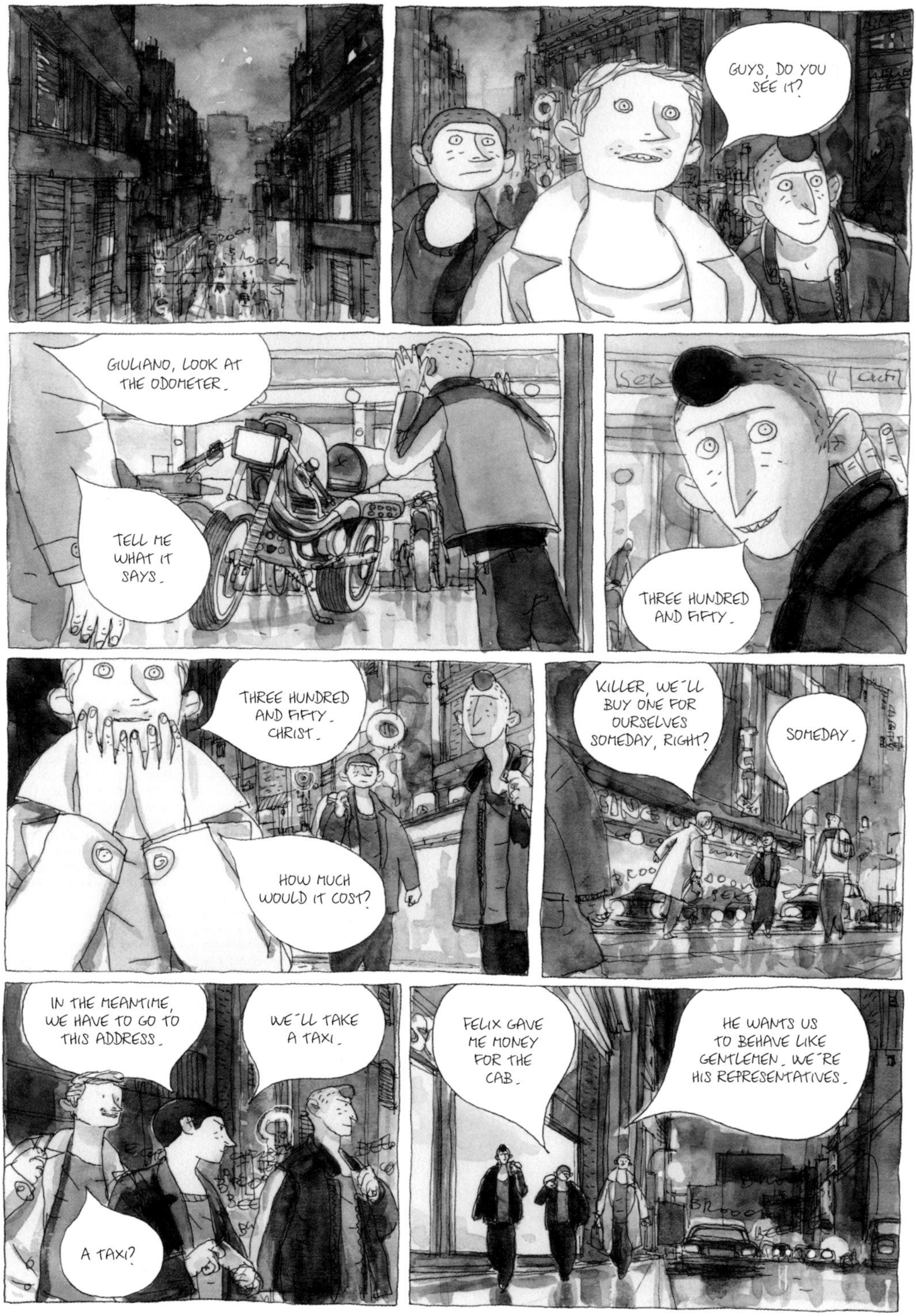
GUYS, DO YOU SEE IT?
GIULIANO, LOOK AT THE ODOMETER.
TELL ME WHAT IT SAYS.
THREE HUNDRED AND FIFTY.
THREE HUNDRED AND FIFTY. CHRIST.
HOW MUCH WOULD IT COST?
KILLER, WE'LL BUY ONE FOR OURSELVES SOMEDAY, RIGHT?
SOMEDAY.
IN THE MEANTIME, WE HAVE TO GO TO THIS ADDRESS.
WE'LL TAKE A TAXI.
A TAXI?
FELIX GAVE ME MONEY FOR THE CAB.
HE WANTS US TO BEHAVE LIKE GENTLEMEN. WE'RE HIS REPRESENTATIVES.

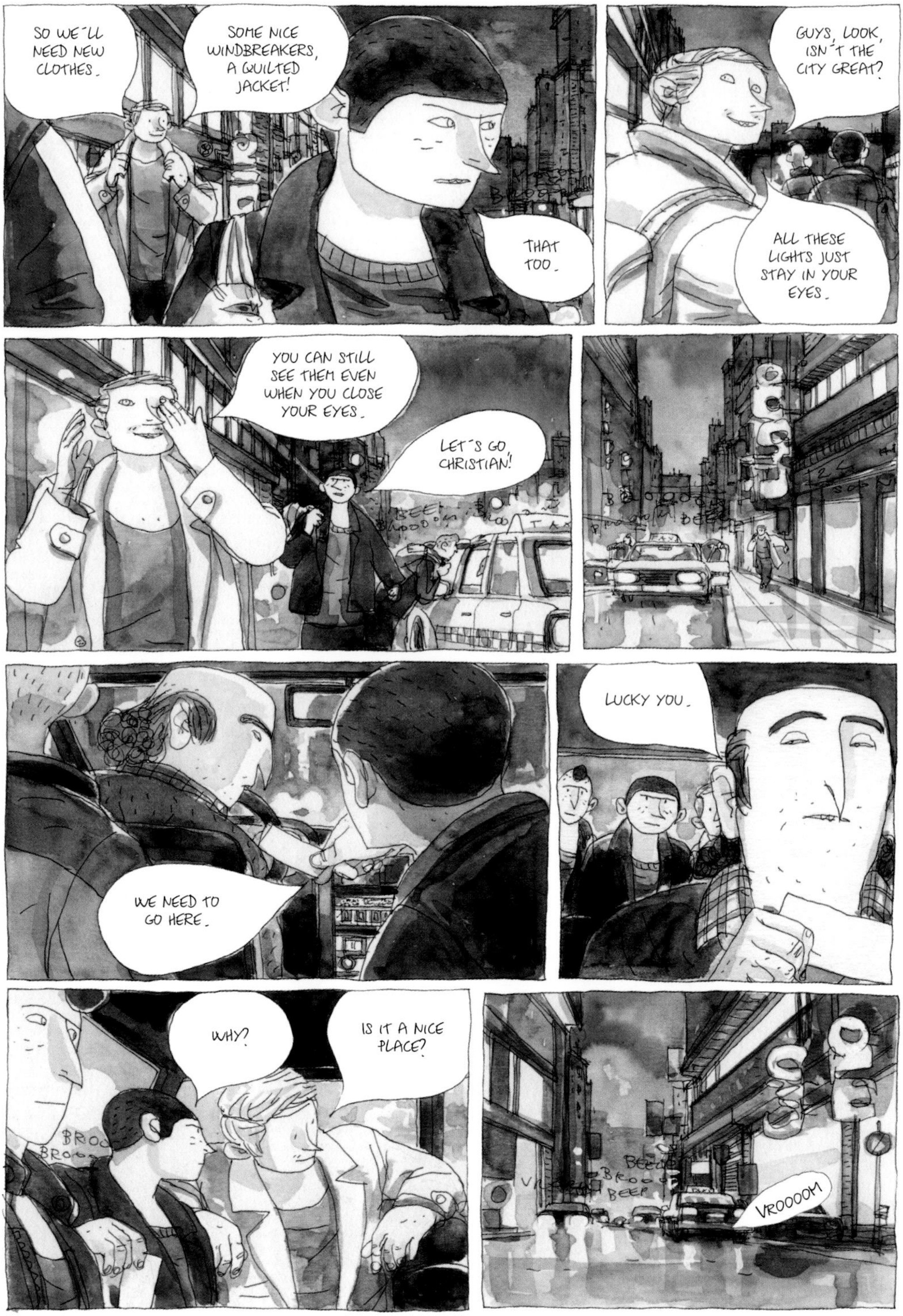
SO WE'LL NEED NEW CLOTHES.
SOME NICE WINDBREAKERS, A QUILTED JACKET!
THAT TOO.
GUYS, LOOK, ISN'T THE CITY GREAT?
ALL THESE LIGHTS JUST STAY IN YOUR EYES.
YOU CAN STILL SEE THEM EVEN WHEN YOU CLOSE YOUR EYES.
LET'S GO, CHRISTIAN!
WE NEED TO GO HERE.
LUCKY YOU.
WHY?
IS IT A NICE PLACE?
VROOOOM

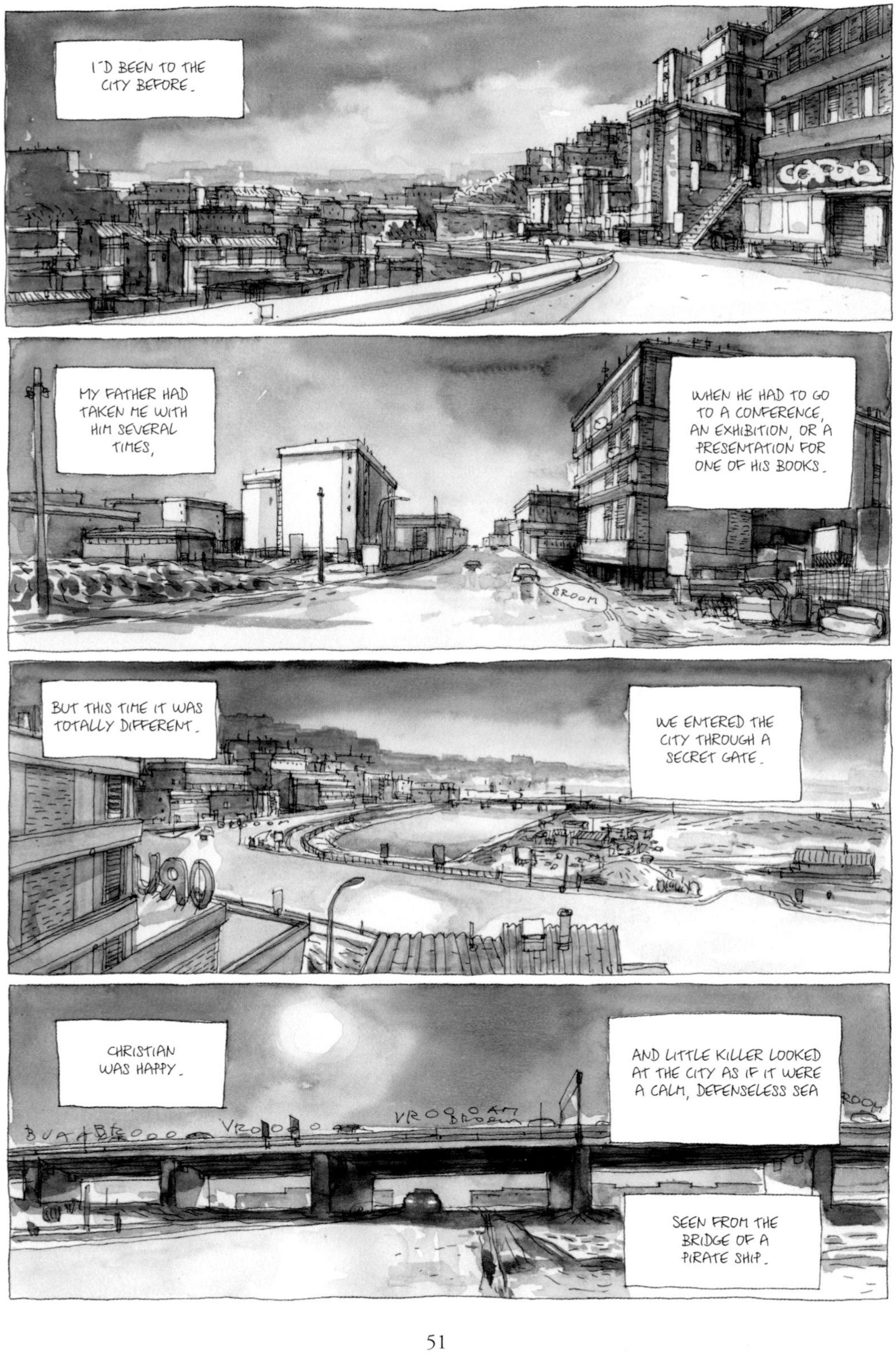
I'D BEEN TO THE CITY BEFORE.
MY FATHER HAD TAKEN ME WITH HIM SEVERAL TIMES,
WHEN HE HAD TO GO TO A CONFERENCE, AN EXHIBITION, OR A PRESENTATION FOR ONE OF HIS BOOKS.
BROOM
BUT THIS TIME IT WAS TOTALLY DIFFERENT.
WE ENTERED THE CITY THROUGH A SECRET GATE.
CHRISTIAN WAS HAPPY.
AND LITTLE KILLER LOOKED AT THE CITY AS IF IT WERE A CALM, DEFENSELESS SEA
SEEN FROM THE BRIDGE OF A PIRATE SHIP.

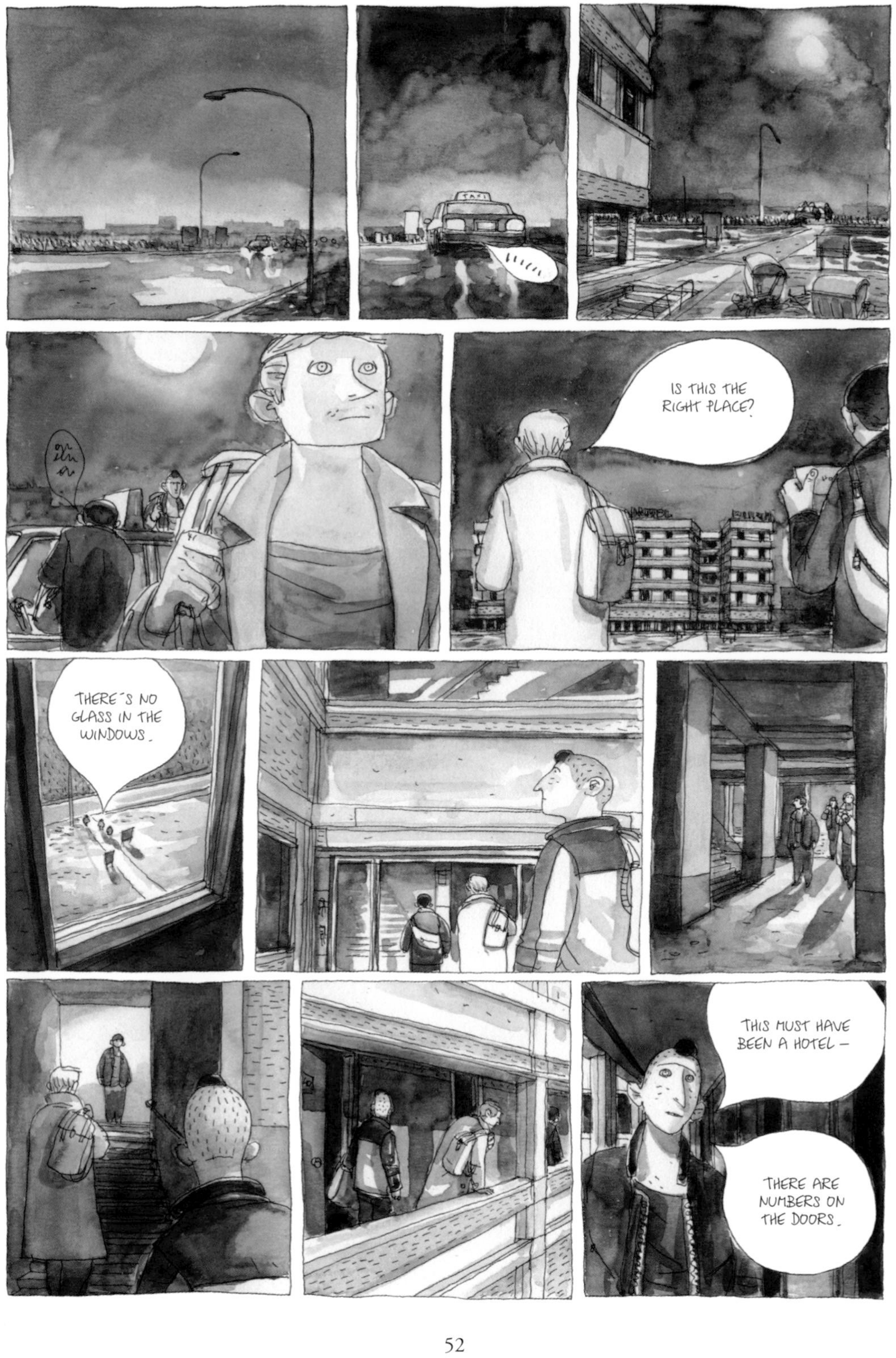
IS THIS THE RIGHT PLACE?
THERE´S NO GLASS IN THE WINDOWS.
THIS MUST HAVE BEEN A HOTEL –
THERE ARE NUMBERS ON THE DOORS.

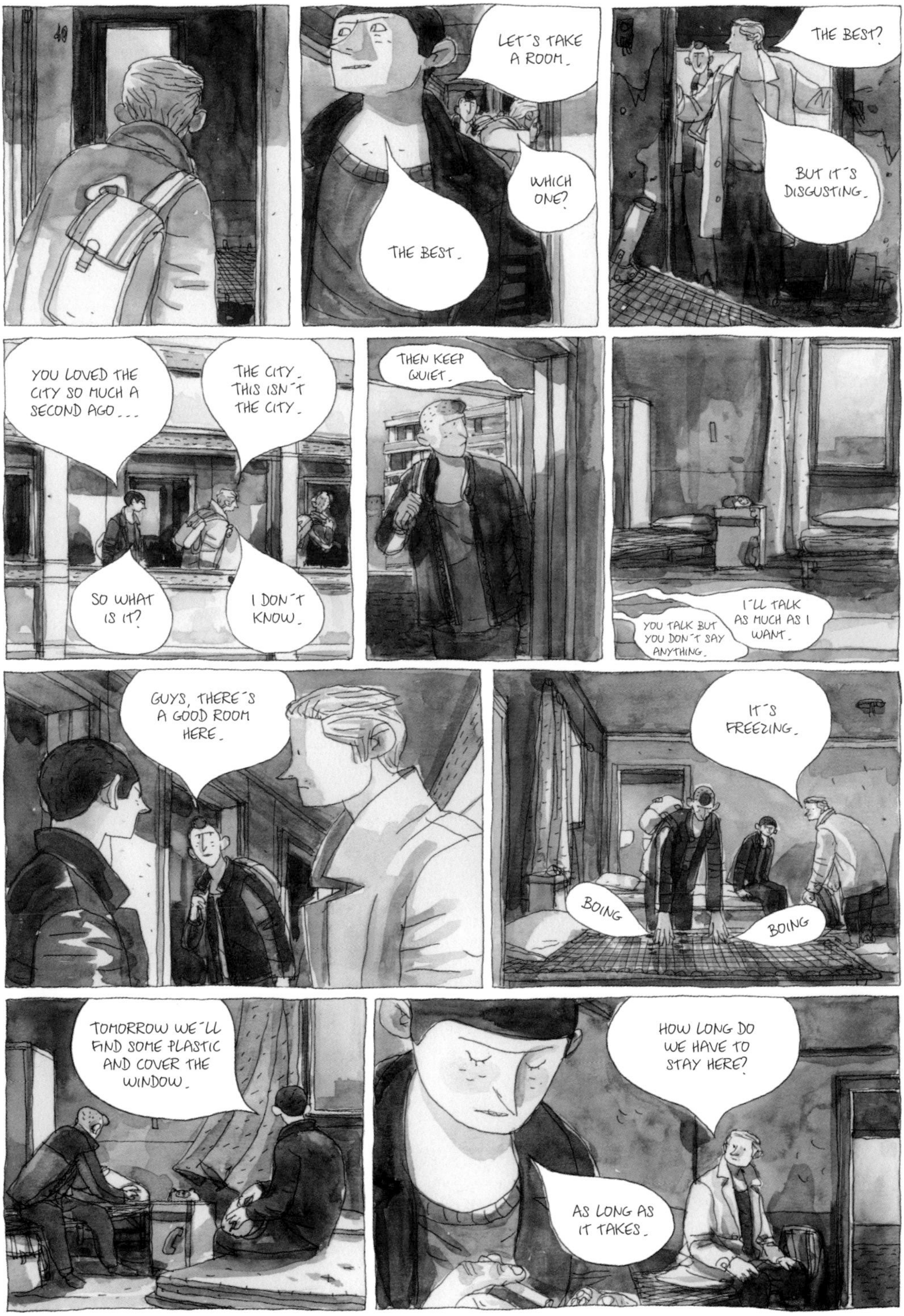
LET´S TAKE A ROOM.
WHICH ONE?
THE BEST.
THE BEST?
BUT IT´S DISGUSTING.
YOU LOVED THE CITY SO MUCH A SECOND AGO...
THE CITY. THIS ISN´T THE CITY.
SO WHAT IS IT?
I DON´T KNOW.
THEN KEEP QUIET.
YOU TALK BUT YOU DON´T SAY ANYTHING.
I´LL TALK AS MUCH AS I WANT.
GUYS, THERE´S A GOOD ROOM HERE.
IT´S FREEZING.
BOING
BOING
TOMORROW WE´LL FIND SOME PLASTIC AND COVER THE WINDOW.
HOW LONG DO WE HAVE TO STAY HERE?
AS LONG AS IT TAKES.

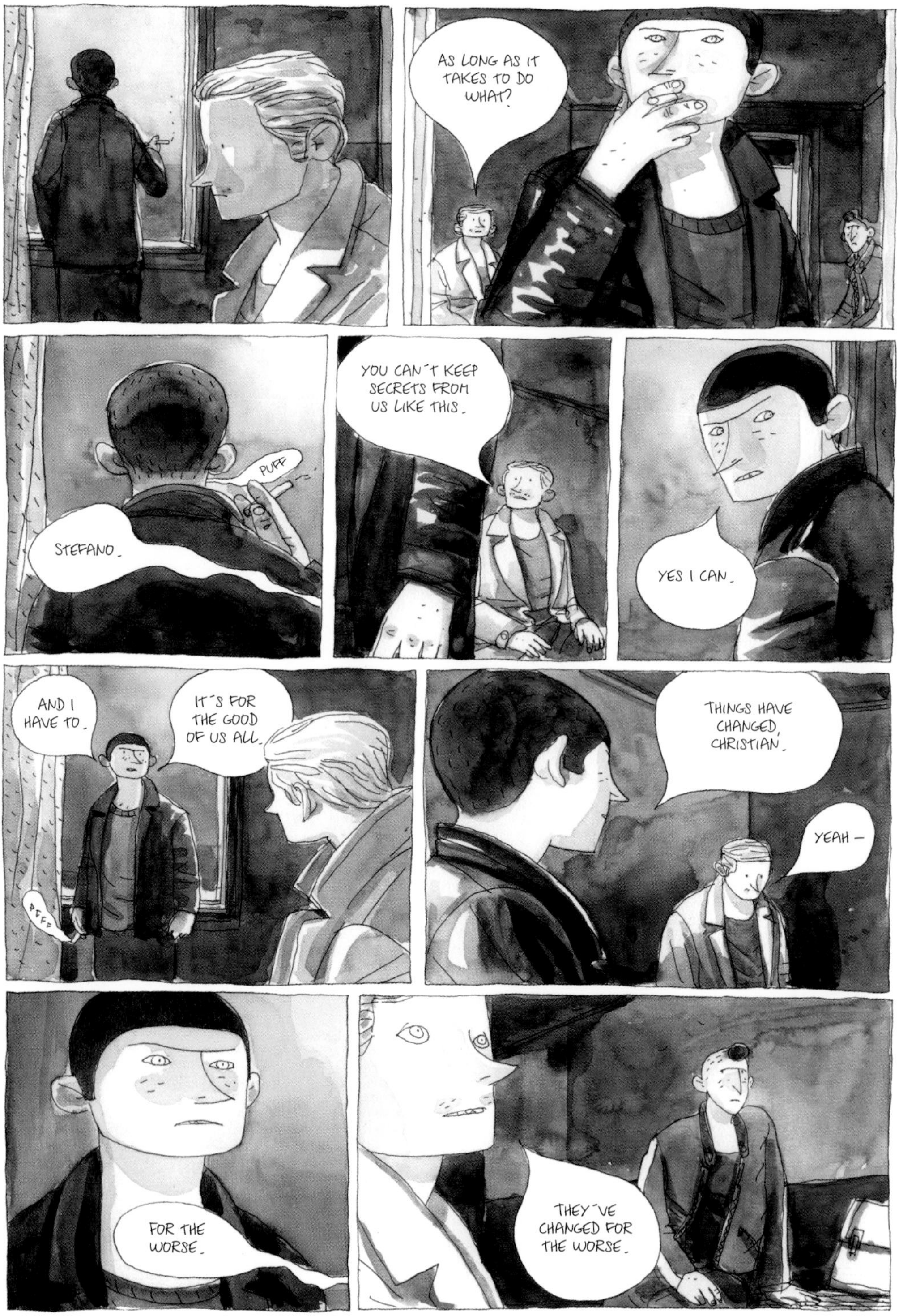
AS LONG AS IT TAKES TO DO WHAT?
PUFF
STEFANO.
YOU CAN'T KEEP SECRETS FROM US LIKE THIS.
YES I CAN.
AND I HAVE TO.
IT'S FOR THE GOOD OF US ALL.
PFFF
THINGS HAVE CHANGED, CHRISTIAN.
YEAH —
FOR THE WORSE.
THEY'VE CHANGED FOR THE WORSE.

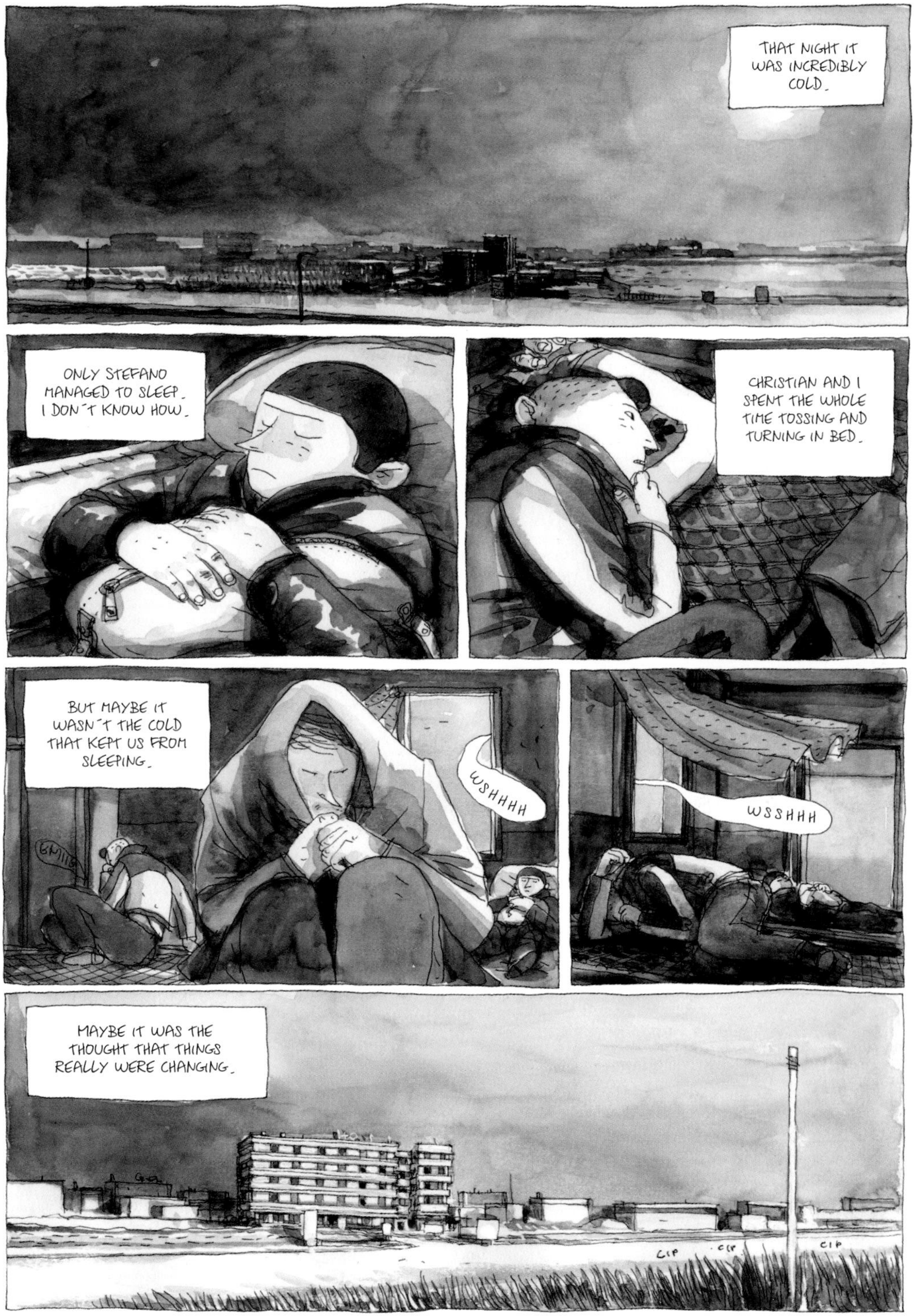
THAT NIGHT IT WAS INCREDIBLY COLD.
ONLY STEFANO MANAGED TO SLEEP. I DON'T KNOW HOW.
CHRISTIAN AND I SPENT THE WHOLE TIME TOSSING AND TURNING IN BED.
BUT MAYBE IT WASN'T THE COLD THAT KEPT US FROM SLEEPING.
WSHHHH
WSSHHH
MAYBE IT WAS THE THOUGHT THAT THINGS REALLY WERE CHANGING.

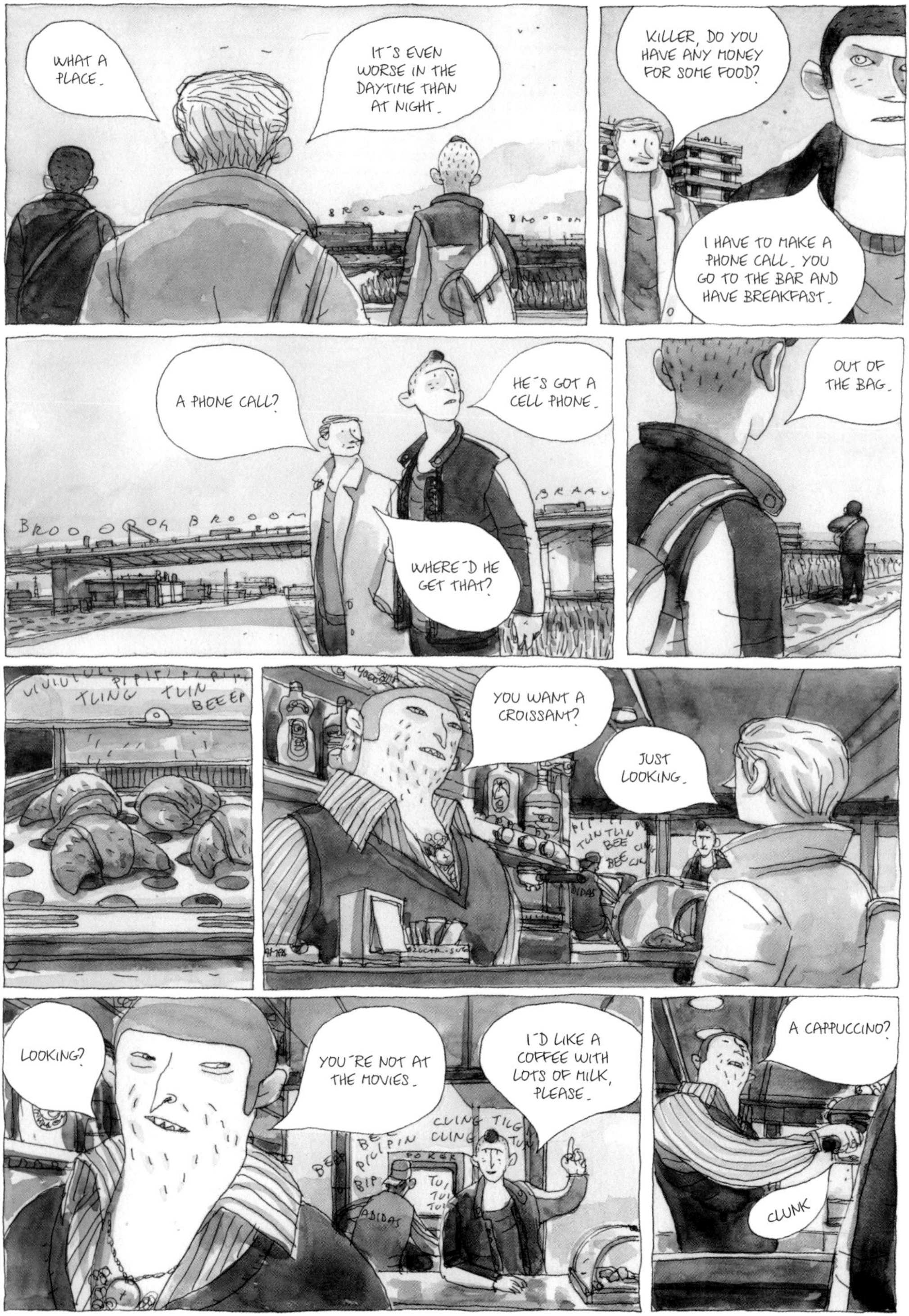
WHAT A PLACE.
IT'S EVEN WORSE IN THE DAYTIME THAN AT NIGHT.
KILLER, DO YOU HAVE ANY MONEY FOR SOME FOOD?
I HAVE TO MAKE A PHONE CALL. YOU GO TO THE BAR AND HAVE BREAKFAST.
A PHONE CALL?
HE'S GOT A CELL PHONE.
WHERE'D HE GET THAT?
OUT OF THE BAG.
TLING TLIN BEEEP
YOU WANT A CROISSANT?
JUST LOOKING.
LOOKING?
YOU'RE NOT AT THE MOVIES.
I'D LIKE A COFFEE WITH LOTS OF MILK, PLEASE.
A CAPPUCCINO?
CLUNK

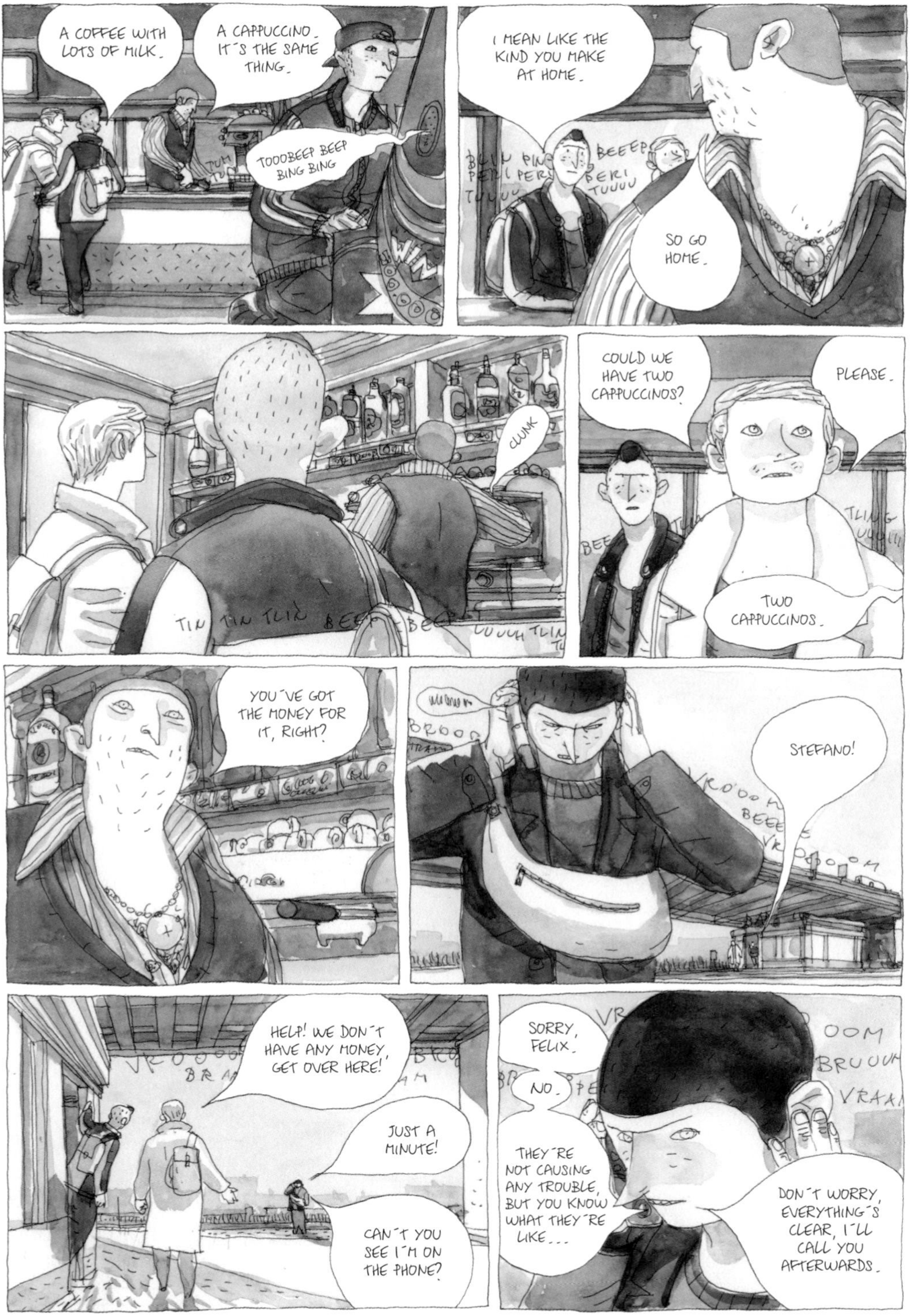
A COFFEE WITH LOTS OF MILK.
A CAPPUCCINO. IT'S THE SAME THING.
TOOOBEEP BEEP BING BING
I MEAN LIKE THE KIND YOU MAKE AT HOME.
SO GO HOME.
CLUNK
TIN TIN TLIN BEEP BEEP
COULD WE HAVE TWO CAPPUCCINOS?
PLEASE.
TWO CAPPUCCINOS.
YOU'VE GOT THE MONEY FOR IT, RIGHT?
STEFANO!
HELP! WE DON'T HAVE ANY MONEY, GET OVER HERE!
JUST A MINUTE!
CAN'T YOU SEE I'M ON THE PHONE?
SORRY, FELIX.
NO.
THEY'RE NOT CAUSING ANY TROUBLE, BUT YOU KNOW WHAT THEY'RE LIKE...
DON'T WORRY, EVERYTHING'S CLEAR, I'LL CALL YOU AFTERWARDS.

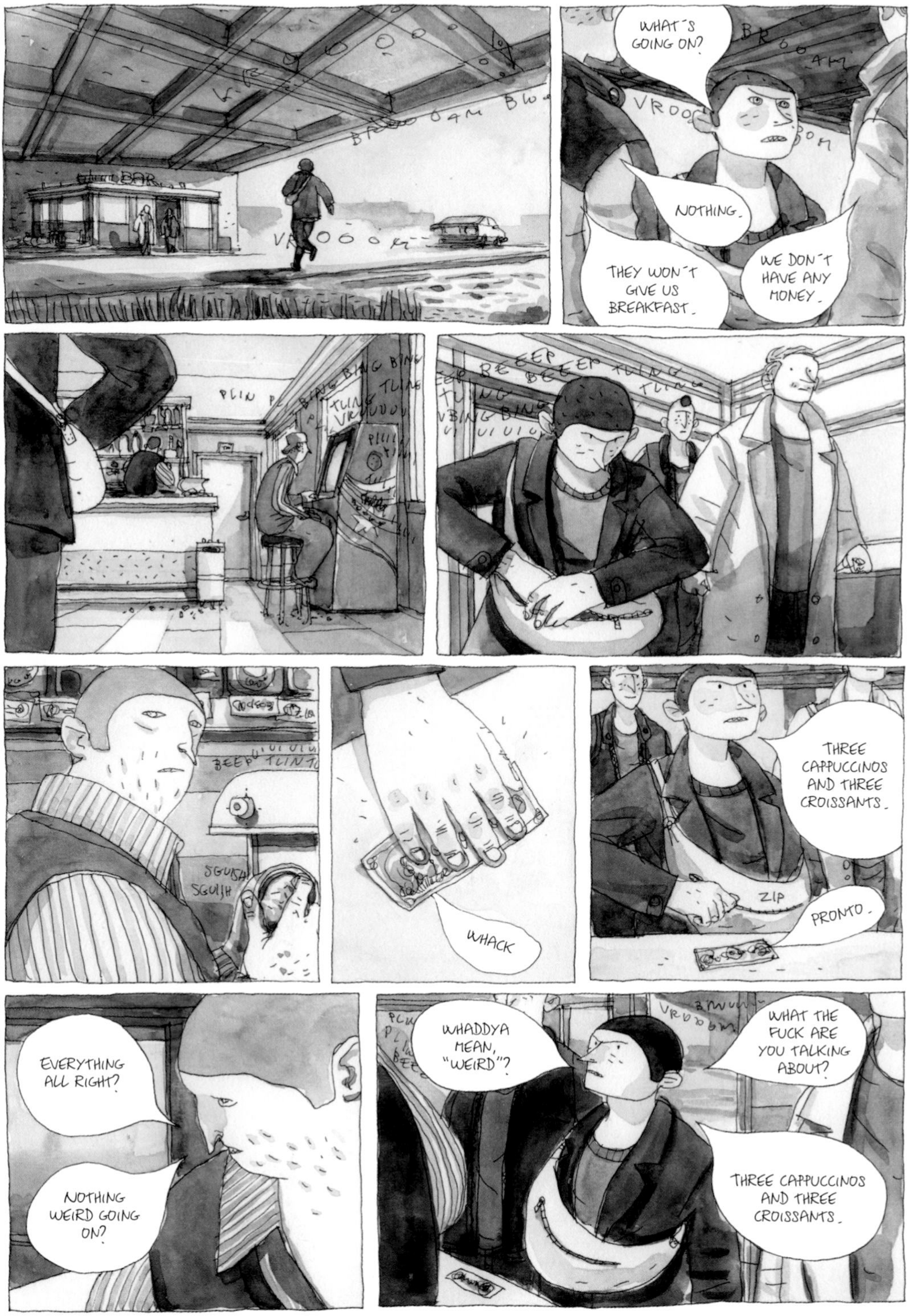
BAR
VROOOOM
WHAT'S GOING ON?
NOTHING.
THEY WON'T GIVE US BREAKFAST.
WE DON'T HAVE ANY MONEY.
PLIN
BING BING
BEEP BEEP TLING
BEEP
WHACK
THREE CAPPUCCINOS AND THREE CROISSANTS.
ZIP
PRONTO.
EVERYTHING ALL RIGHT?
NOTHING WEIRD GOING ON?
WHADDYA MEAN, "WEIRD"?
WHAT THE FUCK ARE YOU TALKING ABOUT?
THREE CAPPUCCINOS AND THREE CROISSANTS.

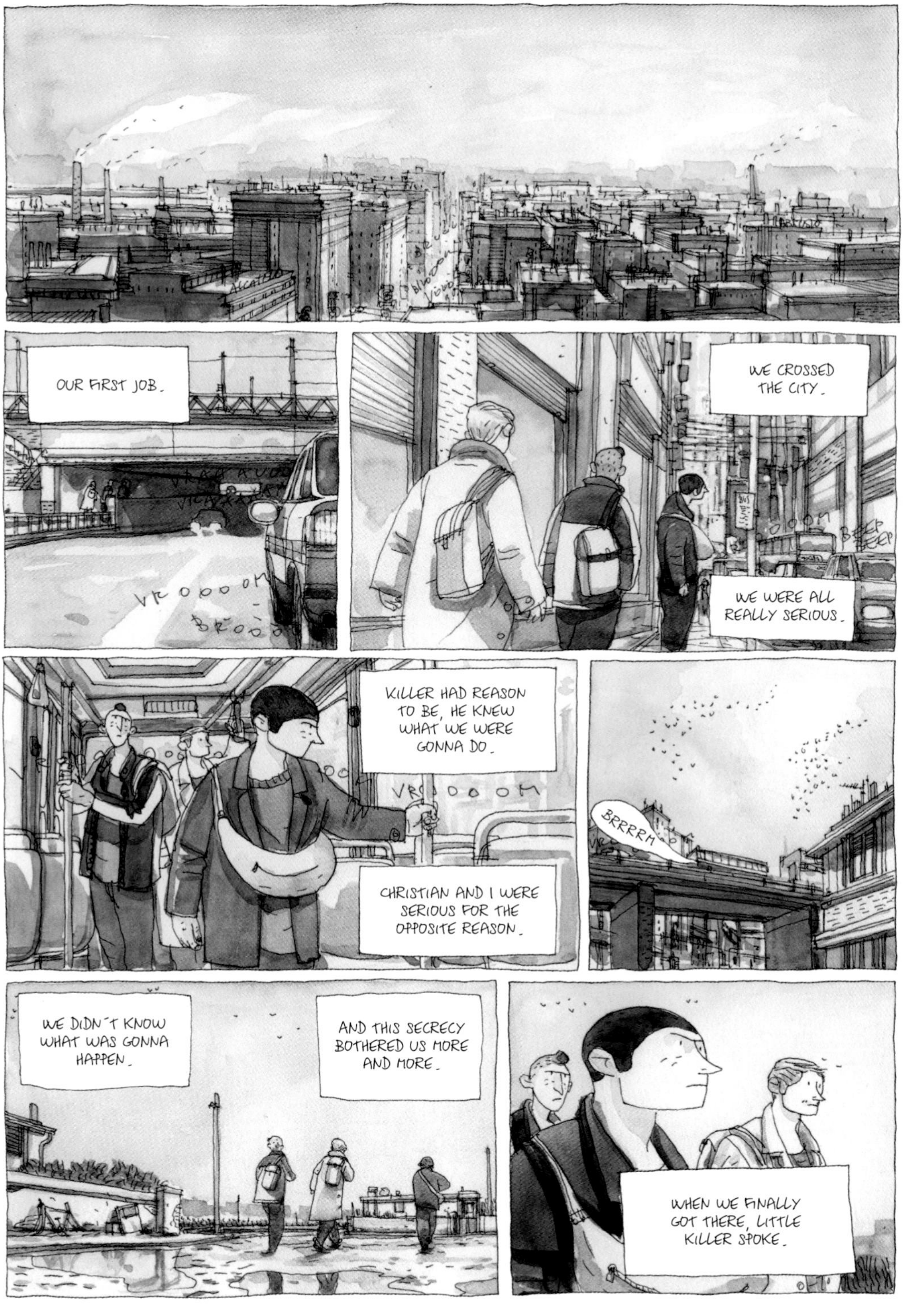
OUR FIRST JOB.
VROOOOM
WE CROSSED THE CITY.
WE WERE ALL REALLY SERIOUS.
KILLER HAD REASON TO BE, HE KNEW WHAT WE WERE GONNA DO.
VROOOOM
CHRISTIAN AND I WERE SERIOUS FOR THE OPPOSITE REASON.
BRRRRM
WE DIDN'T KNOW WHAT WAS GONNA HAPPEN.
AND THIS SECRECY BOTHERED US MORE AND MORE.
WHEN WE FINALLY GOT THERE, LITTLE KILLER SPOKE.

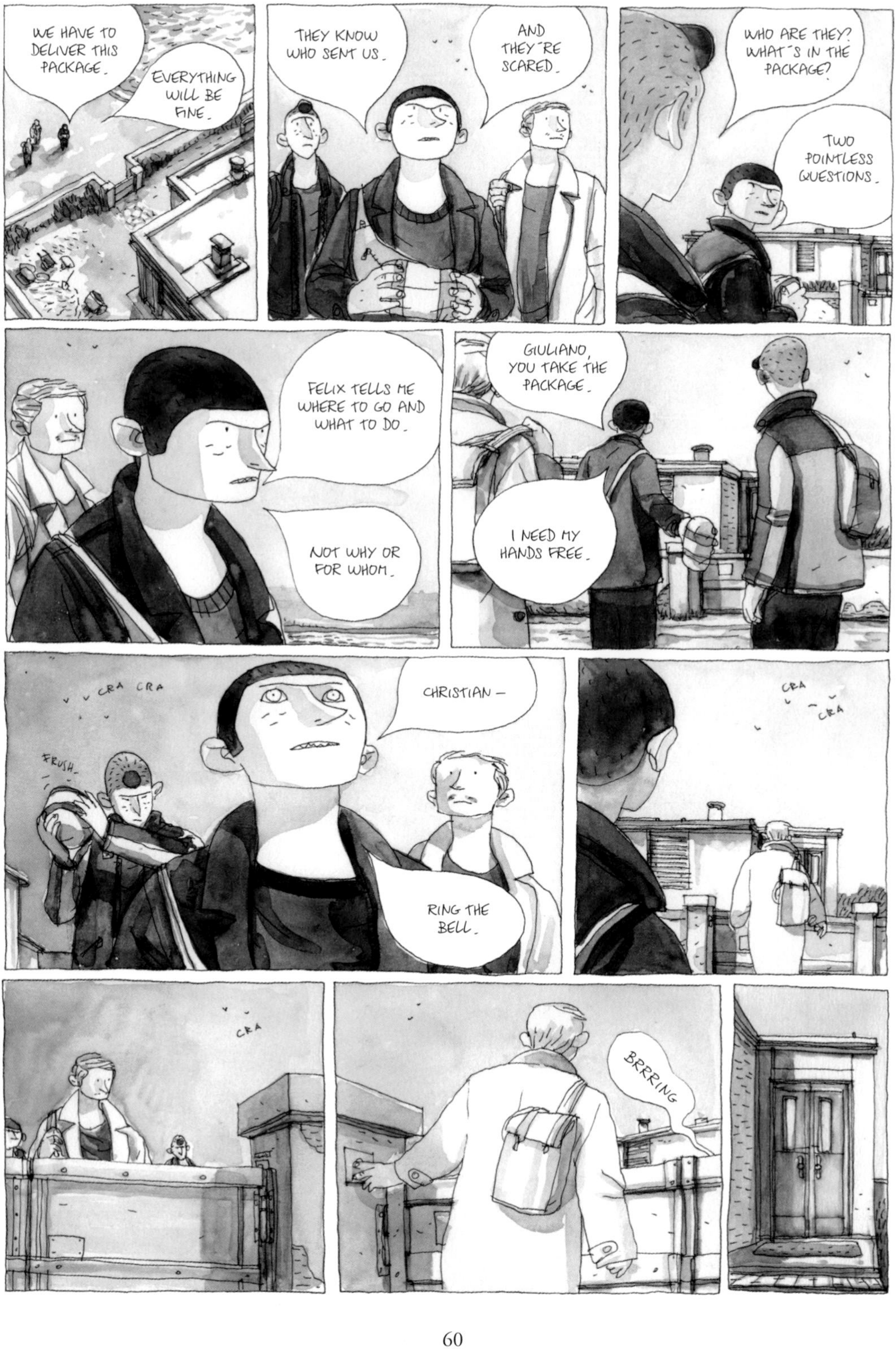
WE HAVE TO DELIVER THIS PACKAGE.
EVERYTHING WILL BE FINE.
THEY KNOW WHO SENT US.
AND THEY'RE SCARED.
WHO ARE THEY? WHAT'S IN THE PACKAGE?
TWO POINTLESS QUESTIONS.
FELIX TELLS ME WHERE TO GO AND WHAT TO DO.
NOT WHY OR FOR WHOM.
GIULIANO, YOU TAKE THE PACKAGE.
I NEED MY HANDS FREE.
CRA CRA
FRUSH
CHRISTIAN —
RING THE BELL.
CRA
CRA
CRA
BRRRING

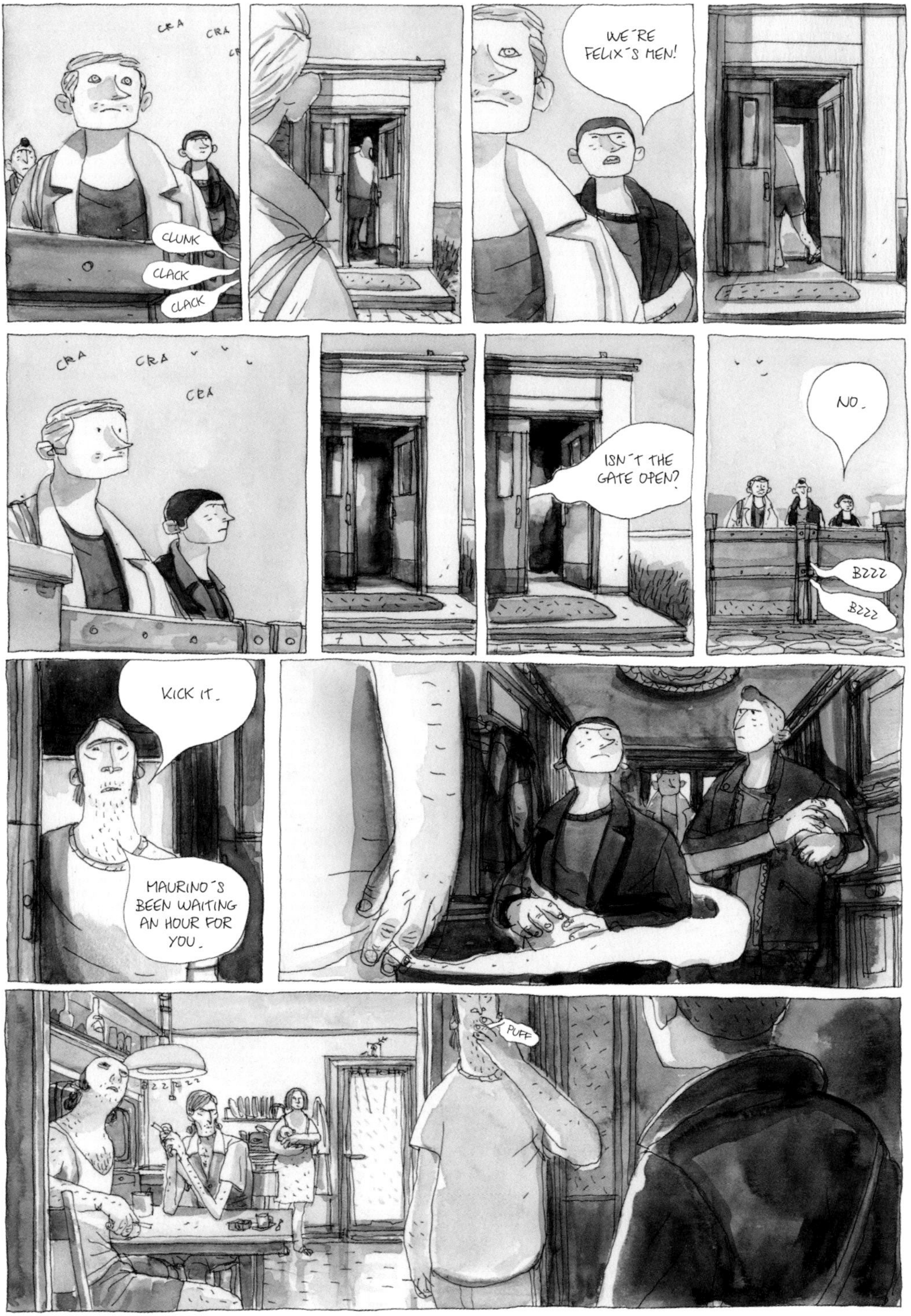
CRA
CRA
CLUNK
CLACK
CLACK
WE'RE FELIX'S MEN!
CRA
CRA
CRA
ISN'T THE GATE OPEN?
NO.
BZZZ
BZZZ
KICK IT.
MAURINO'S BEEN WAITING AN HOUR FOR YOU.
PUFF

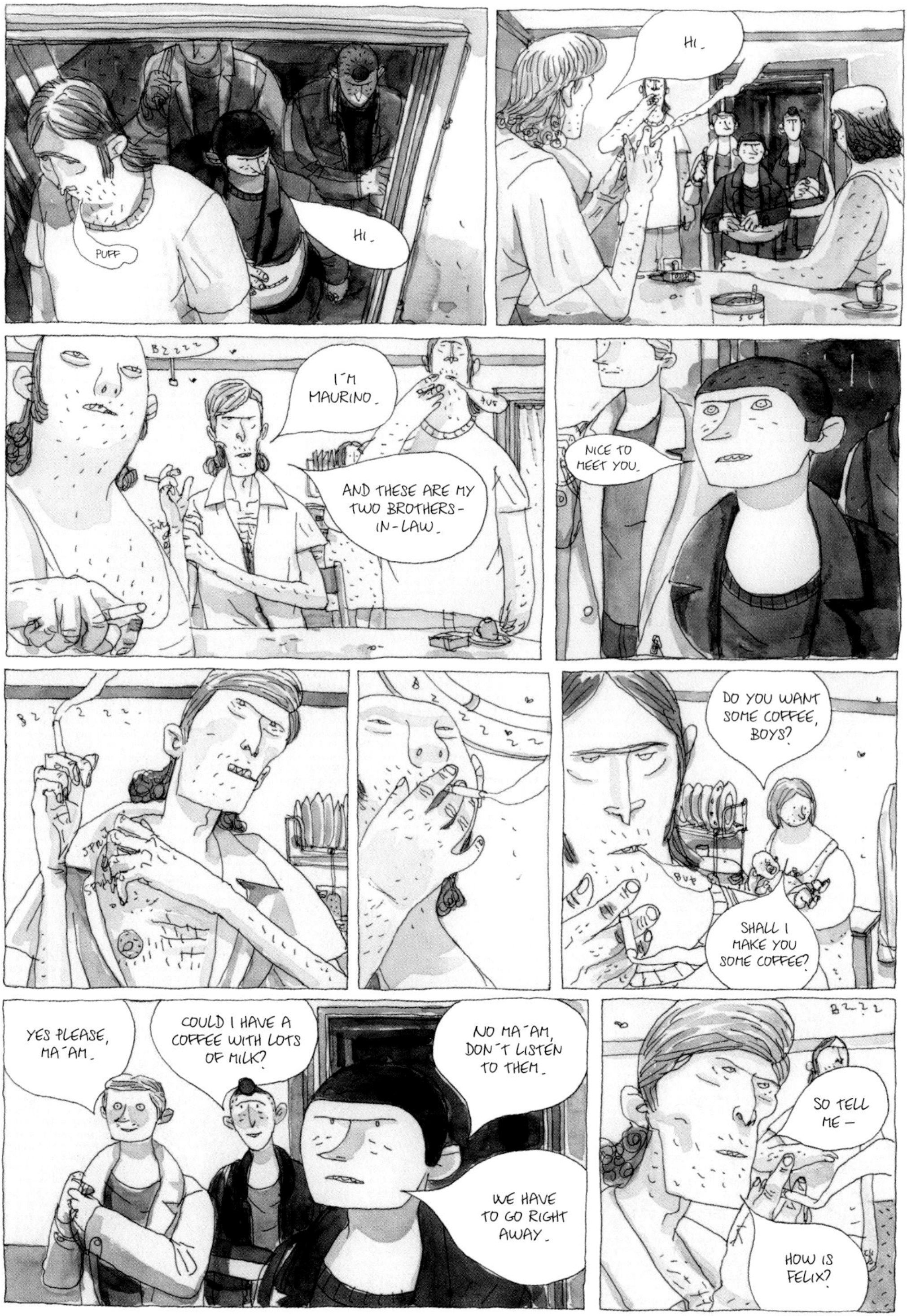
PUFF
HI.
HI.
BZZZZ
I'M MAURINO.
AND THESE ARE MY TWO BROTHERS-IN-LAW.
NICE TO MEET YOU.
BZZ ZZZ
DO YOU WANT SOME COFFEE, BOYS?
SHALL I MAKE YOU SOME COFFEE?
YES PLEASE, MA'AM.
COULD I HAVE A COFFEE WITH LOTS OF MILK?
NO MA'AM, DON'T LISTEN TO THEM.
WE HAVE TO GO RIGHT AWAY.
BZZZZ
SO TELL ME—
HOW IS FELIX?

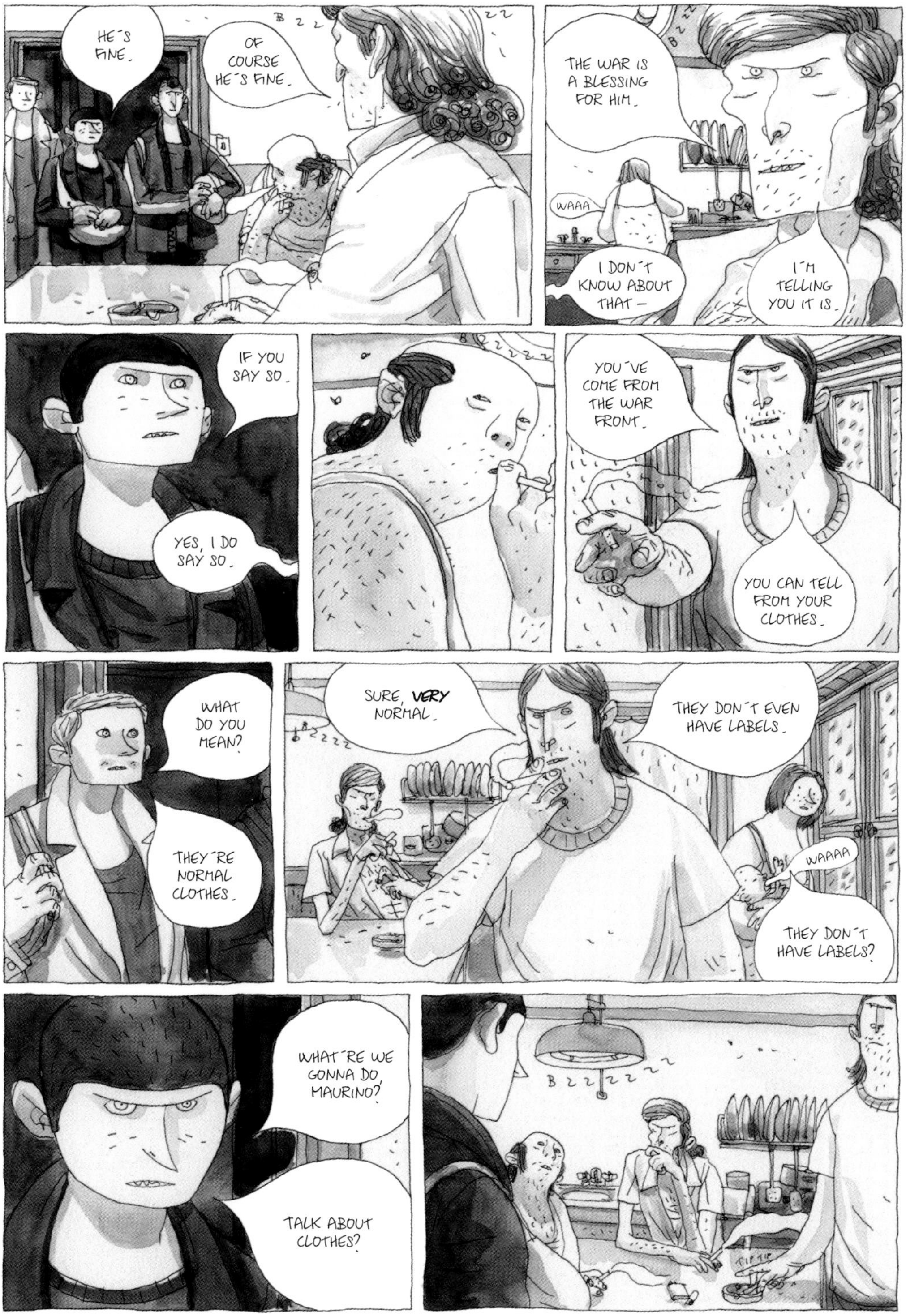
HE'S FINE.
B Z Z Z
OF COURSE HE'S FINE.
THE WAR IS A BLESSING FOR HIM.
WAAA
I DON'T KNOW ABOUT THAT —
I'M TELLING YOU IT IS.
IF YOU SAY SO.
YES, I DO SAY SO.
B Z Z Z Z Z
YOU'VE COME FROM THE WAR FRONT.
YOU CAN TELL FROM YOUR CLOTHES.
WHAT DO YOU MEAN?
THEY'RE NORMAL CLOTHES.
SURE, **VERY** NORMAL.
THEY DON'T EVEN HAVE LABELS.
WAAAA
THEY DON'T HAVE LABELS?
WHAT'RE WE GONNA DO, MAURINO?
TALK ABOUT CLOTHES?
B Z Z Z Z Z Z
TIP TIP

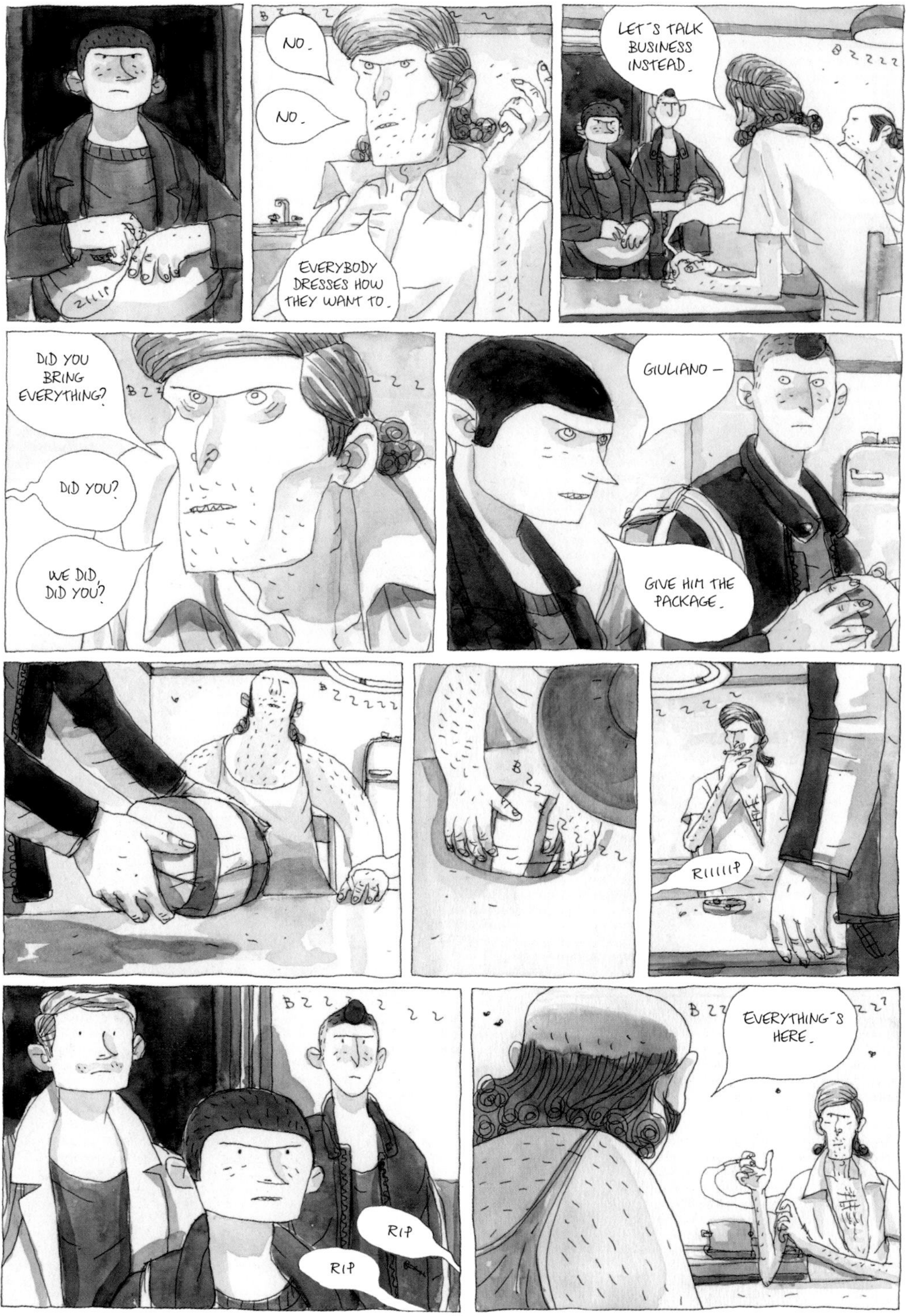
ZIIIP
BZZZZ
NO.
NO.
EVERYBODY DRESSES HOW THEY WANT TO.
LET'S TALK BUSINESS INSTEAD.
BZZZZ
DID YOU BRING EVERYTHING?
BZZ ZZZ
DID YOU?
WE DID, DID YOU?
GIULIANO —
GIVE HIM THE PACKAGE.
BZZZZZ
BZZ ZZ
ZZZ
RIIIIIP
BZZZ ZZZ
RIP
RIP
BZZ ZZZ
EVERYTHING'S HERE.

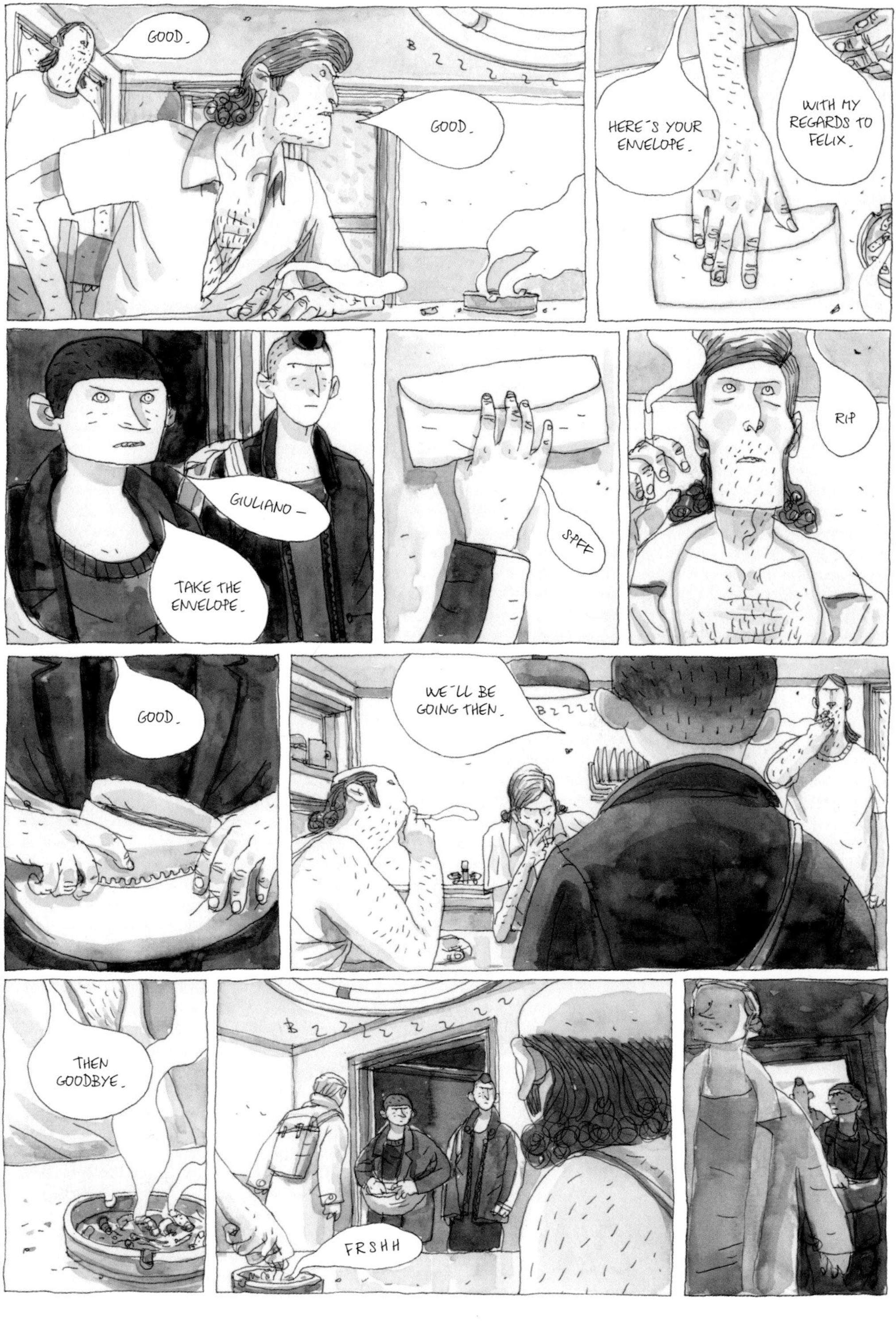
GOOD.
BZZZZZZZ
GOOD.
HERE'S YOUR ENVELOPE.
WITH MY REGARDS TO FELIX.
GIULIANO—
TAKE THE ENVELOPE.
SPFF
RIP
GOOD.
WE'LL BE GOING THEN.
BZZZZ
THEN GOODBYE.
BZZZZZZZZ
FRSHH

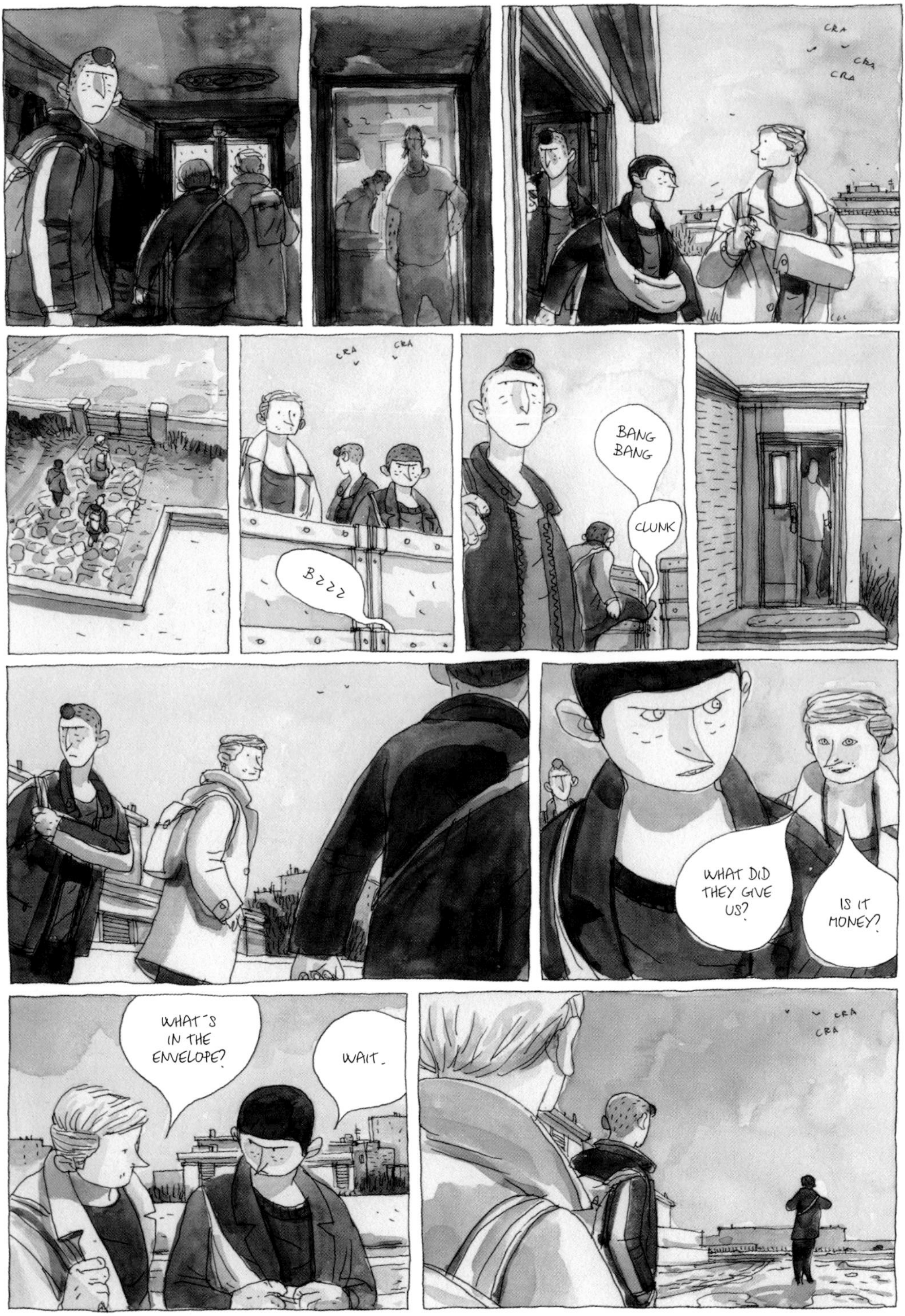
CRA
CRA
CRA
CRA
CRA
BZZZ
BANG BANG
CLUNK
WHAT DID THEY GIVE US?
IS IT MONEY?
WHAT'S IN THE ENVELOPE?
WAIT.
CRA
CRA

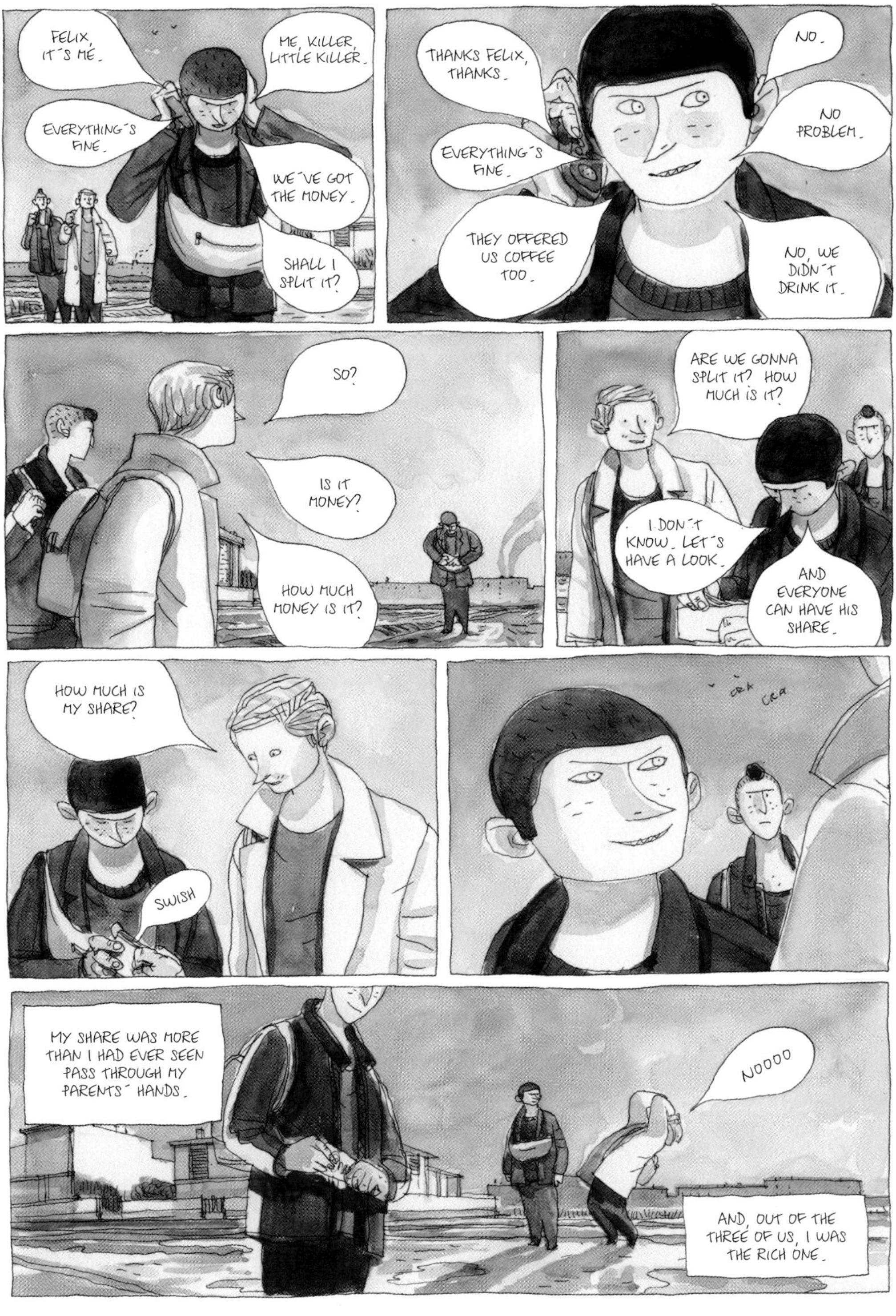
FELIX, IT'S ME.
ME, KILLER, LITTLE KILLER.
EVERYTHING'S FINE.
WE'VE GOT THE MONEY.
SHALL I SPLIT IT?
THANKS FELIX, THANKS.
NO.
NO PROBLEM.
EVERYTHING'S FINE.
THEY OFFERED US COFFEE TOO.
NO, WE DIDN'T DRINK IT.
SO?
IS IT MONEY?
HOW MUCH MONEY IS IT?
ARE WE GONNA SPLIT IT? HOW MUCH IS IT?
I DON'T KNOW. LET'S HAVE A LOOK.
AND EVERYONE CAN HAVE HIS SHARE.
HOW MUCH IS MY SHARE?
SWISH
CRA
CRA
MY SHARE WAS MORE THAN I HAD EVER SEEN PASS THROUGH MY PARENTS' HANDS.
NOOOO
AND, OUT OF THE THREE OF US, I WAS THE RICH ONE.

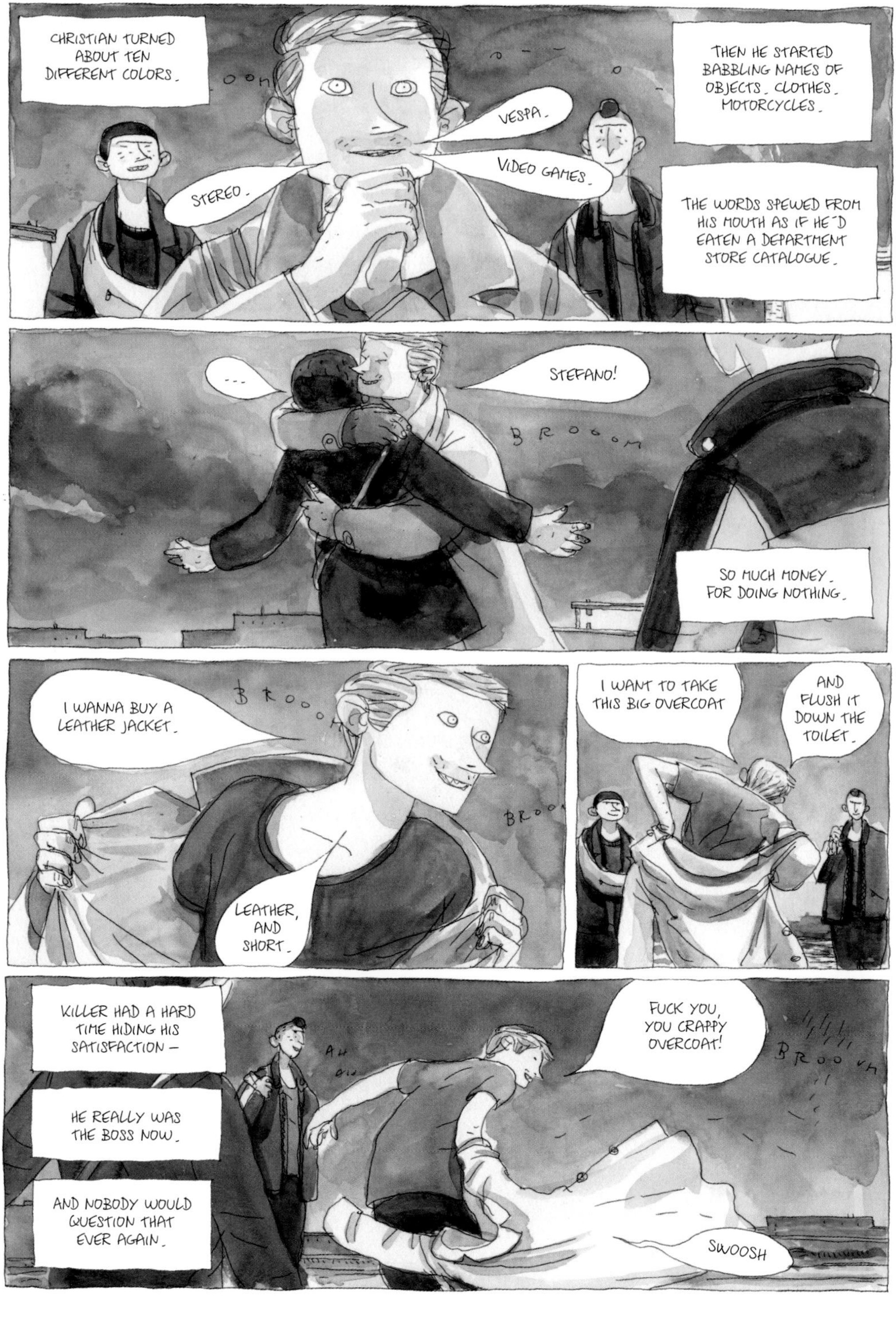
CHRISTIAN TURNED ABOUT TEN DIFFERENT COLORS.
OOH
VESPA.
VIDEO GAMES.
STEREO.
THEN HE STARTED BABBLING NAMES OF OBJECTS, CLOTHES, MOTORCYCLES.
THE WORDS SPEWED FROM HIS MOUTH AS IF HE'D EATEN A DEPARTMENT STORE CATALOGUE.
...
STEFANO!
BROOOOM
SO MUCH MONEY. FOR DOING NOTHING.
I WANNA BUY A LEATHER JACKET.
BROOOM
BROO
LEATHER, AND SHORT.
I WANT TO TAKE THIS BIG OVERCOAT
AND FLUSH IT DOWN THE TOILET.
KILLER HAD A HARD TIME HIDING HIS SATISFACTION —
HE REALLY WAS THE BOSS NOW.
AND NOBODY WOULD QUESTION THAT EVER AGAIN.
FUCK YOU, YOU CRAPPY OVERCOAT!
BROOOM
SWOOSH

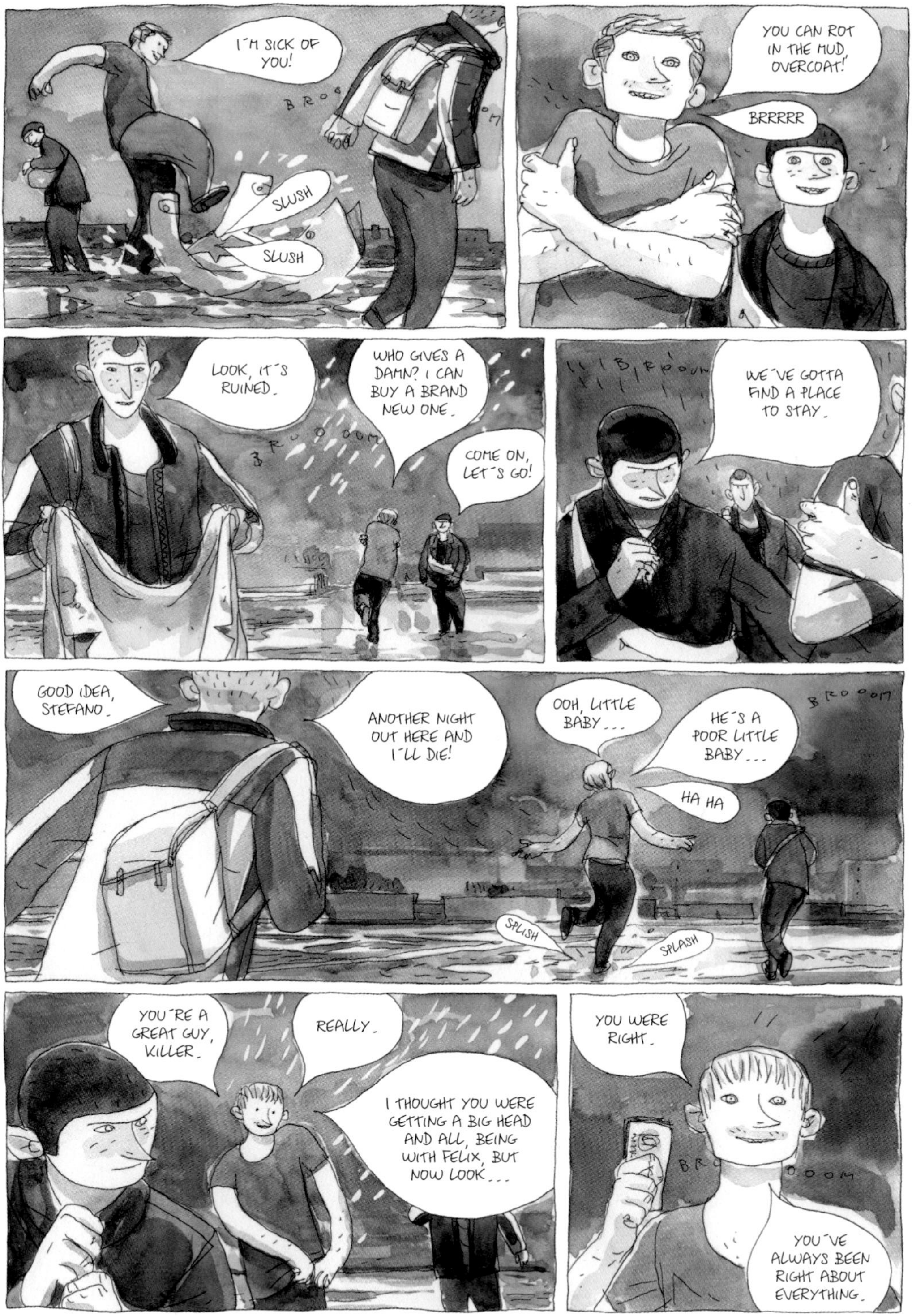
I'M SICK OF YOU!
BROOOM
SLUSH
SLUSH
YOU CAN ROT IN THE MUD, OVERCOAT!
BRRRRR
LOOK, IT'S RUINED.
WHO GIVES A DAMN? I CAN BUY A BRAND NEW ONE.
BROOOOM
COME ON, LET'S GO!
BROOOM
WE'VE GOTTA FIND A PLACE TO STAY.
GOOD IDEA, STEFANO.
ANOTHER NIGHT OUT HERE AND I'LL DIE!
OOH, LITTLE BABY...
HE'S A POOR LITTLE BABY...
BROOOM
HA HA
SPLISH
SPLASH
YOU'RE A GREAT GUY, KILLER.
REALLY.
I THOUGHT YOU WERE GETTING A BIG HEAD AND ALL, BEING WITH FELIX, BUT NOW LOOK...
YOU WERE RIGHT.
BROOOOM
YOU'VE ALWAYS BEEN RIGHT ABOUT EVERYTHING.

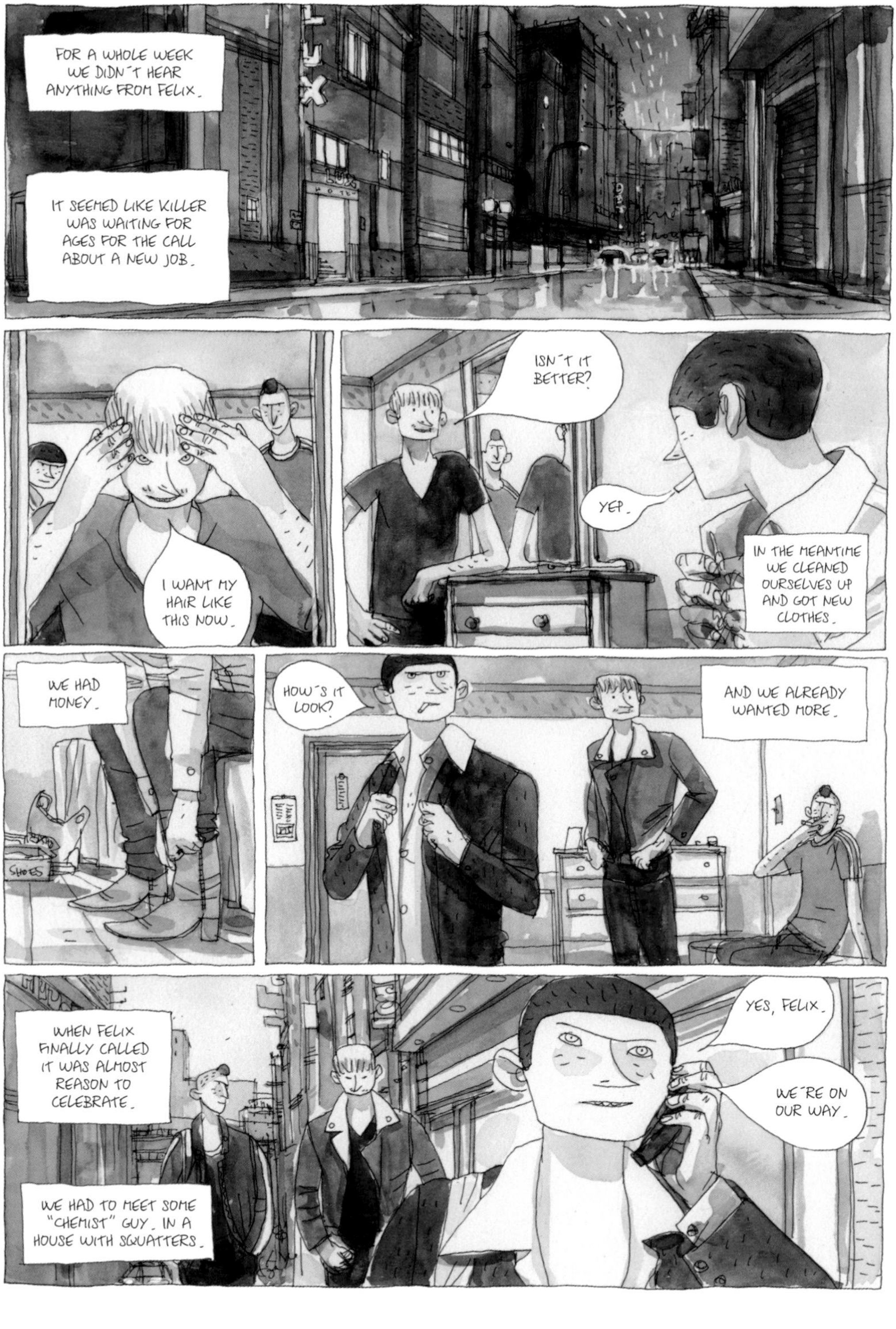
FOR A WHOLE WEEK WE DIDN'T HEAR ANYTHING FROM FELIX.
IT SEEMED LIKE KILLER WAS WAITING FOR AGES FOR THE CALL ABOUT A NEW JOB.
I WANT MY HAIR LIKE THIS NOW.
ISN'T IT BETTER?
YEP.
IN THE MEANTIME WE CLEANED OURSELVES UP AND GOT NEW CLOTHES.
WE HAD MONEY.
HOW'S IT LOOK?
AND WE ALREADY WANTED MORE.
SHOES
WHEN FELIX FINALLY CALLED IT WAS ALMOST REASON TO CELEBRATE.
YES, FELIX.
WE'RE ON OUR WAY.
WE HAD TO MEET SOME "CHEMIST" GUY. IN A HOUSE WITH SQUATTERS.

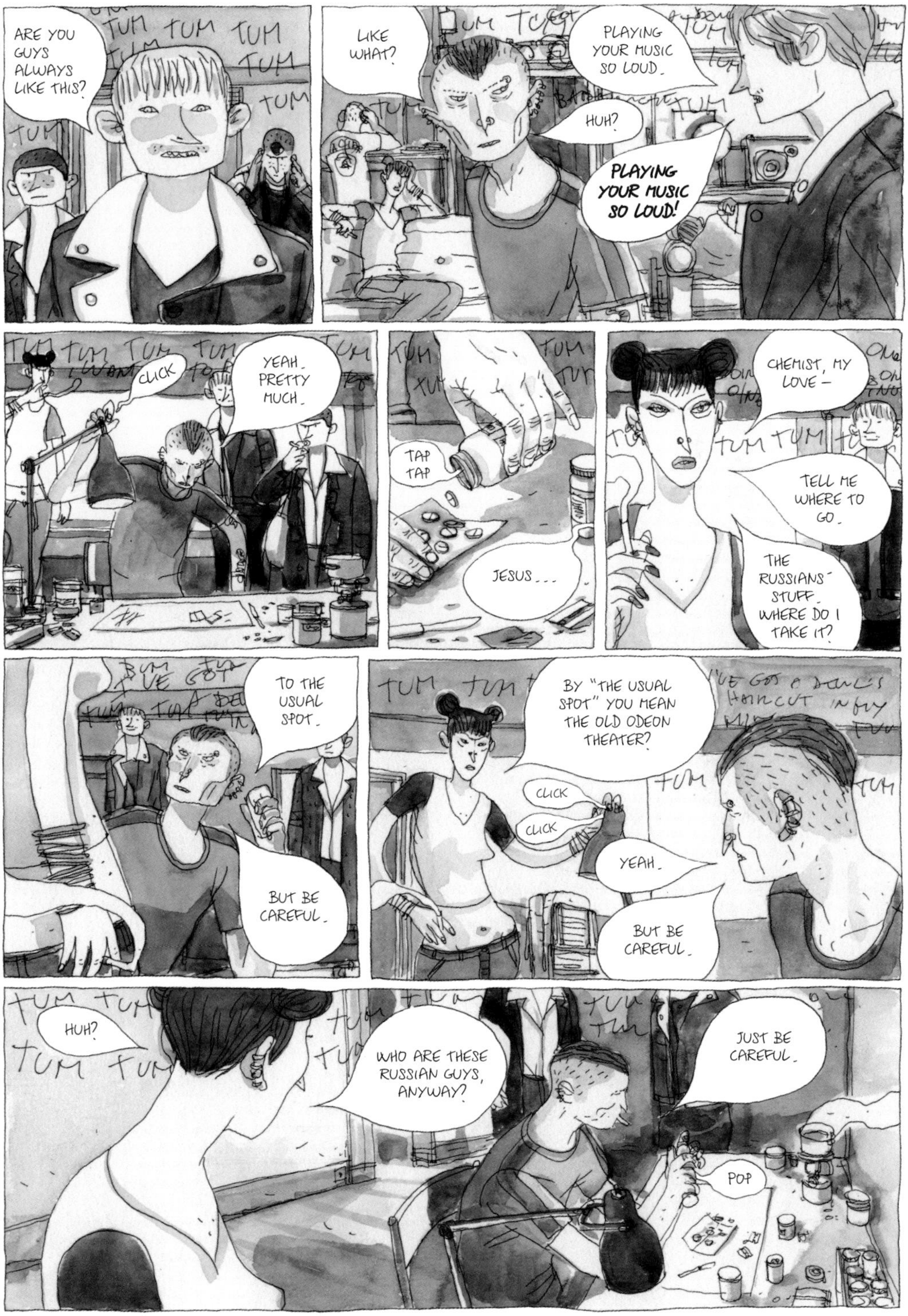
ARE YOU GUYS ALWAYS LIKE THIS?
LIKE WHAT?
PLAYING YOUR MUSIC SO LOUD.
HUH?
PLAYING YOUR MUSIC SO LOUD!
CLICK
YEAH. PRETTY MUCH.
TAP TAP
JESUS...
CHEMIST, MY LOVE —
TELL ME WHERE TO GO.
THE RUSSIANS' STUFF. WHERE DO I TAKE IT?
TO THE USUAL SPOT.
BUT BE CAREFUL.
BY "THE USUAL SPOT" YOU MEAN THE OLD ODEON THEATER?
CLICK
CLICK
YEAH.
BUT BE CAREFUL.
HUH?
WHO ARE THESE RUSSIAN GUYS, ANYWAY?
JUST BE CAREFUL.
POP

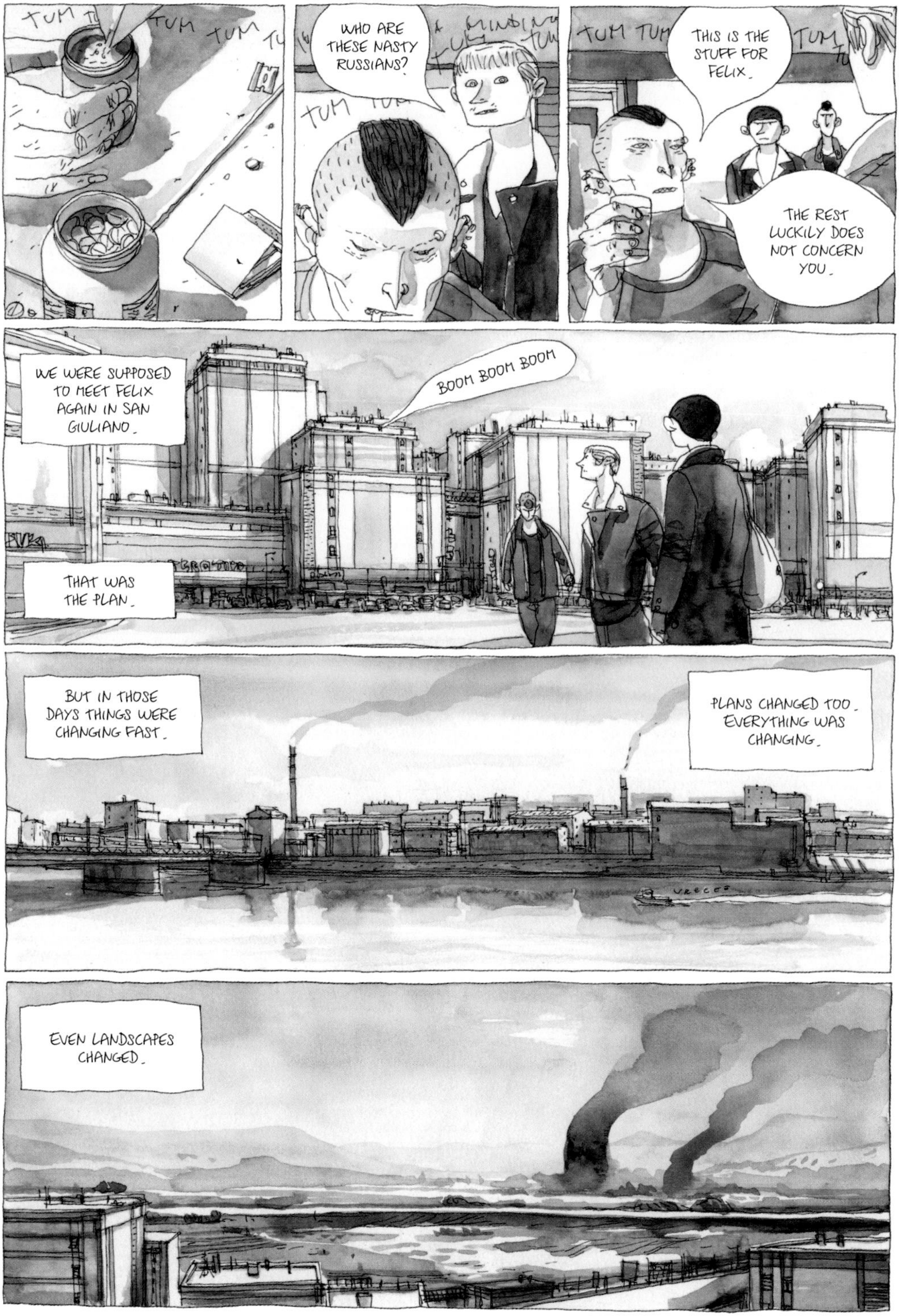
TUM TUM TUM
WHO ARE THESE NASTY RUSSIANS?
TUM
TUM TUM
THIS IS THE STUFF FOR FELIX.
TUM
THE REST LUCKILY DOES NOT CONCERN YOU.
WE WERE SUPPOSED TO MEET FELIX AGAIN IN SAN GIULIANO.
BOOM BOOM BOOM
THAT WAS THE PLAN.
BUT IN THOSE DAYS THINGS WERE CHANGING FAST.
PLANS CHANGED TOO. EVERYTHING WAS CHANGING.
EVEN LANDSCAPES CHANGED.

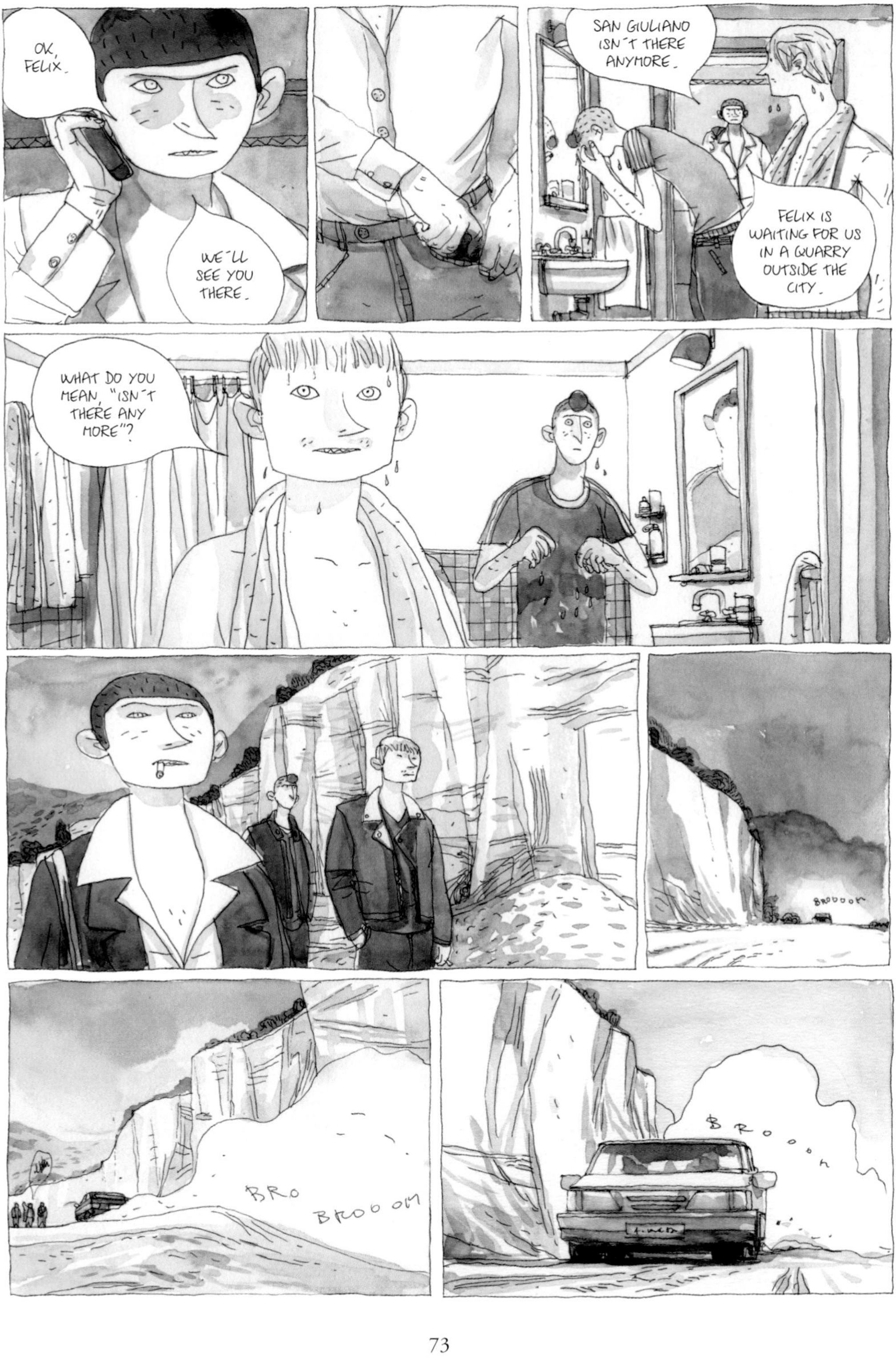
OK, FELIX.
WE'LL SEE YOU THERE.
SAN GIULIANO ISN'T THERE ANYMORE.
FELIX IS WAITING FOR US IN A QUARRY OUTSIDE THE CITY.
WHAT DO YOU MEAN, "ISN'T THERE ANY MORE"?
BRO
BROOOOM
BROOOOh

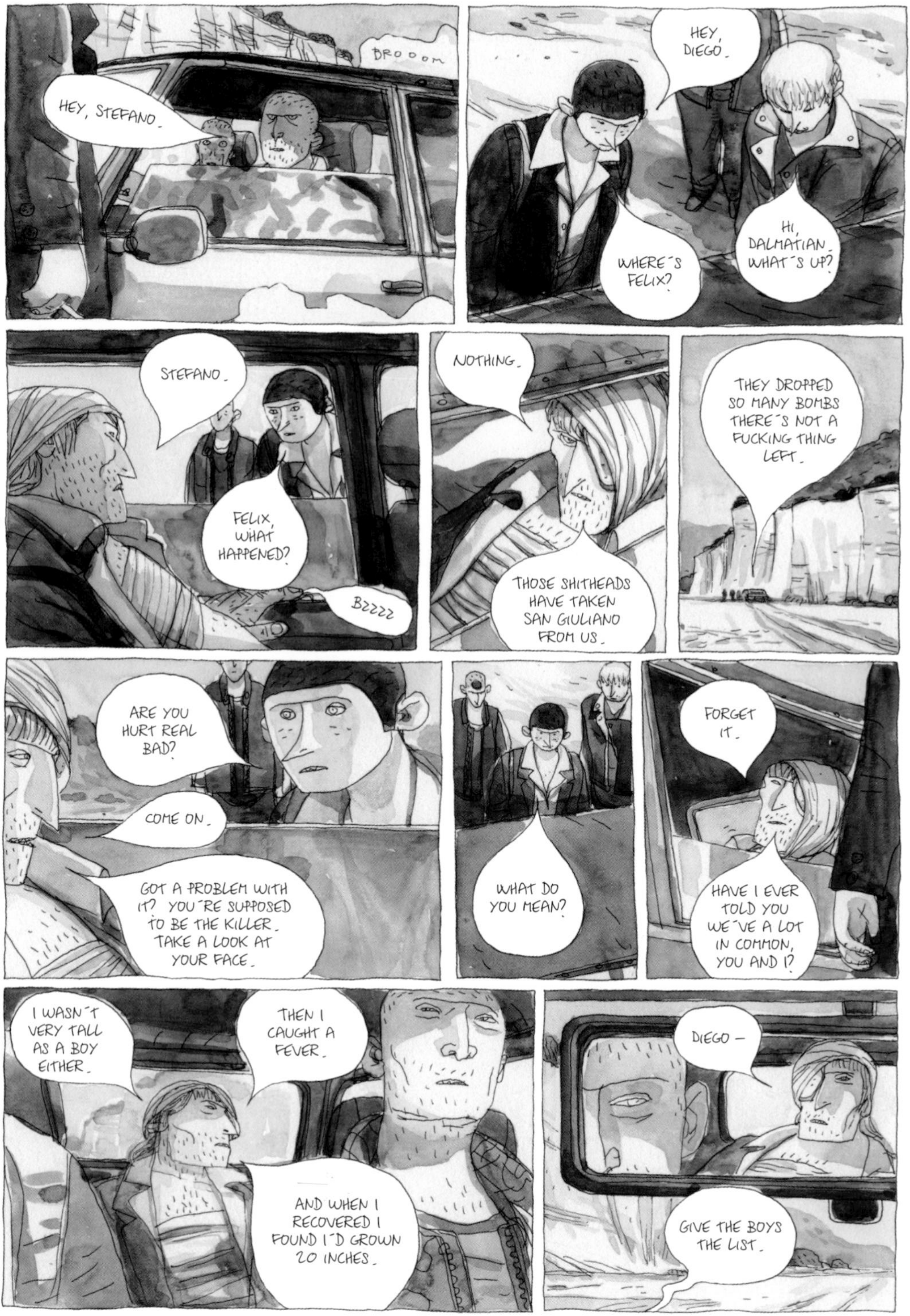
BROOOM
HEY, STEFANO.
HEY, DIEGO.
WHERE'S FELIX?
HI, DALMATIAN. WHAT'S UP?
STEFANO.
FELIX, WHAT HAPPENED?
BZZZZ
NOTHING.
THOSE SHITHEADS HAVE TAKEN SAN GIULIANO FROM US.
THEY DROPPED SO MANY BOMBS THERE'S NOT A FUCKING THING LEFT.
ARE YOU HURT REAL BAD?
COME ON.
GOT A PROBLEM WITH IT? YOU'RE SUPPOSED TO BE THE KILLER. TAKE A LOOK AT YOUR FACE.
WHAT DO YOU MEAN?
FORGET IT.
HAVE I EVER TOLD YOU WE'VE A LOT IN COMMON, YOU AND I?
I WASN'T VERY TALL AS A BOY EITHER.
THEN I CAUGHT A FEVER.
AND WHEN I RECOVERED I FOUND I'D GROWN 20 INCHES.
DIEGO —
GIVE THE BOYS THE LIST.

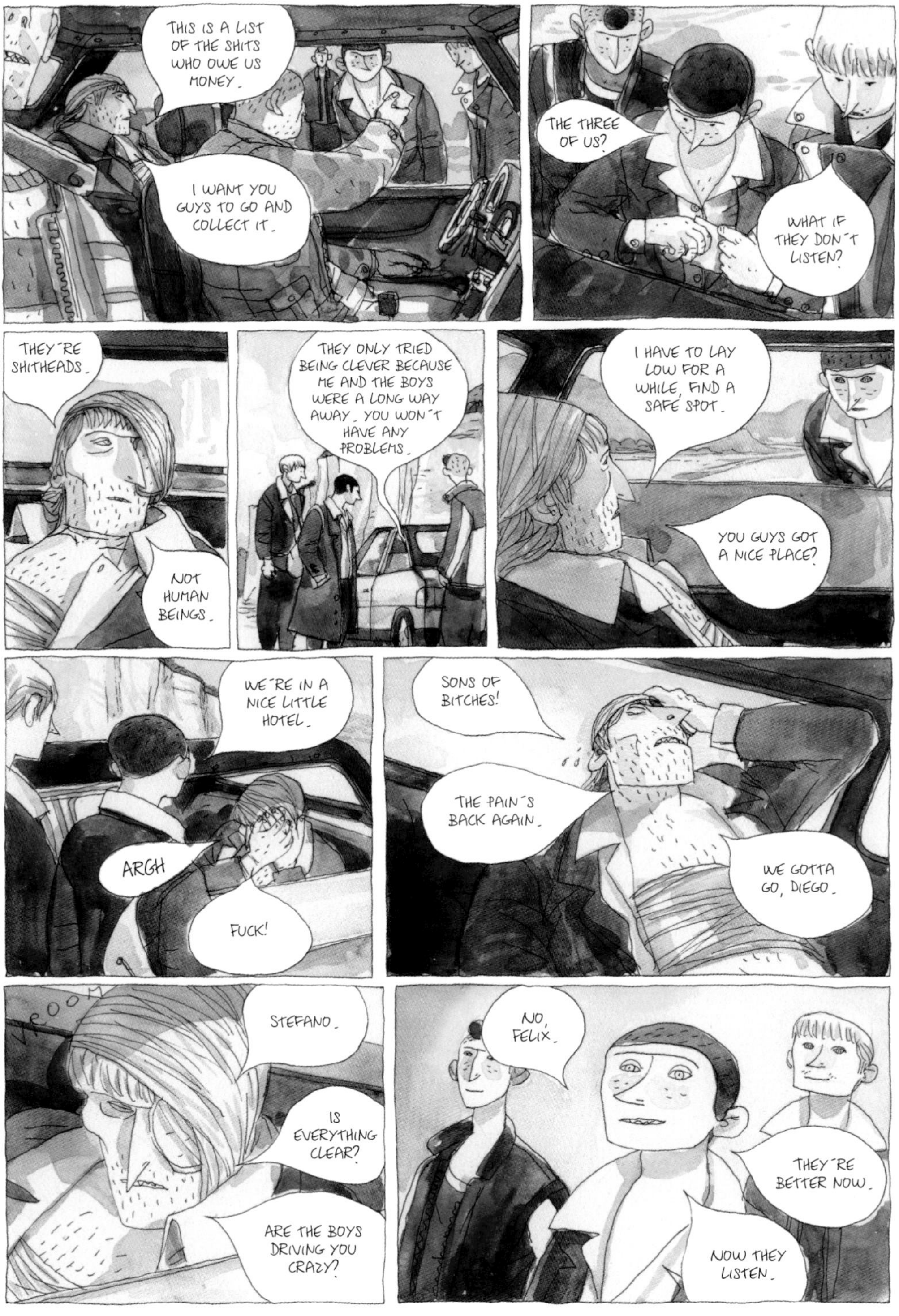
THIS IS A LIST OF THE SHITS WHO OWE US MONEY.
I WANT YOU GUYS TO GO AND COLLECT IT.
THE THREE OF US?
WHAT IF THEY DON'T LISTEN?
THEY'RE SHITHEADS.
NOT HUMAN BEINGS.
THEY ONLY TRIED BEING CLEVER BECAUSE ME AND THE BOYS WERE A LONG WAY AWAY. YOU WON'T HAVE ANY PROBLEMS.
I HAVE TO LAY LOW FOR A WHILE, FIND A SAFE SPOT.
YOU GUYS GOT A NICE PLACE?
WE'RE IN A NICE LITTLE HOTEL.
ARGH
FUCK!
SONS OF BITCHES!
THE PAIN'S BACK AGAIN.
WE GOTTA GO, DIEGO.
VROOM
STEFANO.
IS EVERYTHING CLEAR?
ARE THE BOYS DRIVING YOU CRAZY?
NO, FELIX.
THEY'RE BETTER NOW.
NOW THEY LISTEN.

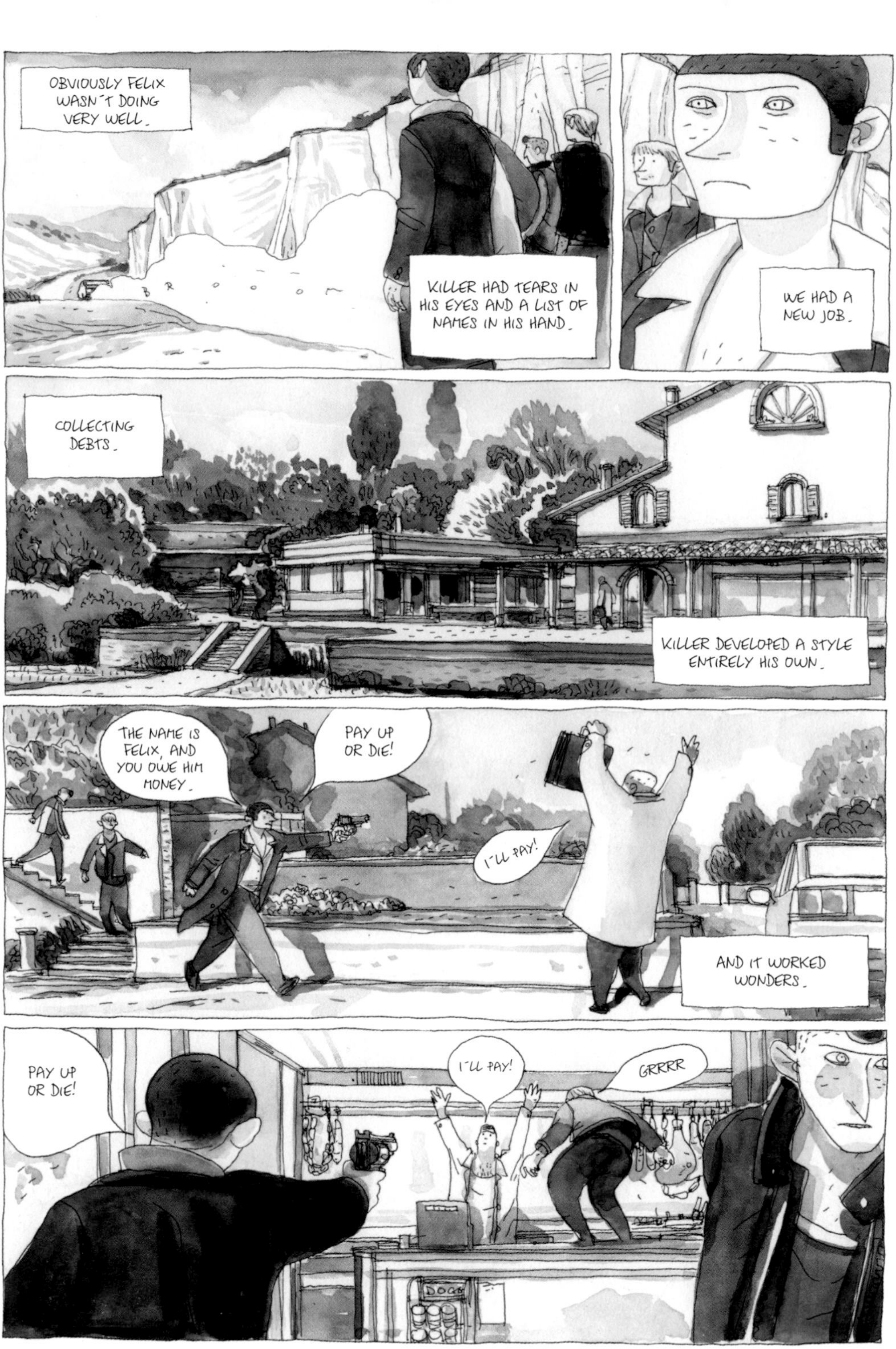
OBVIOUSLY FELIX WASN'T DOING VERY WELL.
B R O O M
KILLER HAD TEARS IN HIS EYES AND A LIST OF NAMES IN HIS HAND.
WE HAD A NEW JOB.
COLLECTING DEBTS.
KILLER DEVELOPED A STYLE ENTIRELY HIS OWN.
THE NAME IS FELIX, AND YOU OWE HIM MONEY.
PAY UP OR DIE!
I'LL PAY!
AND IT WORKED WONDERS.
PAY UP OR DIE!
I'LL PAY!
GRRRR
DOGS

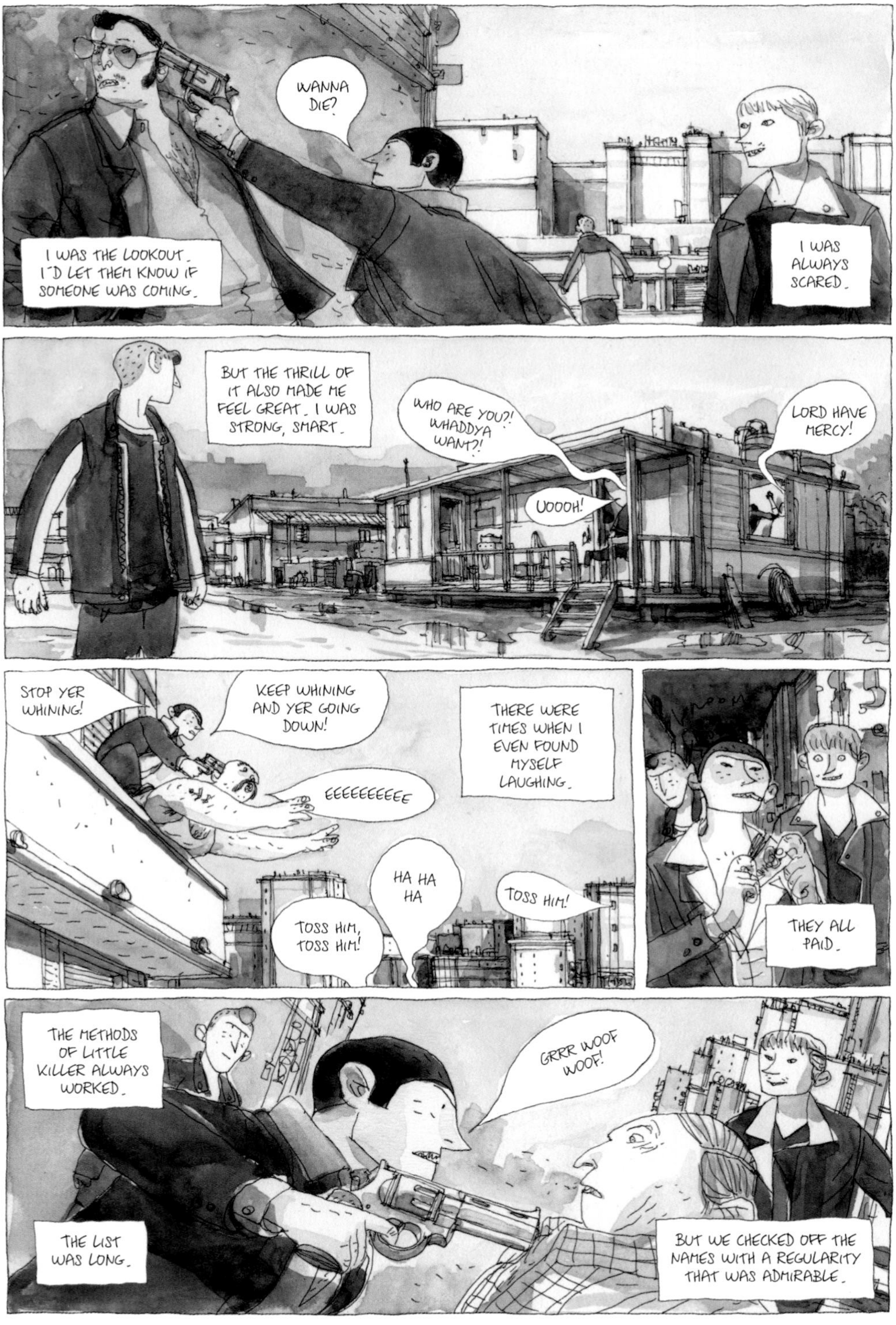
WANNA DIE?
I WAS THE LOOKOUT. I'D LET THEM KNOW IF SOMEONE WAS COMING.
I WAS ALWAYS SCARED.
BUT THE THRILL OF IT ALSO MADE ME FEEL GREAT. I WAS STRONG, SMART.
WHO ARE YOU?! WHADDYA WANT?!
UOOOH!
LORD HAVE MERCY!
STOP YER WHINING!
KEEP WHINING AND YER GOING DOWN!
EEEEEEEEEE
THERE WERE TIMES WHEN I EVEN FOUND MYSELF LAUGHING.
HA HA HA
TOSS HIM, TOSS HIM!
TOSS HIM!
THEY ALL PAID.
THE METHODS OF LITTLE KILLER ALWAYS WORKED.
GRRR WOOF WOOF!
THE LIST WAS LONG.
BUT WE CHECKED OFF THE NAMES WITH A REGULARITY THAT WAS ADMIRABLE.

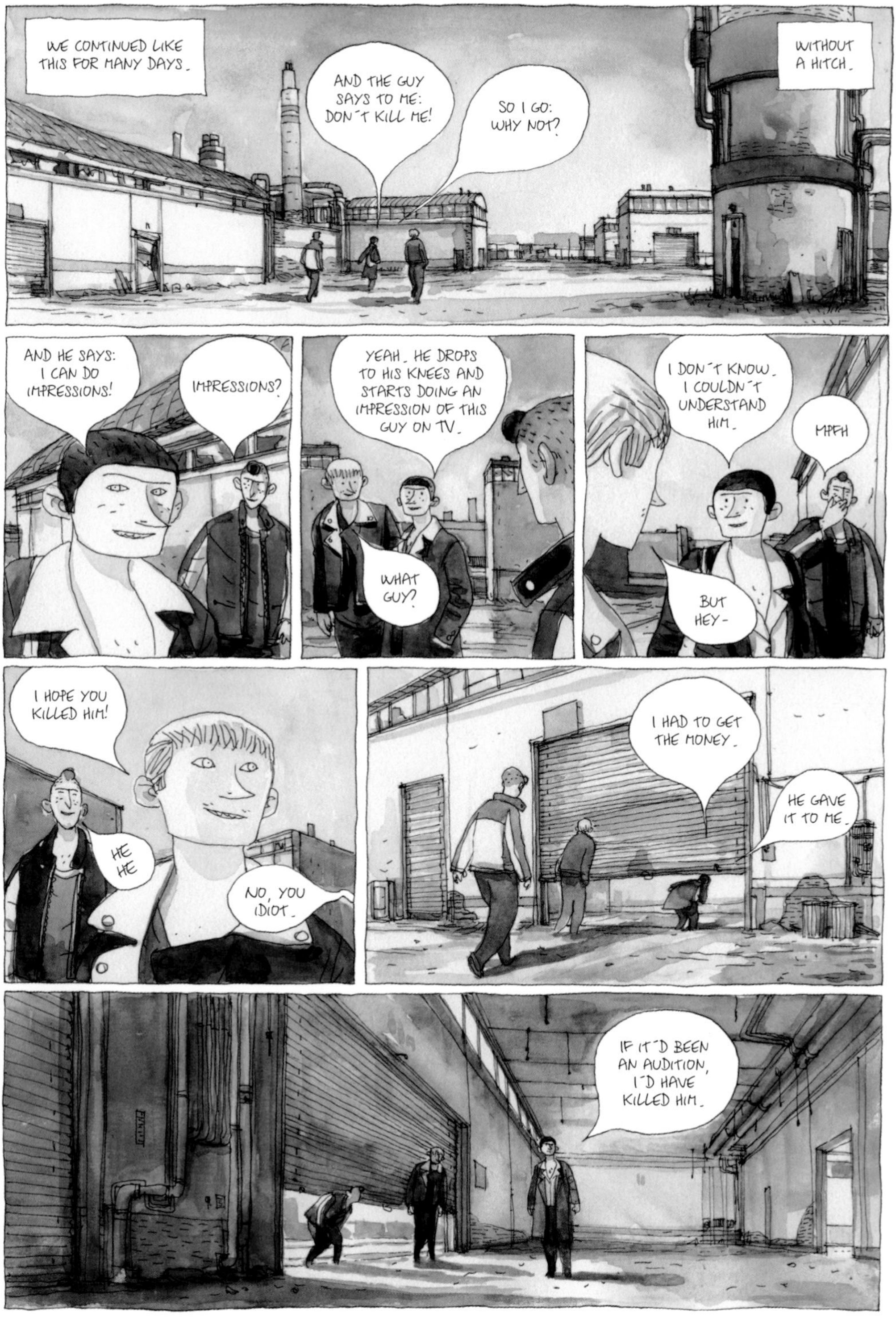
WE CONTINUED LIKE THIS FOR MANY DAYS.
AND THE GUY SAYS TO ME: DON'T KILL ME!
SO I GO: WHY NOT?
WITHOUT A HITCH.
AND HE SAYS: I CAN DO IMPRESSIONS!
IMPRESSIONS?
YEAH. HE DROPS TO HIS KNEES AND STARTS DOING AN IMPRESSION OF THIS GUY ON TV.
WHAT GUY?
I DON'T KNOW. I COULDN'T UNDERSTAND HIM.
MPFH
BUT HEY-
I HOPE YOU KILLED HIM!
HE HE
NO, YOU IDIOT.
I HAD TO GET THE MONEY.
HE GAVE IT TO ME.
IF IT'D BEEN AN AUDITION, I'D HAVE KILLED HIM.

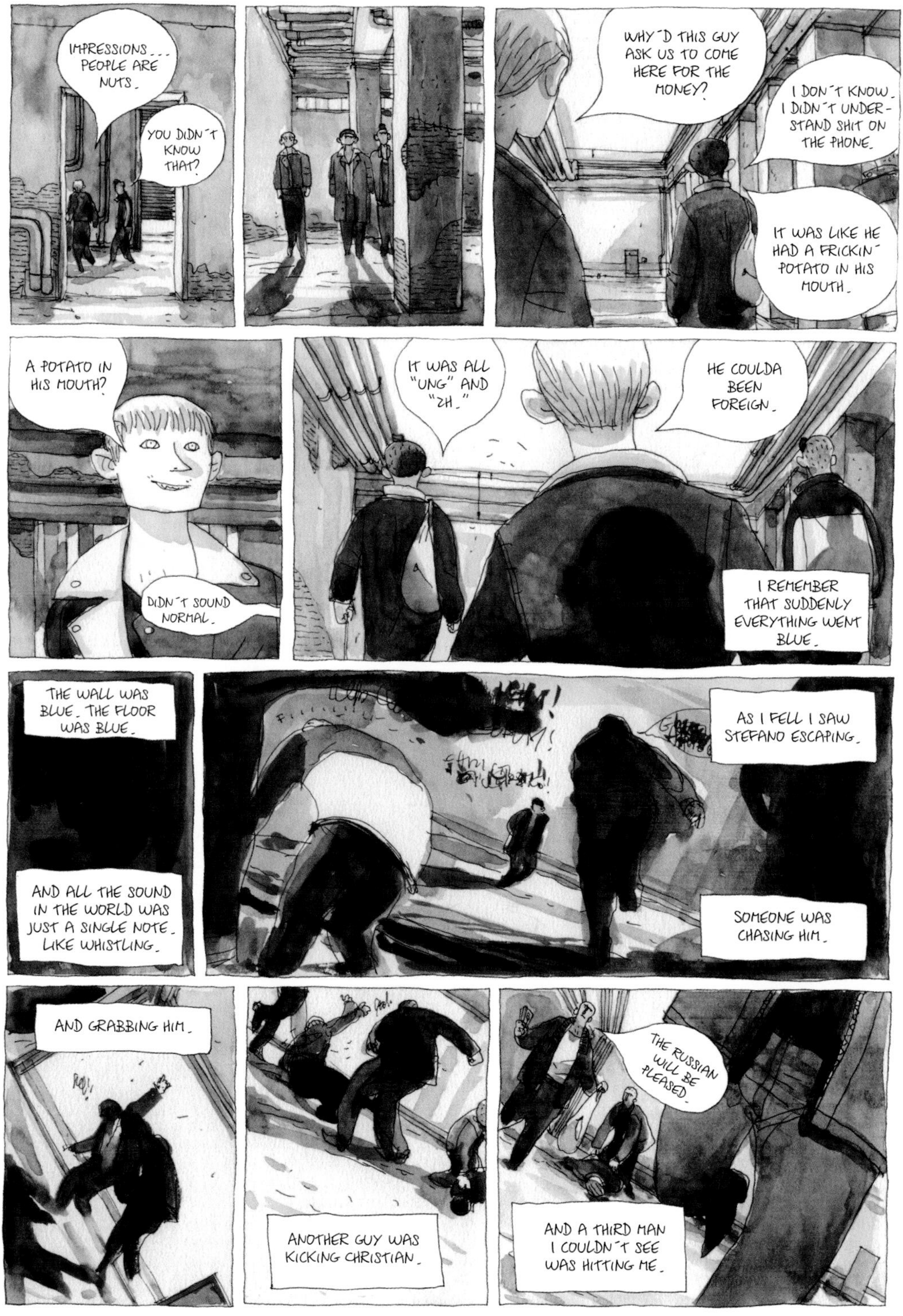
IMPRESSIONS... PEOPLE ARE NUTS.
YOU DIDN'T KNOW THAT?
WHY'D THIS GUY ASK US TO COME HERE FOR THE MONEY?
I DON'T KNOW. I DIDN'T UNDERSTAND SHIT ON THE PHONE.
IT WAS LIKE HE HAD A FRICKIN' POTATO IN HIS MOUTH.
A POTATO IN HIS MOUTH?
DIDN'T SOUND NORMAL.
IT WAS ALL "UNG" AND "ZH."
HE COULDA BEEN FOREIGN.
I REMEMBER THAT SUDDENLY EVERYTHING WENT BLUE.
THE WALL WAS BLUE. THE FLOOR WAS BLUE.
AND ALL THE SOUND IN THE WORLD WAS JUST A SINGLE NOTE. LIKE WHISTLING.
AS I FELL I SAW STEFANO ESCAPING.
SOMEONE WAS CHASING HIM.
AND GRABBING HIM.
ANOTHER GUY WAS KICKING CHRISTIAN.
THE RUSSIAN WILL BE PLEASED.
AND A THIRD MAN I COULDN'T SEE WAS HITTING ME.

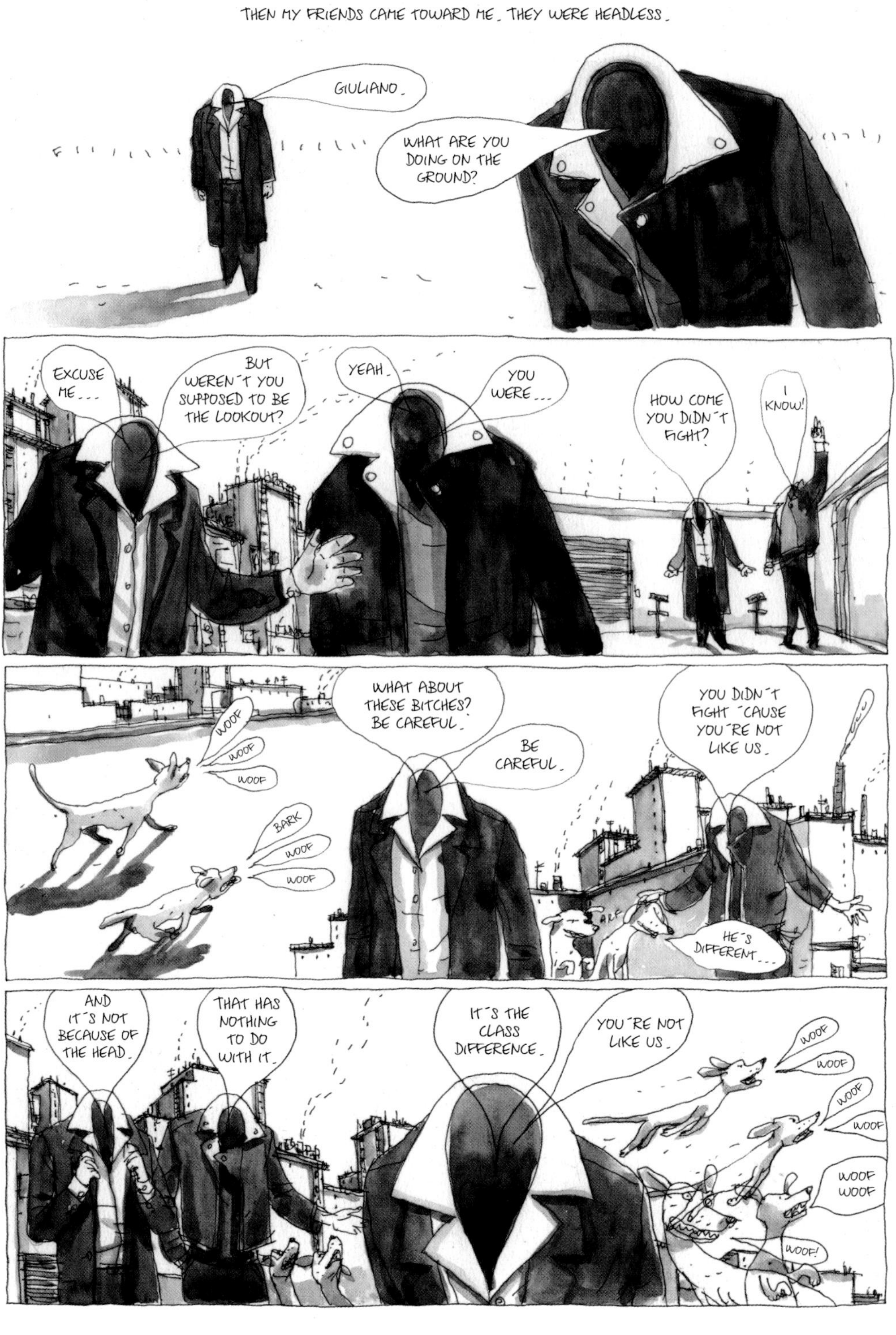
THEN MY FRIENDS CAME TOWARD ME. THEY WERE HEADLESS.
GIULIANO.
WHAT ARE YOU DOING ON THE GROUND?
EXCUSE ME...
BUT WEREN'T YOU SUPPOSED TO BE THE LOOKOUT?
YEAH.
YOU WERE...
HOW COME YOU DIDN'T FIGHT?
I KNOW!
WOOF
WOOF
WOOF
BARK
WOOF
WOOF
WHAT ABOUT THESE BITCHES? BE CAREFUL.
BE CAREFUL.
YOU DIDN'T FIGHT 'CAUSE YOU'RE NOT LIKE US.
ARF
HE'S DIFFERENT...
AND IT'S NOT BECAUSE OF THE HEAD.
THAT HAS NOTHING TO DO WITH IT.
IT'S THE CLASS DIFFERENCE.
YOU'RE NOT LIKE US.
WOOF
WOOF
WOOF
WOOF
WOOF WOOF
WOOF!

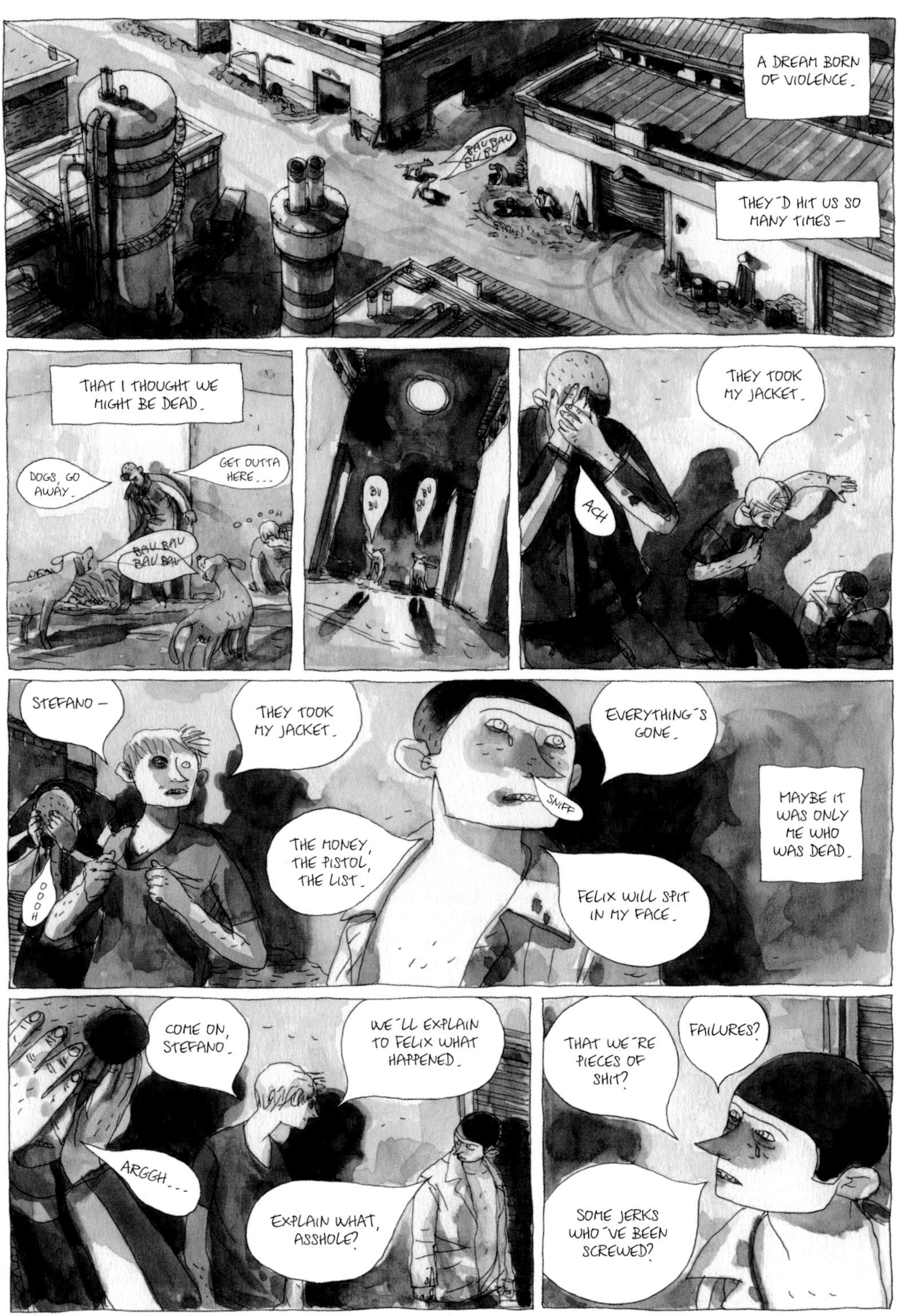
A DREAM BORN OF VIOLENCE.
BAU BAU BU BU
THEY'D HIT US SO MANY TIMES —
THAT I THOUGHT WE MIGHT BE DEAD.
DOGS, GO AWAY.
GET OUTTA HERE...
OOOH
BAU BAU BAU BAU
BU BU
BU BU
THEY TOOK MY JACKET.
ACH
STEFANO —
THEY TOOK MY JACKET.
EVERYTHING'S GONE.
SNIFF
THE MONEY, THE PISTOL, THE LIST.
FELIX WILL SPIT IN MY FACE.
OOOH
MAYBE IT WAS ONLY ME WHO WAS DEAD.
COME ON, STEFANO.
WE'LL EXPLAIN TO FELIX WHAT HAPPENED.
ARGGH...
EXPLAIN WHAT, ASSHOLE?
FAILURES?
THAT WE'RE PIECES OF SHIT?
SOME JERKS WHO'VE BEEN SCREWED?

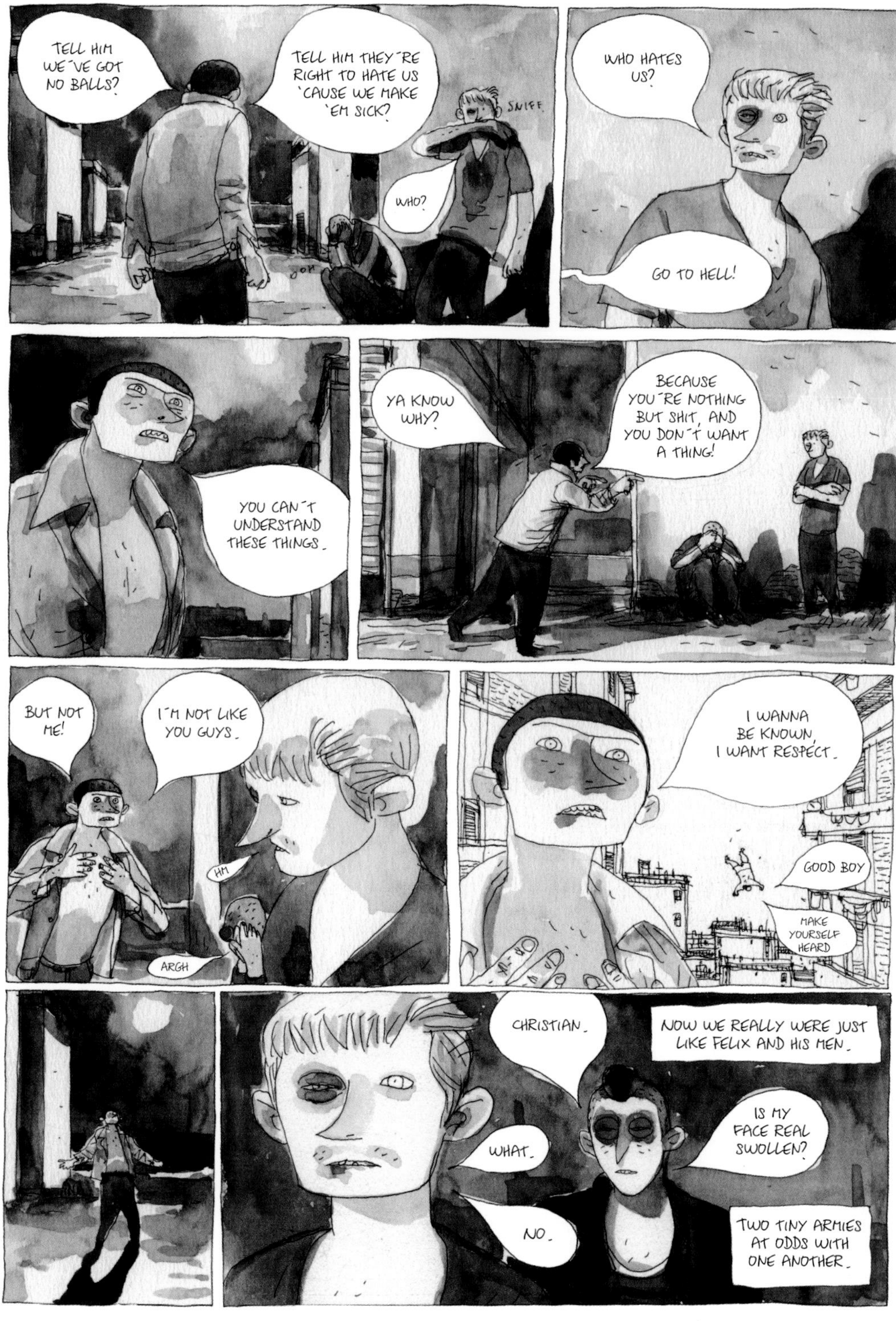
TELL HIM WE'VE GOT NO BALLS?
TELL HIM THEY'RE RIGHT TO HATE US 'CAUSE WE MAKE 'EM SICK?
SNIFF
WHO?
WHO HATES US?
GO TO HELL!
YOU CAN'T UNDERSTAND THESE THINGS.
YA KNOW WHY?
BECAUSE YOU'RE NOTHING BUT SHIT, AND YOU DON'T WANT A THING!
BUT NOT ME!
I'M NOT LIKE YOU GUYS.
HM
ARGH
I WANNA BE KNOWN, I WANT RESPECT.
GOOD BOY
MAKE YOURSELF HEARD
CHRISTIAN.
NOW WE REALLY WERE JUST LIKE FELIX AND HIS MEN.
WHAT.
IS MY FACE REAL SWOLLEN?
NO.
TWO TINY ARMIES AT ODDS WITH ONE ANOTHER.

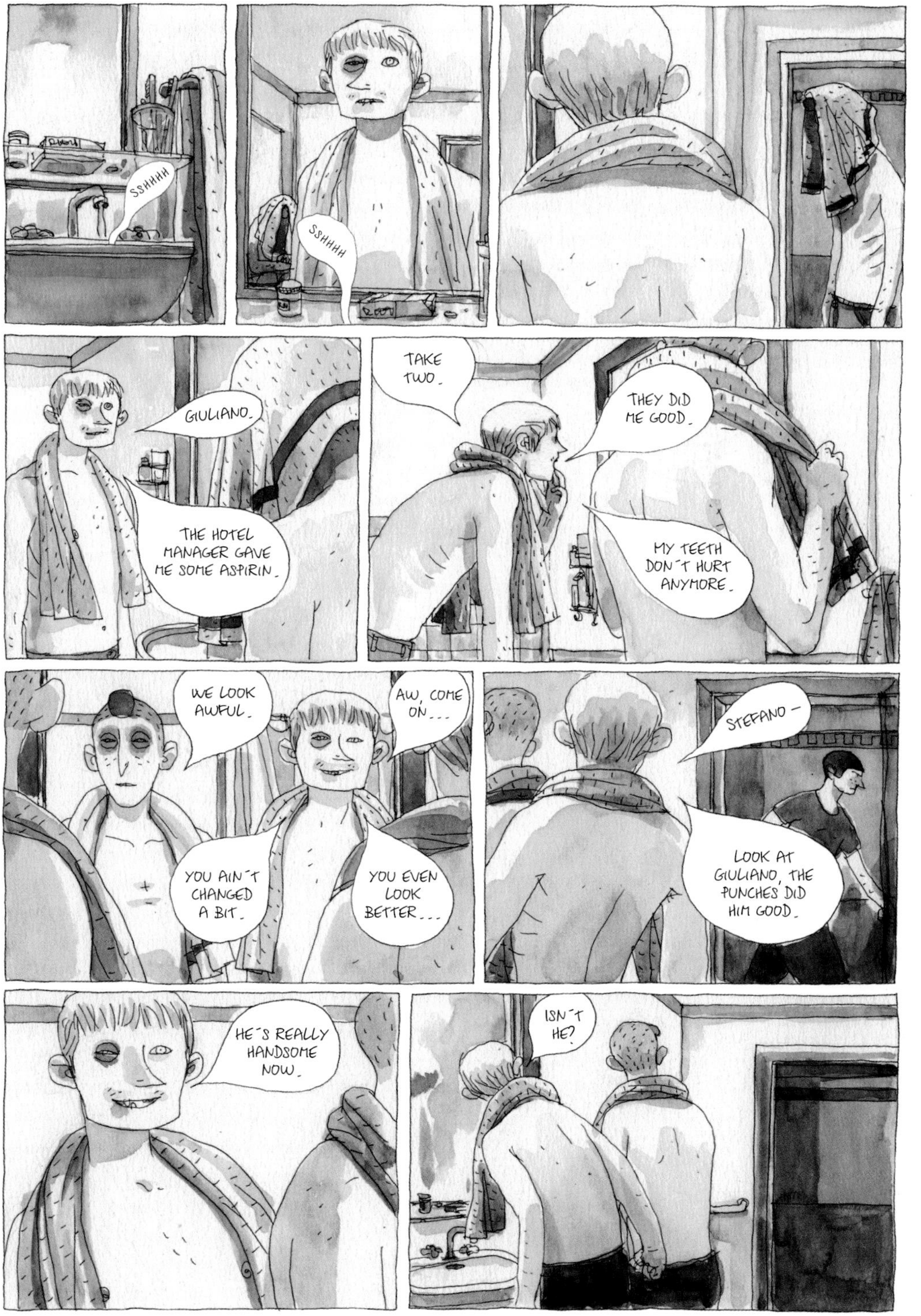
SSHHHH
SSHHHH
GIULIANO.
THE HOTEL MANAGER GAVE ME SOME ASPIRIN.
TAKE TWO.
THEY DID ME GOOD.
MY TEETH DON'T HURT ANYMORE.
WE LOOK AWFUL.
AW, COME ON...
YOU AIN'T CHANGED A BIT.
YOU EVEN LOOK BETTER...
STEFANO —
LOOK AT GIULIANO, THE PUNCHES DID HIM GOOD.
HE'S REALLY HANDSOME NOW.
ISN'T HE?

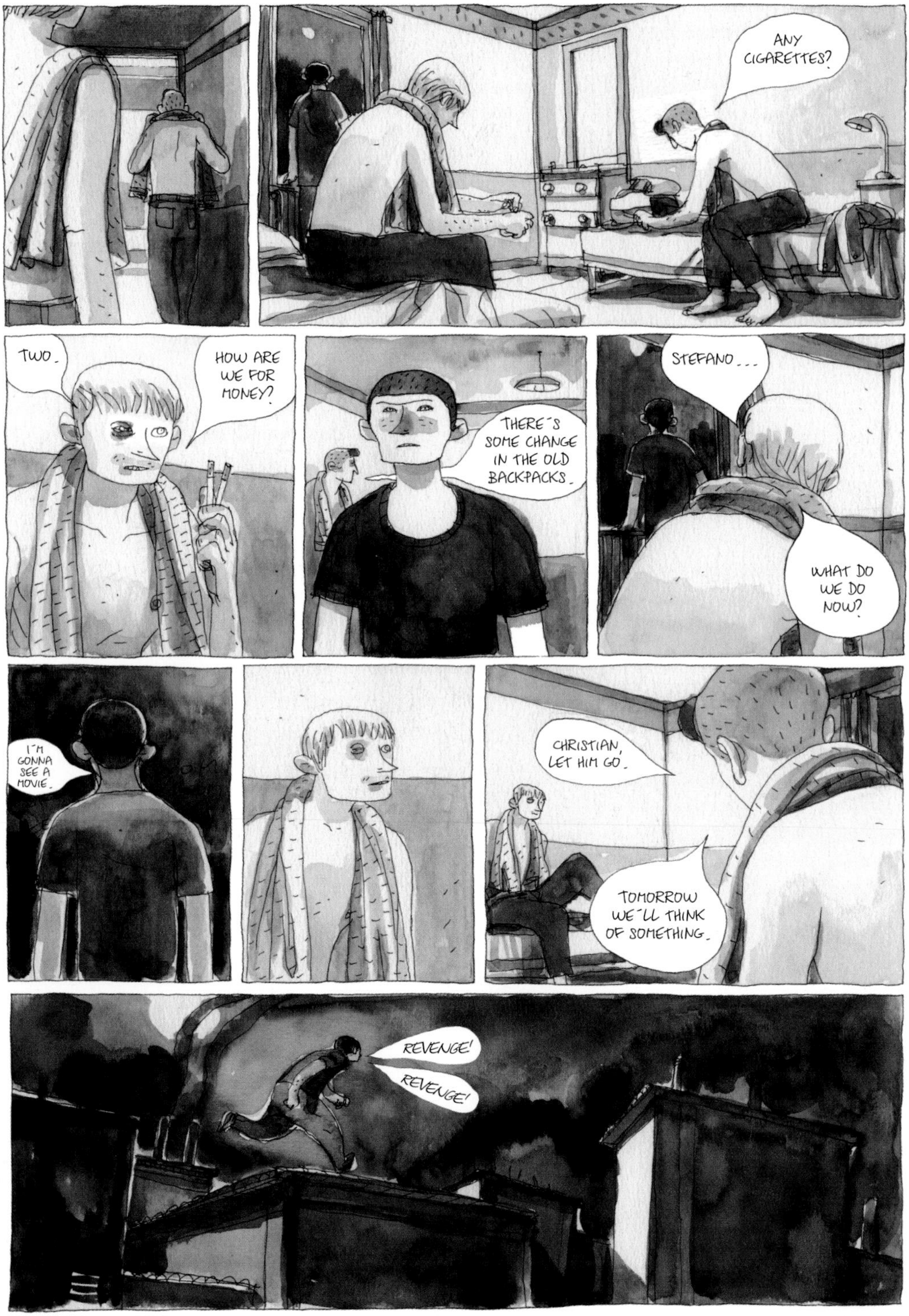
ANY CIGARETTES?
TWO.
HOW ARE WE FOR MONEY?
THERE'S SOME CHANGE IN THE OLD BACKPACKS.
STEFANO...
WHAT DO WE DO NOW?
I'M GONNA SEE A MOVIE.
CHRISTIAN, LET HIM GO.
TOMORROW WE'LL THINK OF SOMETHING.
REVENGE!
REVENGE!

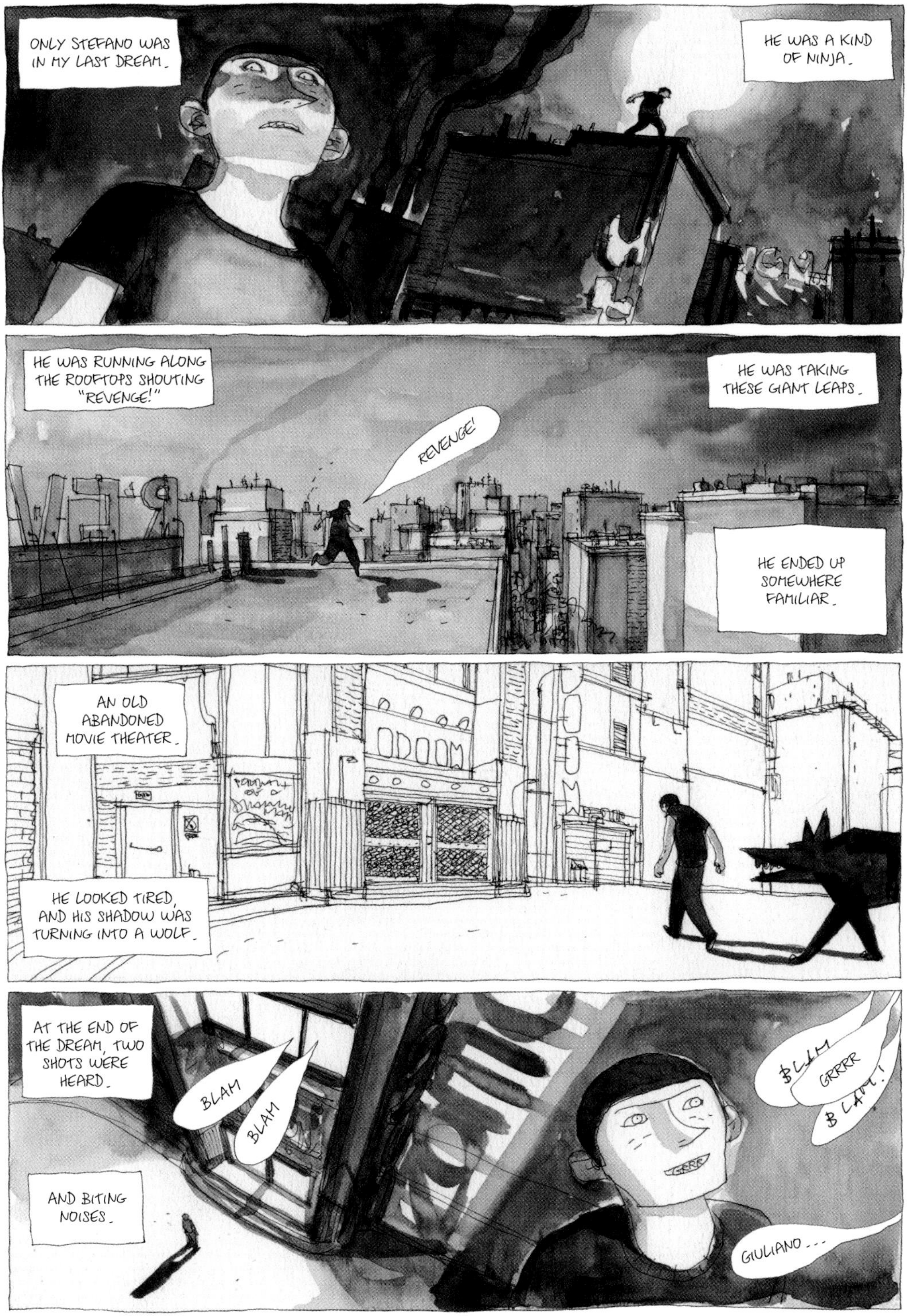
ONLY STEFANO WAS IN MY LAST DREAM.
HE WAS A KIND OF NINJA.
HE WAS RUNNING ALONG THE ROOFTOPS SHOUTING "REVENGE!"
HE WAS TAKING THESE GIANT LEAPS.
REVENGE!
HE ENDED UP SOMEWHERE FAMILIAR.
AN OLD ABANDONED MOVIE THEATER.
ODOOM
HE LOOKED TIRED, AND HIS SHADOW WAS TURNING INTO A WOLF.
AT THE END OF THE DREAM, TWO SHOTS WERE HEARD.
BLAM
BLAM
BLAM
GRRRR
BLAM!
AND BITING NOISES.
GRRR
GIULIANO...

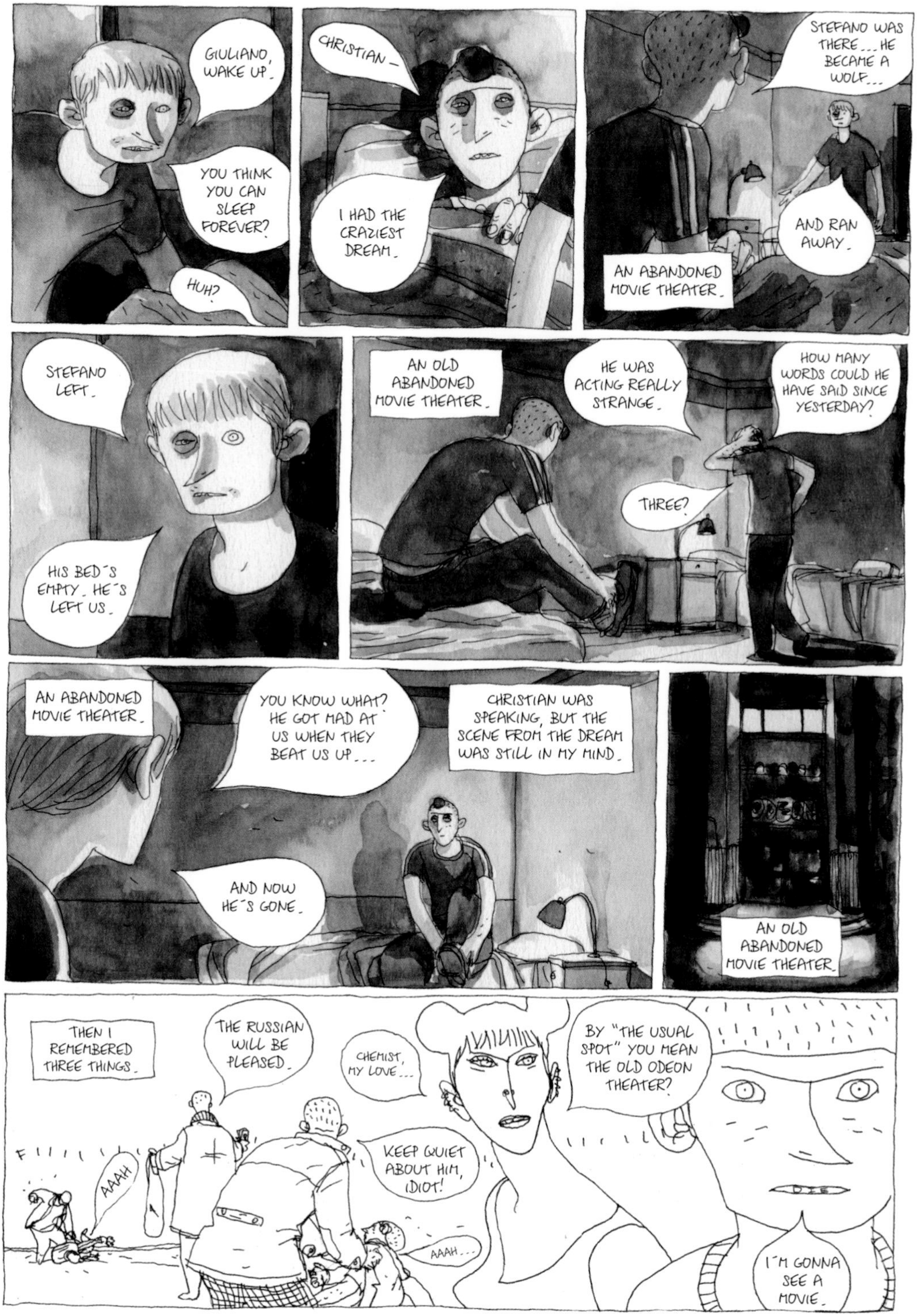
GIULIANO, WAKE UP.
YOU THINK YOU CAN SLEEP FOREVER?
HUH?
CHRISTIAN.
I HAD THE CRAZIEST DREAM.
STEFANO WAS THERE... HE BECAME A WOLF...
AND RAN AWAY.
AN ABANDONED MOVIE THEATER.
STEFANO LEFT.
HIS BED'S EMPTY. HE'S LEFT US.
AN OLD ABANDONED MOVIE THEATER.
HE WAS ACTING REALLY STRANGE.
HOW MANY WORDS COULD HE HAVE SAID SINCE YESTERDAY?
THREE?
AN ABANDONED MOVIE THEATER.
YOU KNOW WHAT? HE GOT MAD AT US WHEN THEY BEAT US UP...
CHRISTIAN WAS SPEAKING, BUT THE SCENE FROM THE DREAM WAS STILL IN MY MIND.
AND NOW HE'S GONE.
AN OLD ABANDONED MOVIE THEATER.
THEN I REMEMBERED THREE THINGS.
THE RUSSIAN WILL BE PLEASED.
AAAH
CHEMIST, MY LOVE...
KEEP QUIET ABOUT HIM, IDIOT!
AAAH...
BY "THE USUAL SPOT" YOU MEAN THE OLD ODEON THEATER?
I'M GONNA SEE A MOVIE.

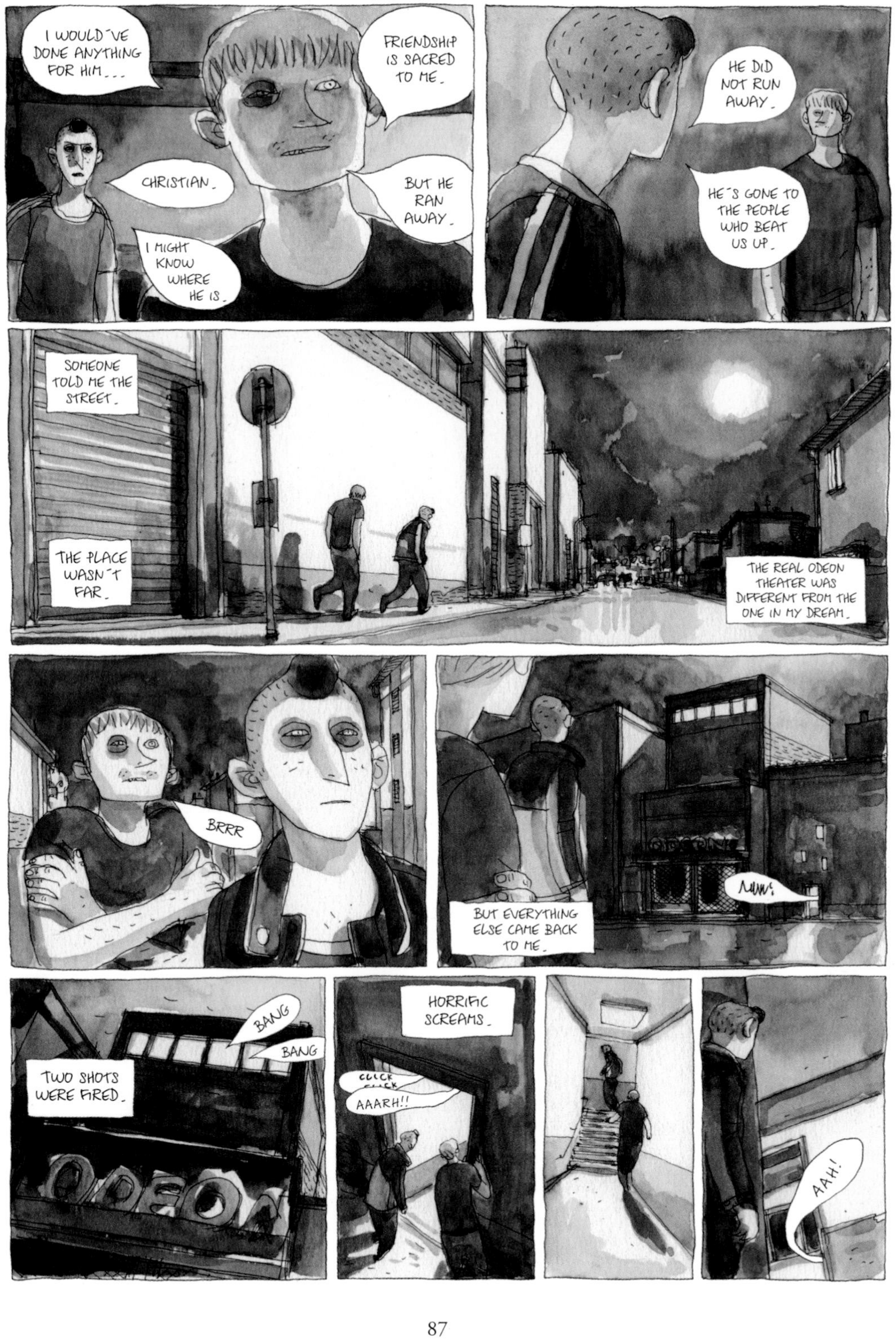
I WOULD'VE DONE ANYTHING FOR HIM...
FRIENDSHIP IS SACRED TO ME.
CHRISTIAN.
BUT HE RAN AWAY.
I MIGHT KNOW WHERE HE IS.
HE DID NOT RUN AWAY.
HE'S GONE TO THE PEOPLE WHO BEAT US UP.
SOMEONE TOLD ME THE STREET.
THE PLACE WASN'T FAR.
THE REAL ODEON THEATER WAS DIFFERENT FROM THE ONE IN MY DREAM.
BRRR
BUT EVERYTHING ELSE CAME BACK TO ME.
BANG
BANG
TWO SHOTS WERE FIRED.
HORRIFIC SCREAMS.
CLICK
AAARH!!
AAH!

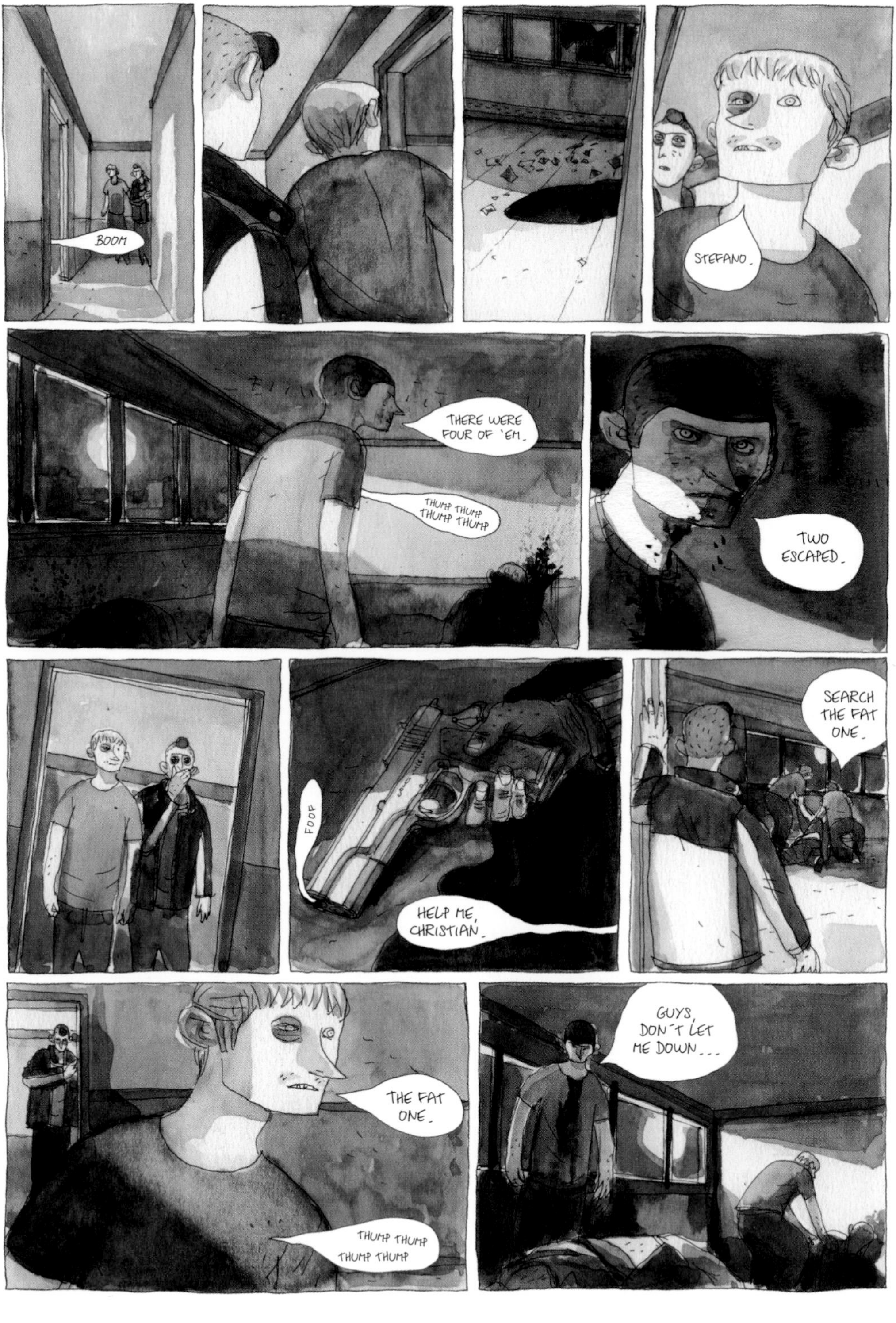
BOOM
STEFANO.
THERE WERE FOUR OF 'EM.
THUMP THUMP THUMP THUMP
TWO ESCAPED.
FOOF
HELP ME, CHRISTIAN.
SEARCH THE FAT ONE.
THE FAT ONE.
THUMP THUMP THUMP THUMP
GUYS, DON'T LET ME DOWN...

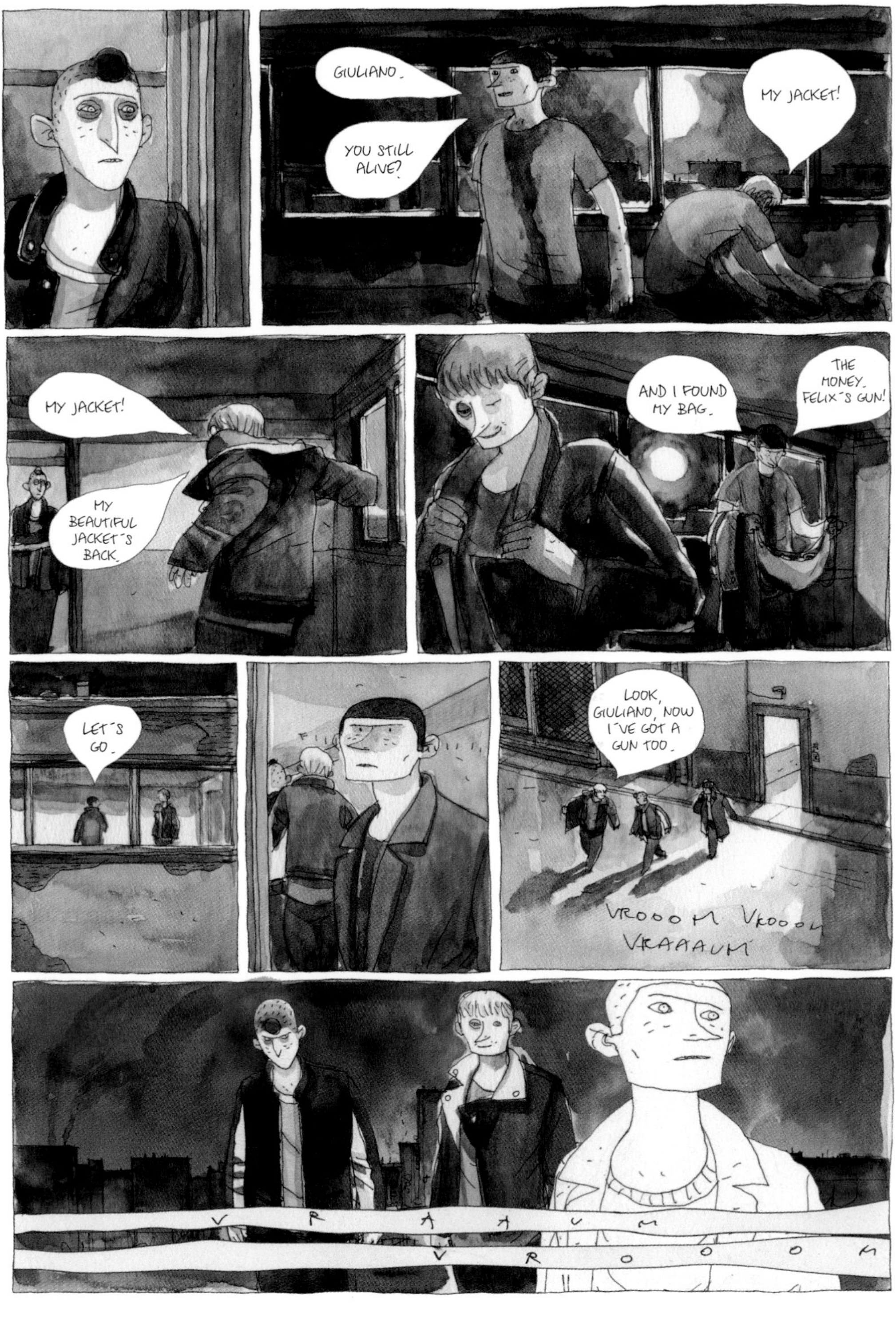
GIULIANO.
YOU STILL ALIVE?
MY JACKET!
MY JACKET!
MY BEAUTIFUL JACKET'S BACK.
AND I FOUND MY BAG.
THE MONEY. FELIX'S GUN!
LET'S GO.
LOOK, GIULIANO, NOW I'VE GOT A GUN TOO.
VROOOM VROOOM
VRAAAUM
VRAAUM
VROOOOM

3

Notes for a War Story

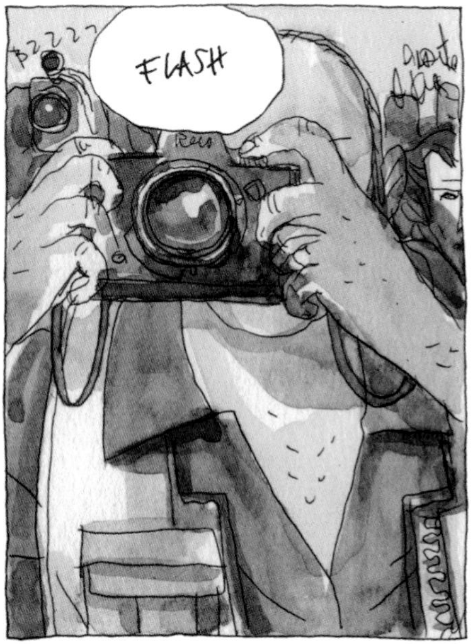
FLASH

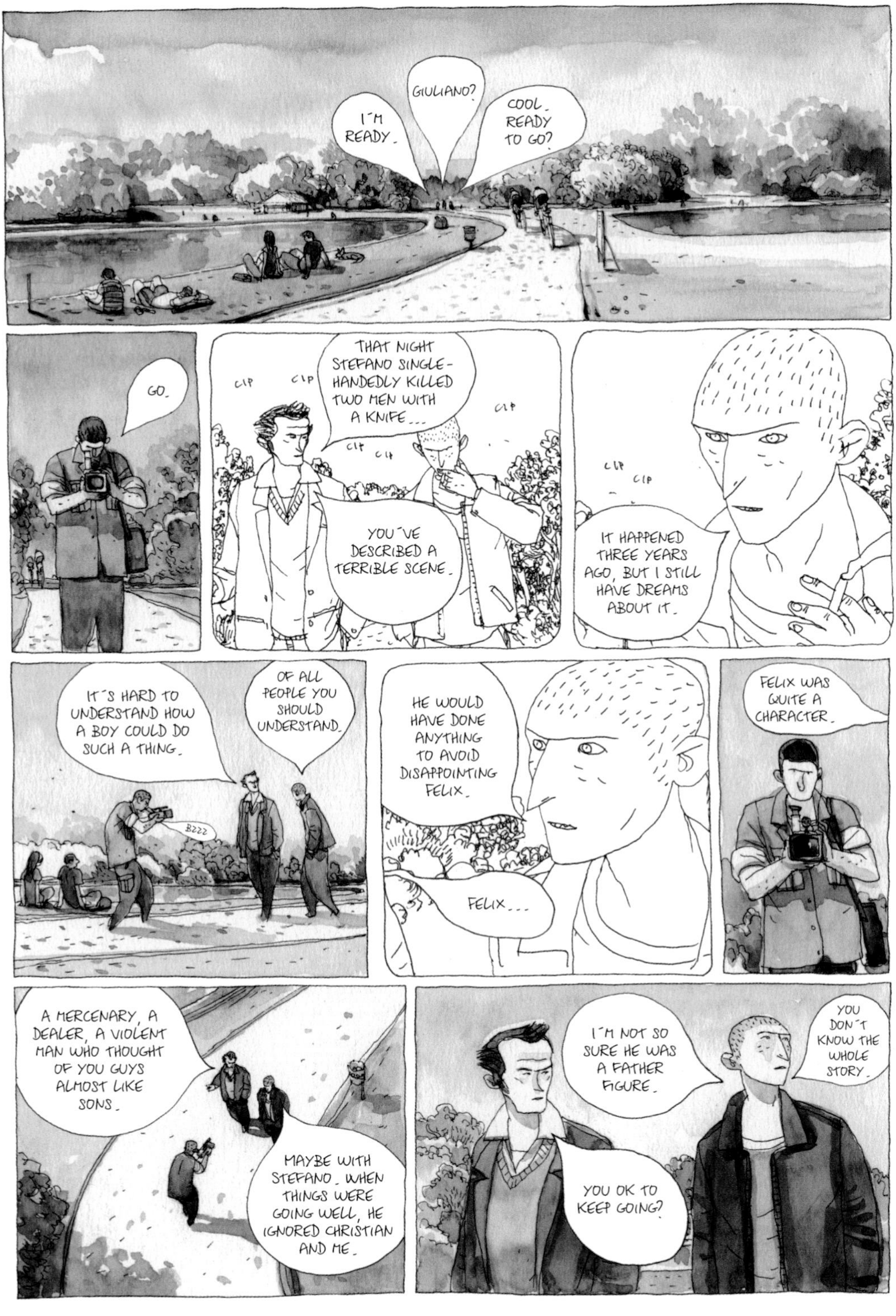
I'M READY.
GIULIANO?
COOL. READY TO GO?
GO.
CIP CIP
THAT NIGHT STEFANO SINGLE-HANDEDLY KILLED TWO MEN WITH A KNIFE...
CIP
CIP CIP
YOU'VE DESCRIBED A TERRIBLE SCENE.
CIP CIP
IT HAPPENED THREE YEARS AGO, BUT I STILL HAVE DREAMS ABOUT IT.
IT'S HARD TO UNDERSTAND HOW A BOY COULD DO SUCH A THING.
OF ALL PEOPLE YOU SHOULD UNDERSTAND.
BZZZ
HE WOULD HAVE DONE ANYTHING TO AVOID DISAPPOINTING FELIX.
FELIX...
FELIX WAS QUITE A CHARACTER.
A MERCENARY, A DEALER, A VIOLENT MAN WHO THOUGHT OF YOU GUYS ALMOST LIKE SONS.
MAYBE WITH STEFANO. WHEN THINGS WERE GOING WELL, HE IGNORED CHRISTIAN AND ME.
I'M NOT SO SURE HE WAS A FATHER FIGURE.
YOU DON'T KNOW THE WHOLE STORY.
YOU OK TO KEEP GOING?

CIP
CIP
CIP
CIP
CIP

BUT WHERE'S THIS FILM GOING?

I TOLD YOU: OUR INTERVIEWS HAVE WAR AS THE MAIN THEME.

EVERY ARTIST BRINGS HIS OWN WORK.

YOU'RE AN ARTIST?

AS A DIRECTOR, I'VE DECIDED TO FILM THE TESTIMONIES OF YOUNG PEOPLE WHO HAVE BEEN PERSONALLY AFFECTED BY THE WAR.

THEN YOU SHOULD SPEAK TO CHRISTIAN AND STEFANO.

HA!

I CAN'T SAY THAT I'VE REALLY BEEN AFFECTED BY IT.

BIP

I WAS ALWAYS OFF TO THE SIDE.

AND THEN, WHEN FELIX CAME BACK FOR THE LAST TIME, I DIDN'T EVEN HAVE THE COURAGE TO FOLLOW THEM.

FOLLOW THEM WHERE?

BZZZZ
2000

AFTER HOW LONG DID FELIX COME BACK?

HE WAS BADLY INJURED, WASN'T HE?

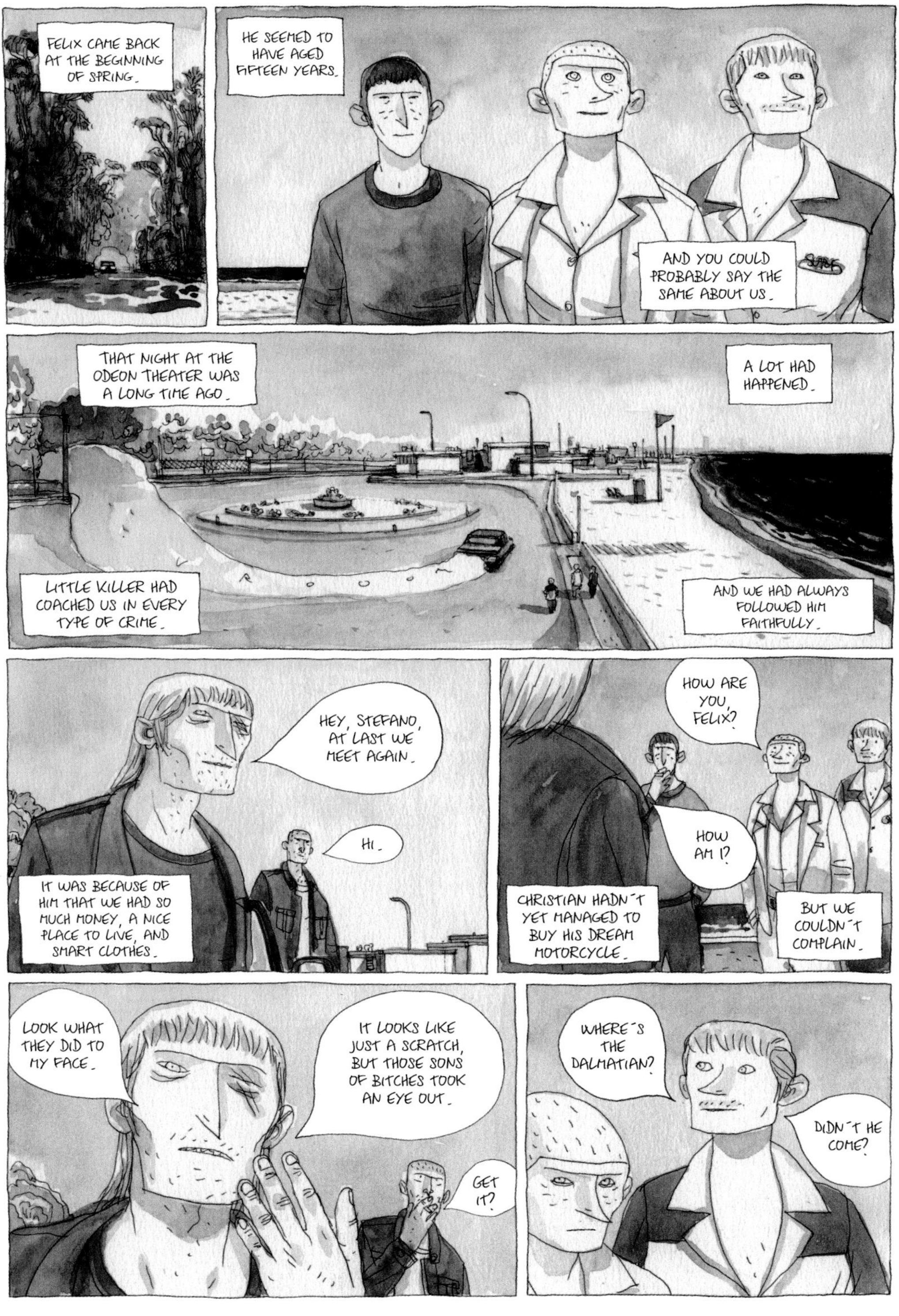
FELIX CAME BACK AT THE BEGINNING OF SPRING.
HE SEEMED TO HAVE AGED FIFTEEN YEARS.
AND YOU COULD PROBABLY SAY THE SAME ABOUT US.
THAT NIGHT AT THE ODEON THEATER WAS A LONG TIME AGO.
A LOT HAD HAPPENED.
LITTLE KILLER HAD COACHED US IN EVERY TYPE OF CRIME.
AND WE HAD ALWAYS FOLLOWED HIM FAITHFULLY.
HEY, STEFANO, AT LAST WE MEET AGAIN.
HI.
IT WAS BECAUSE OF HIM THAT WE HAD SO MUCH MONEY, A NICE PLACE TO LIVE, AND SMART CLOTHES.
HOW ARE YOU, FELIX?
HOW AM I?
CHRISTIAN HADN'T YET MANAGED TO BUY HIS DREAM MOTORCYCLE.
BUT WE COULDN'T COMPLAIN.
LOOK WHAT THEY DID TO MY FACE.
IT LOOKS LIKE JUST A SCRATCH, BUT THOSE SONS OF BITCHES TOOK AN EYE OUT.
GET IT?
WHERE'S THE DALMATIAN?
DIDN'T HE COME?

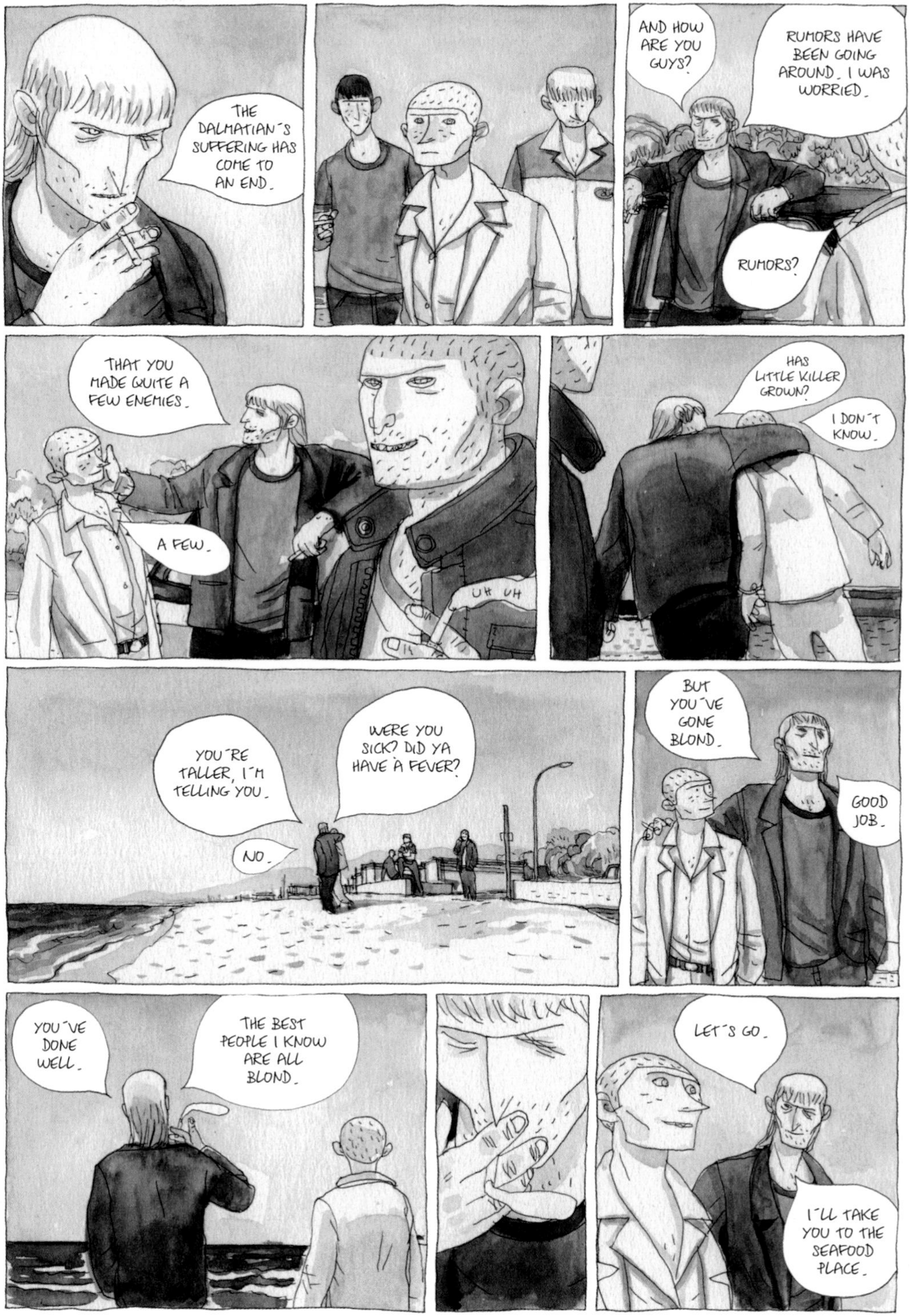
THE DALMATIAN´S SUFFERING HAS COME TO AN END.
AND HOW ARE YOU GUYS?
RUMORS HAVE BEEN GOING AROUND. I WAS WORRIED.
RUMORS?
THAT YOU MADE QUITE A FEW ENEMIES.
A FEW.
UH UH
HAS LITTLE KILLER GROWN?
I DON´T KNOW.
YOU´RE TALLER, I´M TELLING YOU.
WERE YOU SICK? DID YA HAVE A FEVER?
NO.
BUT YOU´VE GONE BLOND.
GOOD JOB.
YOU´VE DONE WELL.
THE BEST PEOPLE I KNOW ARE ALL BLOND.
LET´S GO.
I´LL TAKE YOU TO THE SEAFOOD PLACE.

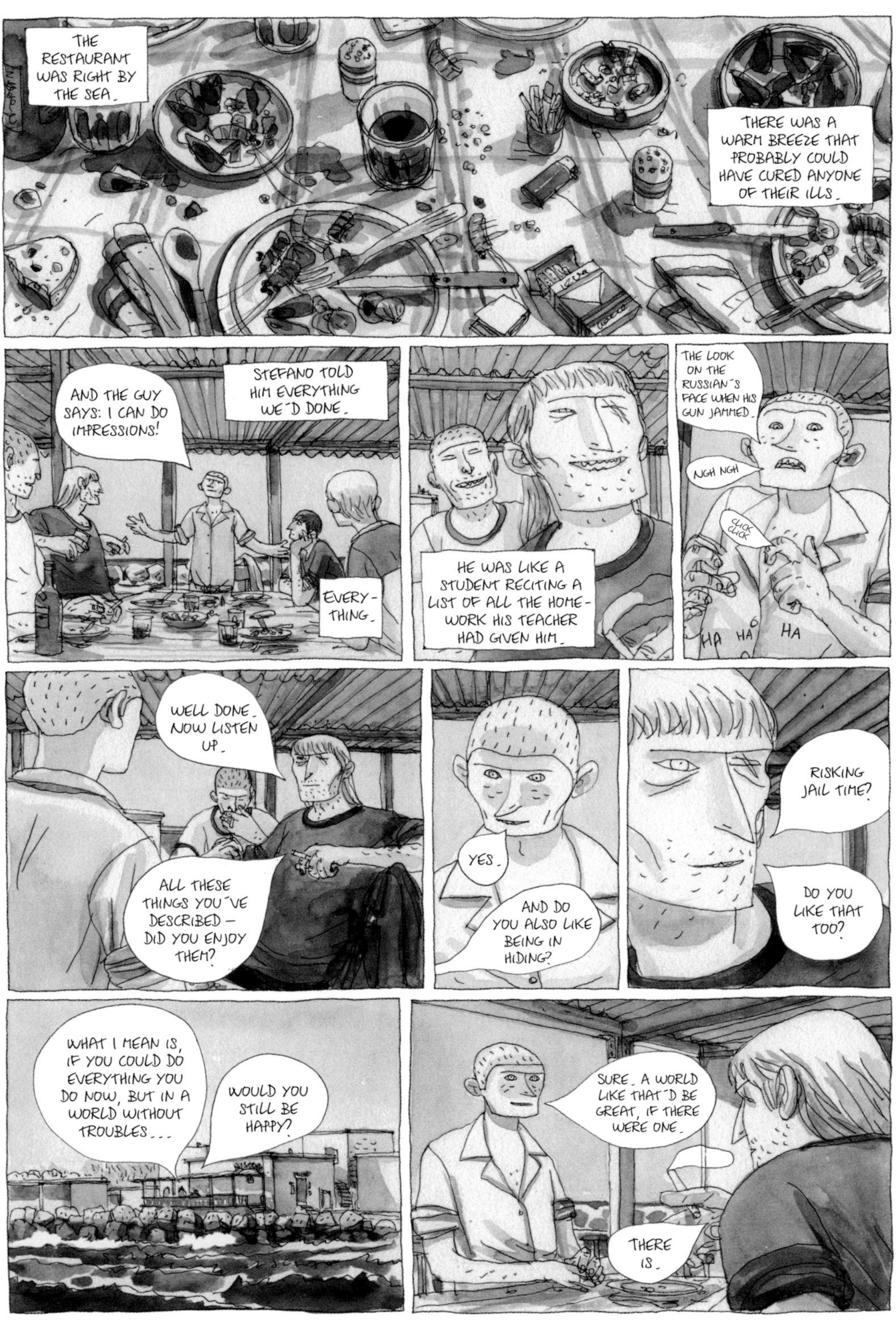
THE RESTAURANT WAS RIGHT BY THE SEA_
THERE WAS A WARM BREEZE THAT PROBABLY COULD HAVE CURED ANYONE OF THEIR ILLS_
AND THE GUY SAYS: I CAN DO IMPRESSIONS!
STEFANO TOLD HIM EVERYTHING WE'D DONE_
EVERY-THING_
HE WAS LIKE A STUDENT RECITING A LIST OF ALL THE HOME-WORK HIS TEACHER HAD GIVEN HIM_
THE LOOK ON THE RUSSIAN'S FACE WHEN HIS GUN JAMMED_
NGH NGH
CLICK CLICK
HA HA HA
WELL DONE_ NOW LISTEN UP_
ALL THESE THINGS YOU'VE DESCRIBED – DID YOU ENJOY THEM?
YES_
AND DO YOU ALSO LIKE BEING IN HIDING?
RISKING JAIL TIME?
DO YOU LIKE THAT TOO?
WHAT I MEAN IS, IF YOU COULD DO EVERYTHING YOU DO NOW, BUT IN A WORLD WITHOUT TROUBLES_ _ _
WOULD YOU STILL BE HAPPY?
SURE_ A WORLD LIKE THAT'D BE GREAT, IF THERE WERE ONE_
THERE IS_

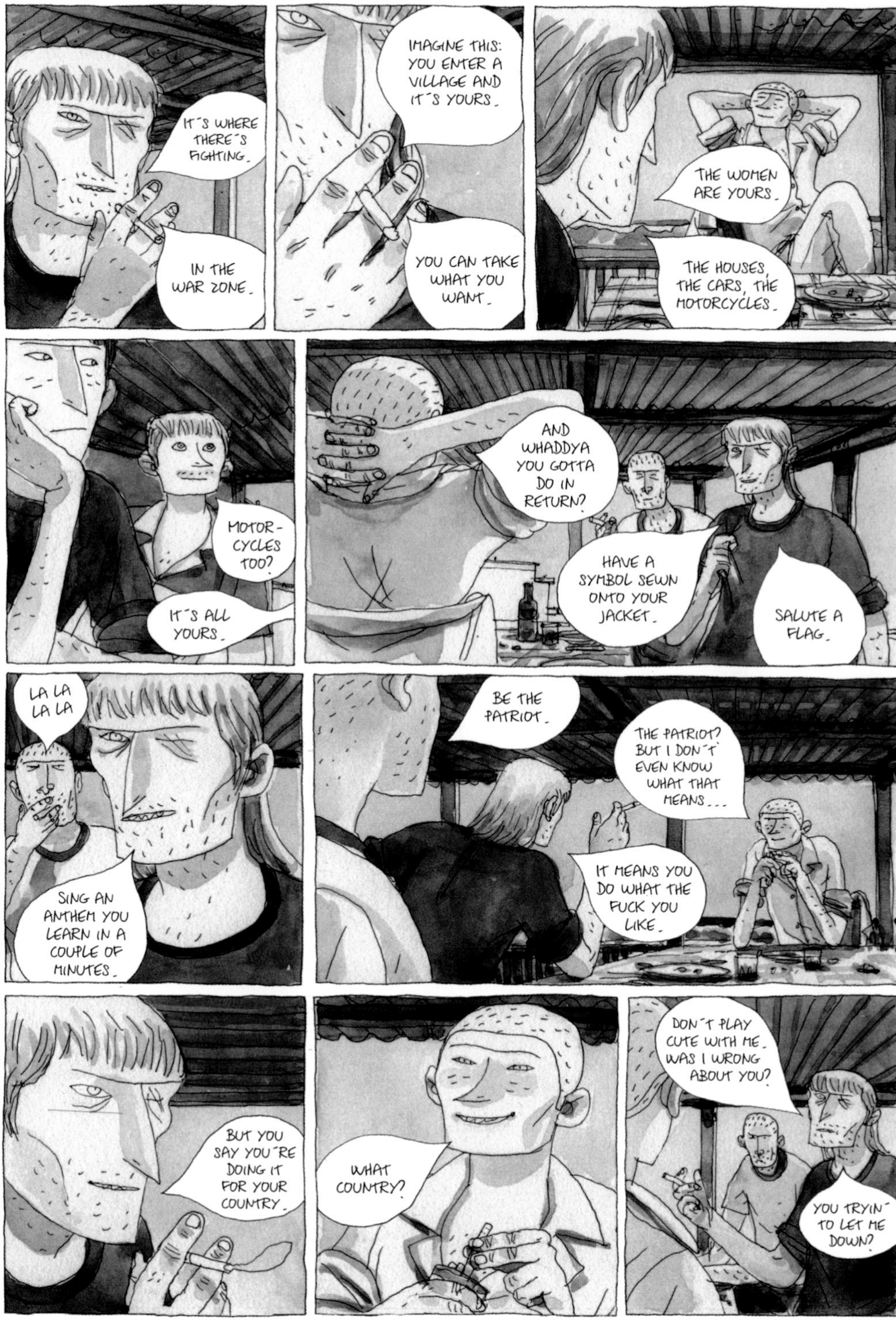

IT´S WHERE THERE´S FIGHTING.
IN THE WAR ZONE.
IMAGINE THIS: YOU ENTER A VILLAGE AND IT´S YOURS.
YOU CAN TAKE WHAT YOU WANT.
THE WOMEN ARE YOURS.
THE HOUSES, THE CARS, THE MOTORCYCLES.
MOTOR-CYCLES TOO?
IT´S ALL YOURS.
AND WHADDYA YOU GOTTA DO IN RETURN?
HAVE A SYMBOL SEWN ONTO YOUR JACKET.
SALUTE A FLAG.
LA LA LA LA
SING AN ANTHEM YOU LEARN IN A COUPLE OF MINUTES.
BE THE PATRIOT.
THE PATRIOT? BUT I DON´T EVEN KNOW WHAT THAT MEANS...
IT MEANS YOU DO WHAT THE FUCK YOU LIKE.
BUT YOU SAY YOU´RE DOING IT FOR YOUR COUNTRY.
WHAT COUNTRY?
DON´T PLAY CUTE WITH ME. WAS I WRONG ABOUT YOU?
YOU TRYIN´ TO LET ME DOWN?

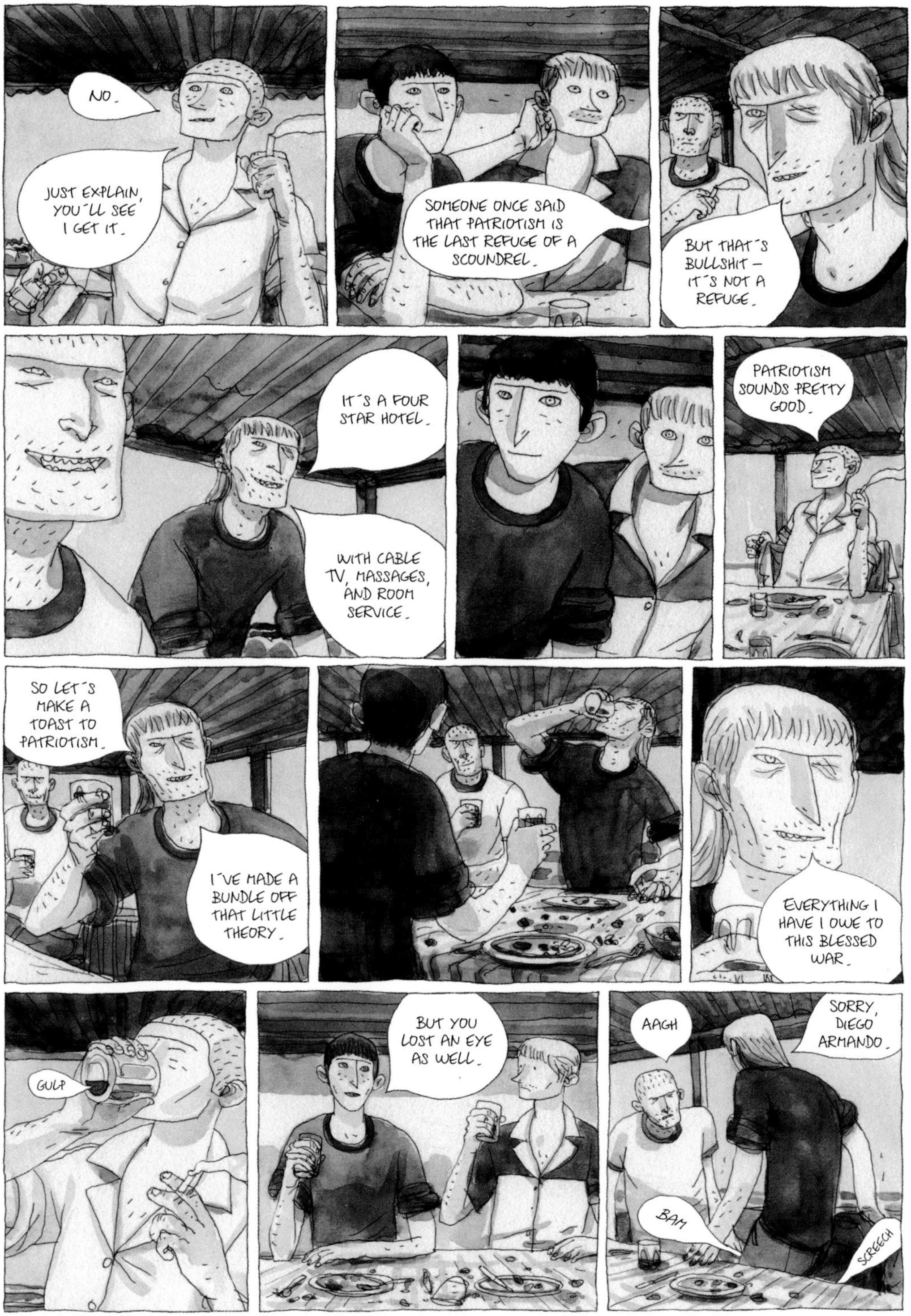
NO.
JUST EXPLAIN, YOU'LL SEE I GET IT.
SOMEONE ONCE SAID THAT PATRIOTISM IS THE LAST REFUGE OF A SCOUNDREL.
BUT THAT'S BULLSHIT — IT'S NOT A REFUGE.
IT'S A FOUR STAR HOTEL.
WITH CABLE TV, MASSAGES, AND ROOM SERVICE.
PATRIOTISM SOUNDS PRETTY GOOD.
SO LET'S MAKE A TOAST TO PATRIOTISM.
I'VE MADE A BUNDLE OFF THAT LITTLE THEORY.
EVERYTHING I HAVE I OWE TO THIS BLESSED WAR.
GULP
BUT YOU LOST AN EYE AS WELL.
AAGH
SORRY, DIEGO ARMANDO.
BAM
SCREECH

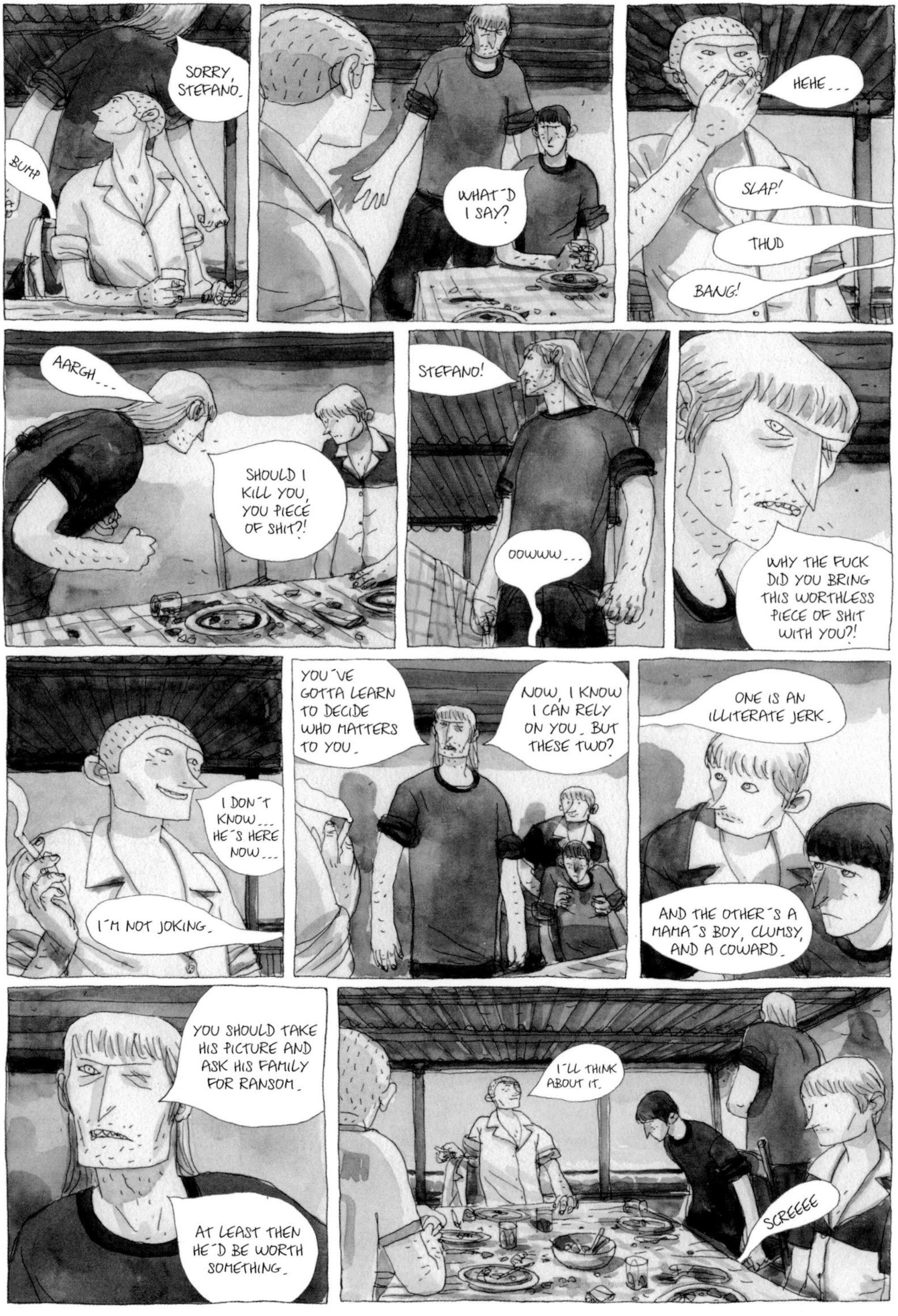
SORRY, STEFANO.
BUMP
WHAT'D I SAY?
HEHE...
SLAP!
THUD
BANG!
AARGH...
SHOULD I KILL YOU, YOU PIECE OF SHIT?!
STEFANO!
OOWWW...
WHY THE FUCK DID YOU BRING THIS WORTHLESS PIECE OF SHIT WITH YOU?!
I DON'T KNOW... HE'S HERE NOW...
I'M NOT JOKING.
YOU'VE GOTTA LEARN TO DECIDE WHO MATTERS TO YOU.
NOW, I KNOW I CAN RELY ON YOU. BUT THESE TWO?
ONE IS AN ILLITERATE JERK.
AND THE OTHER'S A MAMA'S BOY, CLUMSY, AND A COWARD.
YOU SHOULD TAKE HIS PICTURE AND ASK HIS FAMILY FOR RANSOM.
AT LEAST THEN HE'D BE WORTH SOMETHING.
I'LL THINK ABOUT IT.
SCREEEE

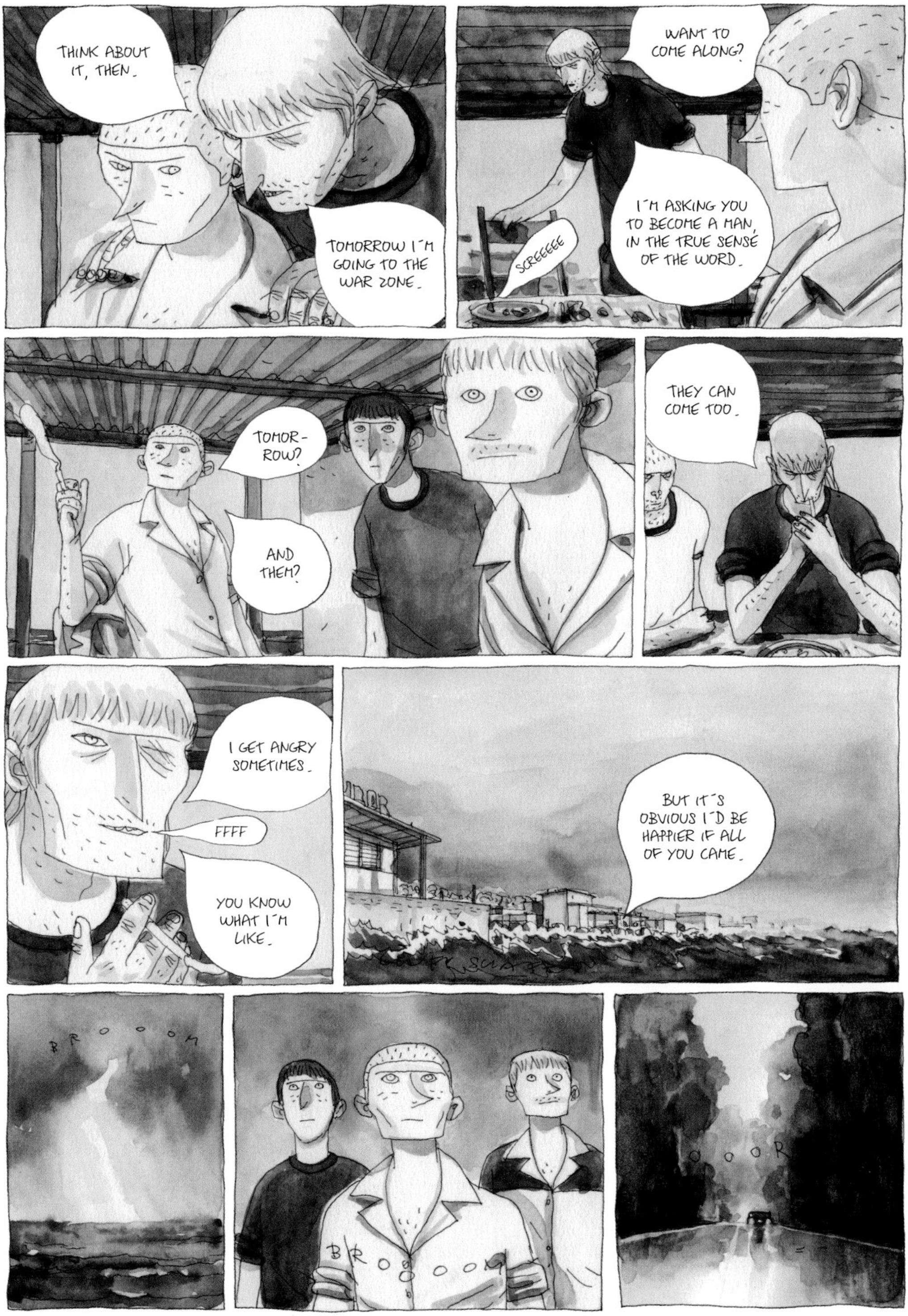
THINK ABOUT IT, THEN.
TOMORROW I'M GOING TO THE WAR ZONE.
WANT TO COME ALONG?
SCREEEEE
I'M ASKING YOU TO BECOME A MAN, IN THE TRUE SENSE OF THE WORD.
TOMOR-ROW?
AND THEM?
THEY CAN COME TOO.
I GET ANGRY SOMETIMES.
FFFF
YOU KNOW WHAT I'M LIKE.
BUT IT'S OBVIOUS I'D BE HAPPIER IF ALL OF YOU CAME.
BROOOOM
BROOOOOM
OOOR

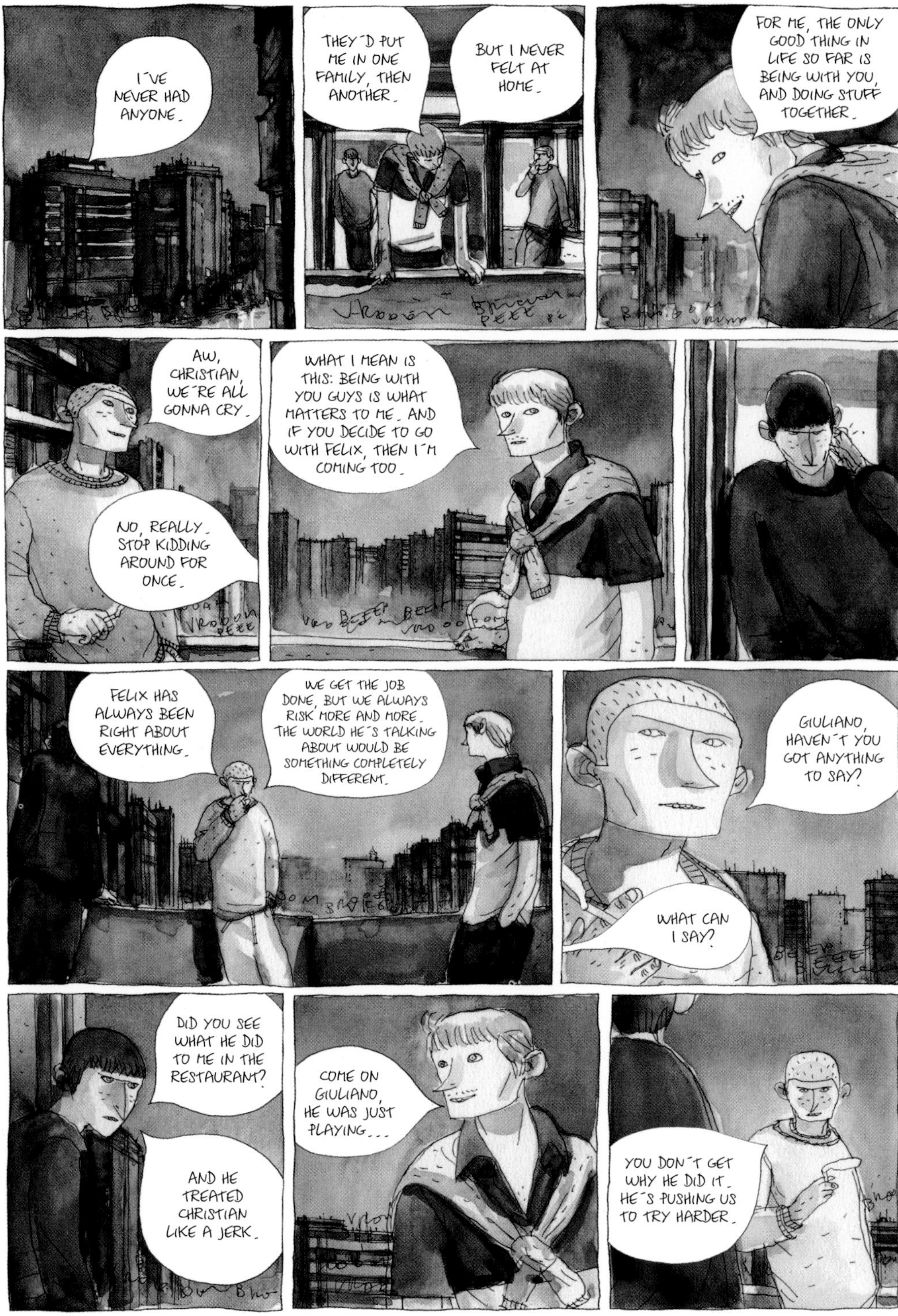
I'VE NEVER HAD ANYONE.
THEY'D PUT ME IN ONE FAMILY, THEN ANOTHER.
BUT I NEVER FELT AT HOME.
FOR ME, THE ONLY GOOD THING IN LIFE SO FAR IS BEING WITH YOU, AND DOING STUFF TOGETHER.
AW, CHRISTIAN, WE'RE ALL GONNA CRY.
NO, REALLY. STOP KIDDING AROUND FOR ONCE.
WHAT I MEAN IS THIS: BEING WITH YOU GUYS IS WHAT MATTERS TO ME. AND IF YOU DECIDE TO GO WITH FELIX, THEN I'M COMING TOO.
FELIX HAS ALWAYS BEEN RIGHT ABOUT EVERYTHING.
WE GET THE JOB DONE, BUT WE ALWAYS RISK MORE AND MORE. THE WORLD HE'S TALKING ABOUT WOULD BE SOMETHING COMPLETELY DIFFERENT.
GIULIANO, HAVEN'T YOU GOT ANYTHING TO SAY?
WHAT CAN I SAY?
DID YOU SEE WHAT HE DID TO ME IN THE RESTAURANT?
AND HE TREATED CHRISTIAN LIKE A JERK.
COME ON GIULIANO, HE WAS JUST PLAYING...
YOU DON'T GET WHY HE DID IT. HE'S PUSHING US TO TRY HARDER.

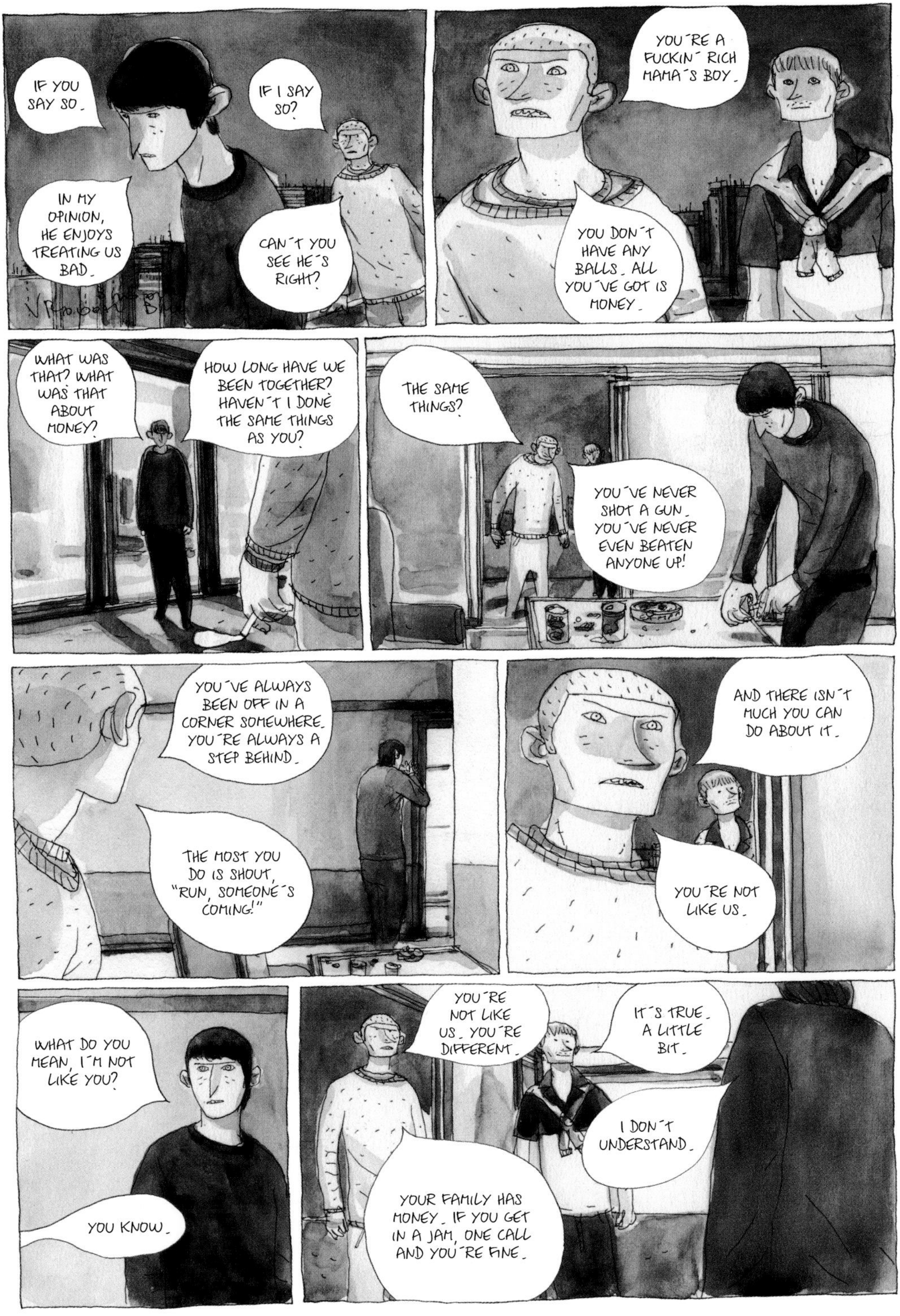
IF YOU SAY SO.
IF I SAY SO?
IN MY OPINION, HE ENJOYS TREATING US BAD.
CAN'T YOU SEE HE'S RIGHT?
YOU'RE A FUCKIN' RICH MAMA'S BOY.
YOU DON'T HAVE ANY BALLS. ALL YOU'VE GOT IS MONEY.
WHAT WAS THAT? WHAT WAS THAT ABOUT MONEY?
HOW LONG HAVE WE BEEN TOGETHER? HAVEN'T I DONE THE SAME THINGS AS YOU?
THE SAME THINGS?
YOU'VE NEVER SHOT A GUN. YOU'VE NEVER EVEN BEATEN ANYONE UP!
YOU'VE ALWAYS BEEN OFF IN A CORNER SOMEWHERE. YOU'RE ALWAYS A STEP BEHIND.
THE MOST YOU DO IS SHOUT, "RUN, SOMEONE'S COMING!"
AND THERE ISN'T MUCH YOU CAN DO ABOUT IT.
YOU'RE NOT LIKE US.
WHAT DO YOU MEAN, I'M NOT LIKE YOU?
YOU KNOW.
YOU'RE NOT LIKE US. YOU'RE DIFFERENT.
IT'S TRUE. A LITTLE BIT.
I DON'T UNDERSTAND.
YOUR FAMILY HAS MONEY. IF YOU GET IN A JAM, ONE CALL AND YOU'RE FINE.

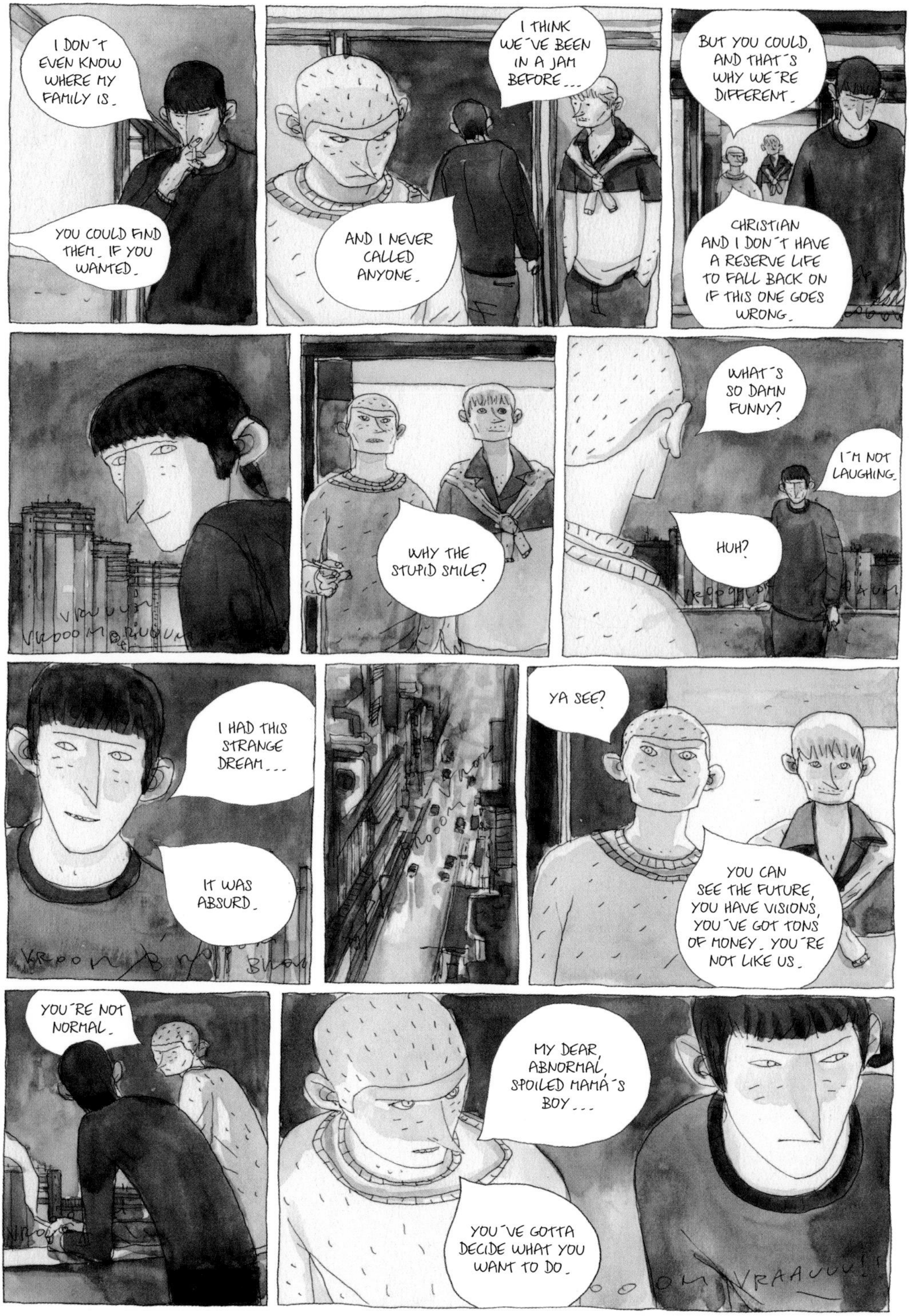
I DON'T EVEN KNOW WHERE MY FAMILY IS.
YOU COULD FIND THEM. IF YOU WANTED.
I THINK WE'VE BEEN IN A JAM BEFORE...
AND I NEVER CALLED ANYONE.
BUT YOU COULD, AND THAT'S WHY WE'RE DIFFERENT.
CHRISTIAN AND I DON'T HAVE A RESERVE LIFE TO FALL BACK ON IF THIS ONE GOES WRONG.
WHY THE STUPID SMILE?
WHAT'S SO DAMN FUNNY?
HUH?
I'M NOT LAUGHING.
I HAD THIS STRANGE DREAM...
IT WAS ABSURD.
YA SEE?
YOU CAN SEE THE FUTURE, YOU HAVE VISIONS, YOU'VE GOT TONS OF MONEY. YOU'RE NOT LIKE US.
YOU'RE NOT NORMAL.
MY DEAR, ABNORMAL, SPOILED MAMÁ'S BOY...
YOU'VE GOTTA DECIDE WHAT YOU WANT TO DO.

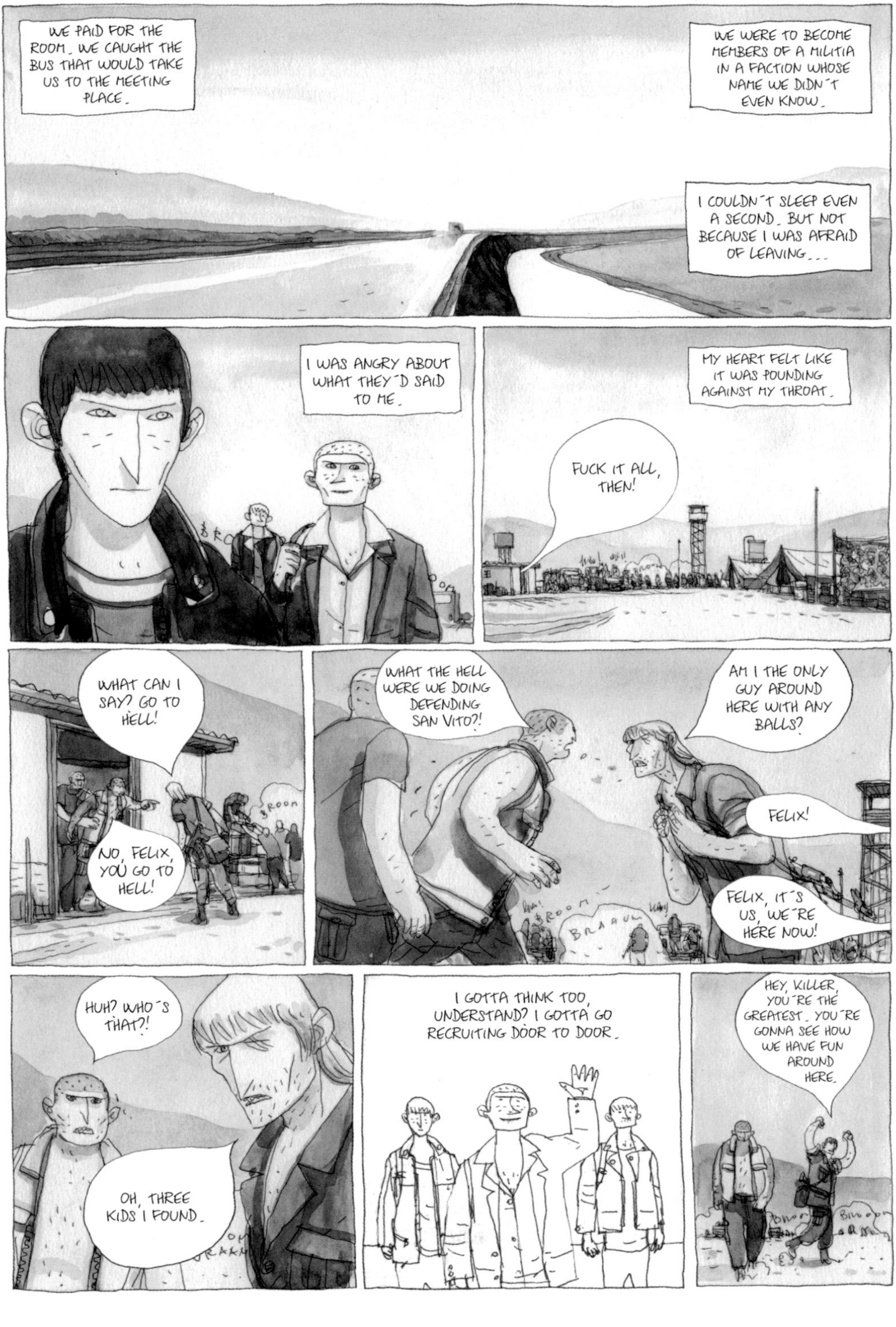

WE PAID FOR THE ROOM. WE CAUGHT THE BUS THAT WOULD TAKE US TO THE MEETING PLACE.
WE WERE TO BECOME MEMBERS OF A MILITIA IN A FACTION WHOSE NAME WE DIDN'T EVEN KNOW.
I COULDN'T SLEEP EVEN A SECOND. BUT NOT BECAUSE I WAS AFRAID OF LEAVING...
I WAS ANGRY ABOUT WHAT THEY'D SAID TO ME.
MY HEART FELT LIKE IT WAS POUNDING AGAINST MY THROAT.
FUCK IT ALL, THEN!
WHAT CAN I SAY? GO TO HELL!
NO, FELIX, YOU GO TO HELL!
WHAT THE HELL WERE WE DOING DEFENDING SAN VITO?!
AM I THE ONLY GUY AROUND HERE WITH ANY BALLS?
FELIX!
FELIX, IT'S US, WE'RE HERE NOW!
HUH? WHO'S THAT?!
OH, THREE KIDS I FOUND.
I GOTTA THINK TOO, UNDERSTAND? I GOTTA GO RECRUITING DOOR TO DOOR.
HEY, KILLER, YOU'RE THE GREATEST. YOU'RE GONNA SEE HOW WE HAVE FUN AROUND HERE.

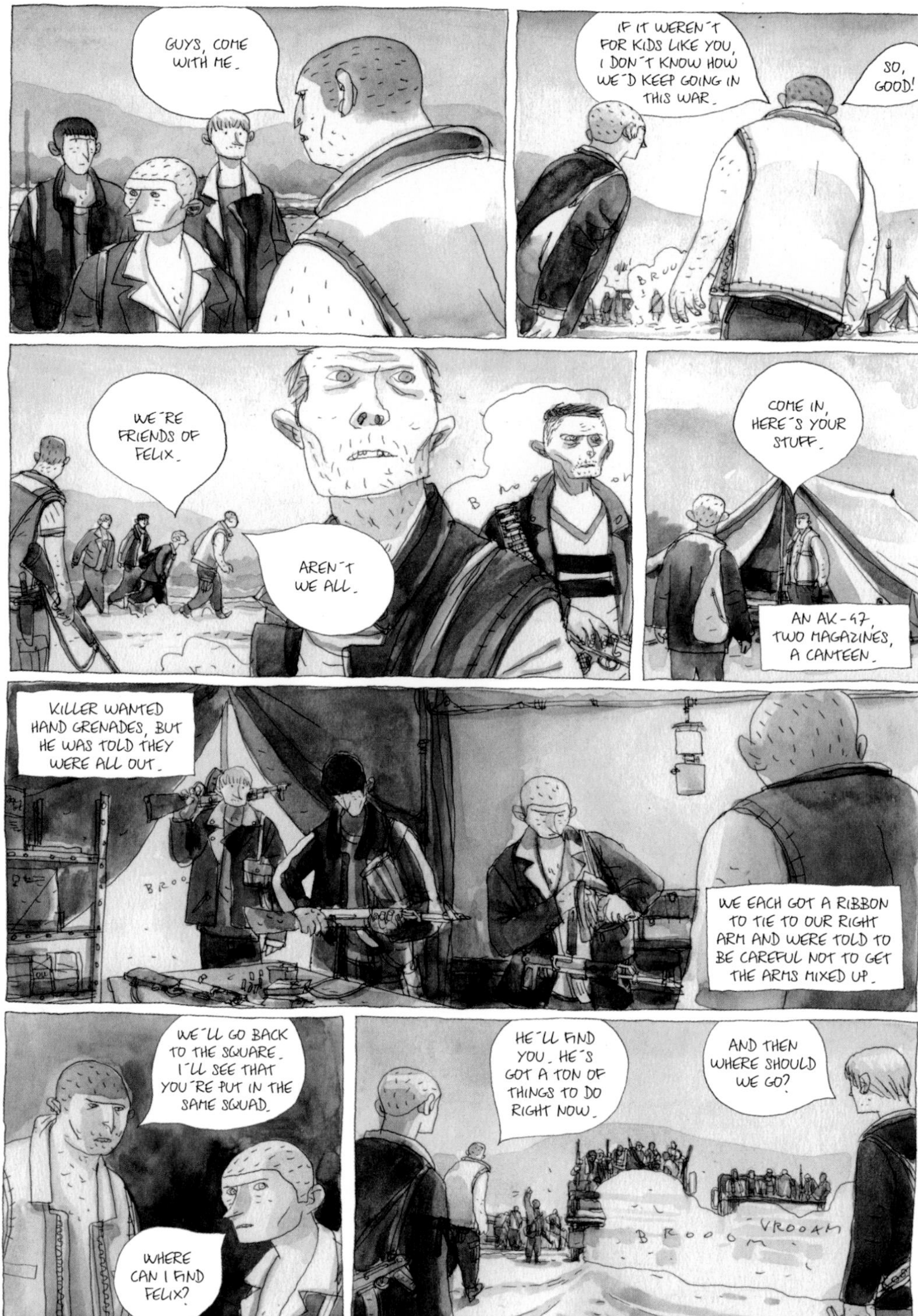
GUYS, COME WITH ME.
IF IT WEREN'T FOR KIDS LIKE YOU, I DON'T KNOW HOW WE'D KEEP GOING IN THIS WAR.
SO, GOOD!
BROU
WE'RE FRIENDS OF FELIX.
AREN'T WE ALL.
BROOOOM
COME IN, HERE'S YOUR STUFF.
AN AK-47, TWO MAGAZINES, A CANTEEN.
KILLER WANTED HAND GRENADES, BUT HE WAS TOLD THEY WERE ALL OUT.
BROO
WE EACH GOT A RIBBON TO TIE TO OUR RIGHT ARM AND WERE TOLD TO BE CAREFUL NOT TO GET THE ARMS MIXED UP.
WE'LL GO BACK TO THE SQUARE. I'LL SEE THAT YOU'RE PUT IN THE SAME SQUAD.
WHERE CAN I FIND FELIX?
HE'LL FIND YOU. HE'S GOT A TON OF THINGS TO DO RIGHT NOW.
AND THEN WHERE SHOULD WE GO?
BROOOM
VROOAM

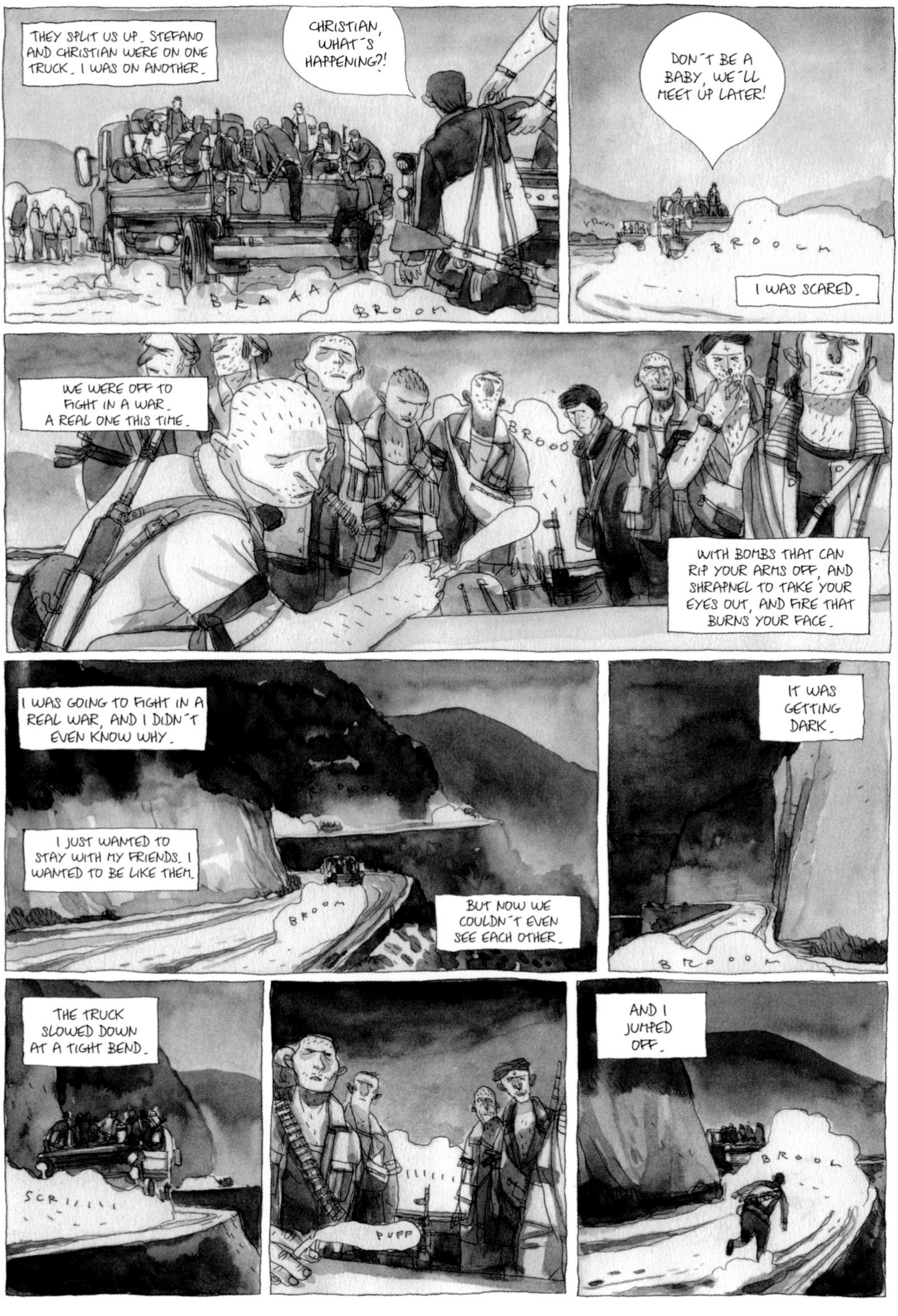
THEY SPLIT US UP. STEFANO AND CHRISTIAN WERE ON ONE TRUCK. I WAS ON ANOTHER.
CHRISTIAN, WHAT'S HAPPENING?!
BRAAAA
BROOM
DON'T BE A BABY, WE'LL MEET UP LATER!
BROOOM
I WAS SCARED.
WE WERE OFF TO FIGHT IN A WAR. A REAL ONE THIS TIME.
BROOOM
WITH BOMBS THAT CAN RIP YOUR ARMS OFF, AND SHRAPNEL TO TAKE YOUR EYES OUT, AND FIRE THAT BURNS YOUR FACE.
I WAS GOING TO FIGHT IN A REAL WAR, AND I DIDN'T EVEN KNOW WHY.
I JUST WANTED TO STAY WITH MY FRIENDS. I WANTED TO BE LIKE THEM.
BROOM
BUT NOW WE COULDN'T EVEN SEE EACH OTHER.
IT WAS GETTING DARK.
BROOOM
THE TRUCK SLOWED DOWN AT A TIGHT BEND.
SCRIIIII
PUFF
AND I JUMPED OFF.
BROOM

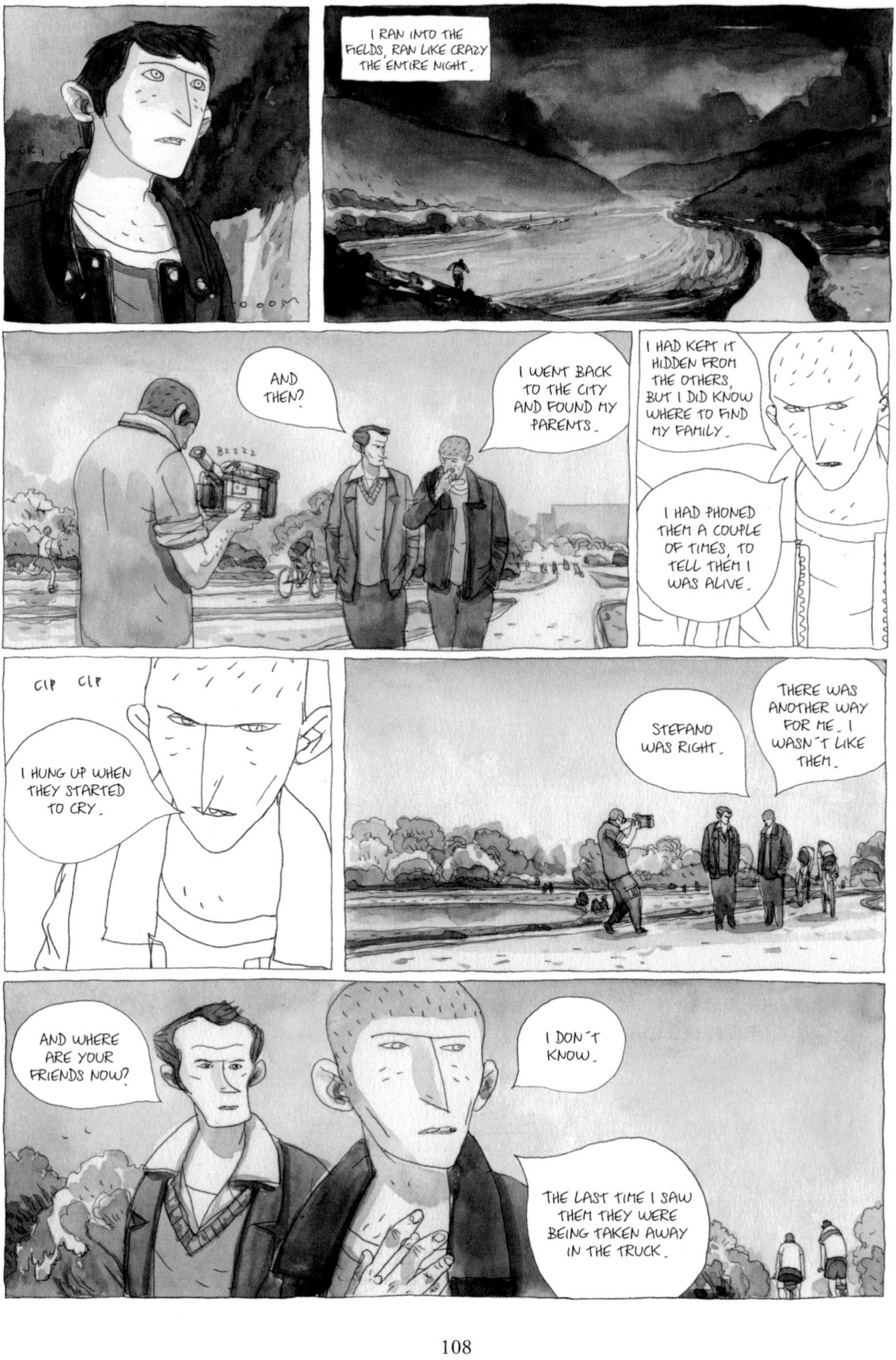
I RAN INTO THE FIELDS, RAN LIKE CRAZY THE ENTIRE NIGHT.
BZZZZ
AND THEN?
I WENT BACK TO THE CITY AND FOUND MY PARENTS.
I HAD KEPT IT HIDDEN FROM THE OTHERS, BUT I DID KNOW WHERE TO FIND MY FAMILY.
I HAD PHONED THEM A COUPLE OF TIMES, TO TELL THEM I WAS ALIVE.
CIP CIP
I HUNG UP WHEN THEY STARTED TO CRY.
STEFANO WAS RIGHT.
THERE WAS ANOTHER WAY FOR ME. I WASN'T LIKE THEM.
AND WHERE ARE YOUR FRIENDS NOW?
I DON'T KNOW.
THE LAST TIME I SAW THEM THEY WERE BEING TAKEN AWAY IN THE TRUCK.

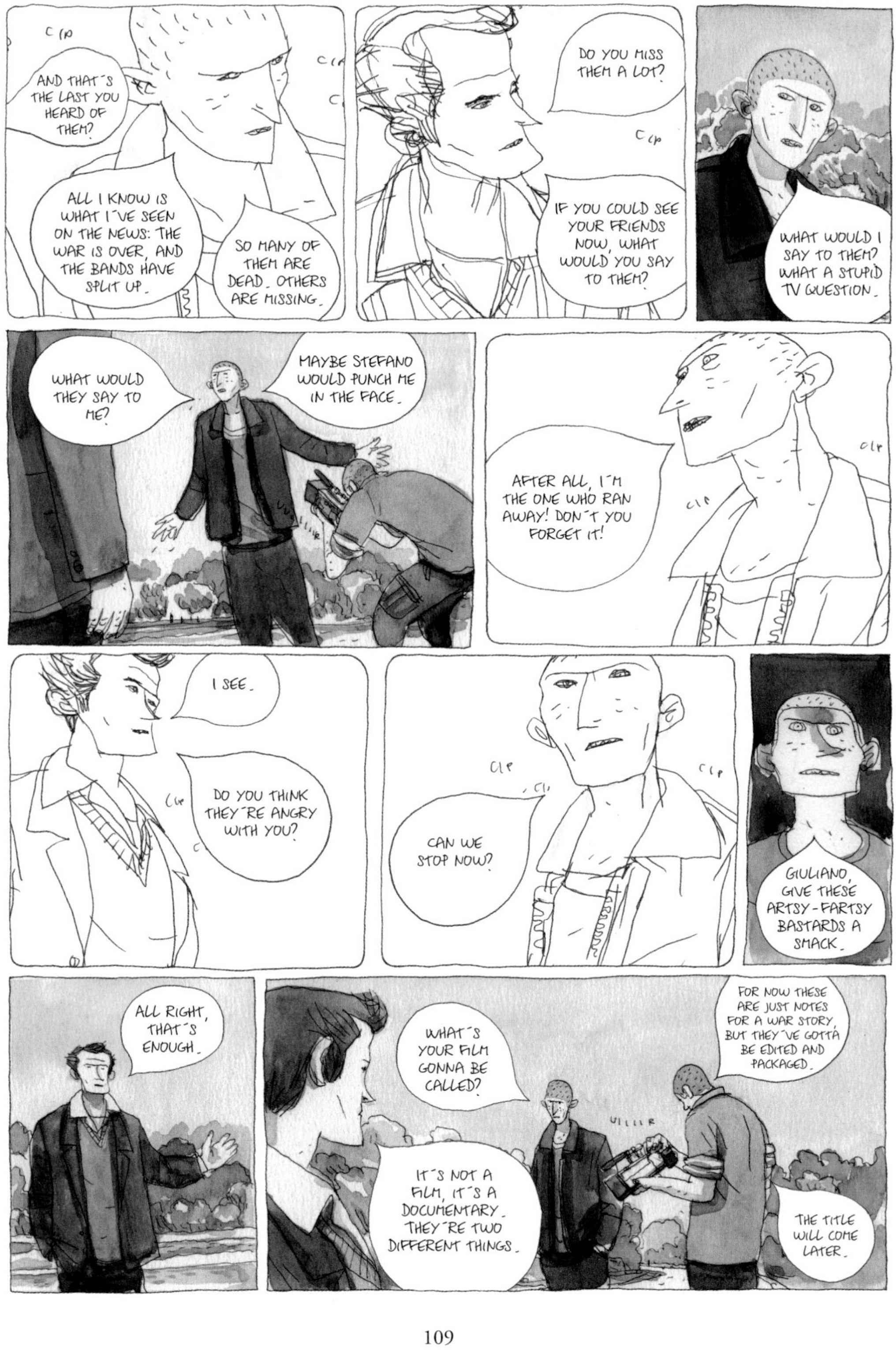

AND THAT'S THE LAST YOU HEARD OF THEM?
ALL I KNOW IS WHAT I'VE SEEN ON THE NEWS: THE WAR IS OVER, AND THE BANDS HAVE SPLIT UP.
SO MANY OF THEM ARE DEAD. OTHERS ARE MISSING.
DO YOU MISS THEM A LOT?
IF YOU COULD SEE YOUR FRIENDS NOW, WHAT WOULD YOU SAY TO THEM?
WHAT WOULD I SAY TO THEM? WHAT A STUPID TV QUESTION.
WHAT WOULD THEY SAY TO ME?
MAYBE STEFANO WOULD PUNCH ME IN THE FACE.
AFTER ALL, I'M THE ONE WHO RAN AWAY! DON'T YOU FORGET IT!
I SEE.
DO YOU THINK THEY'RE ANGRY WITH YOU?
CAN WE STOP NOW?
GIULIANO, GIVE THESE ARTSY-FARTSY BASTARDS A SMACK.
ALL RIGHT, THAT'S ENOUGH.
WHAT'S YOUR FILM GONNA BE CALLED?
FOR NOW THESE ARE JUST NOTES FOR A WAR STORY, BUT THEY'VE GOTTA BE EDITED AND PACKAGED.
IT'S NOT A FILM, IT'S A DOCUMENTARY. THEY'RE TWO DIFFERENT THINGS.
THE TITLE WILL COME LATER.

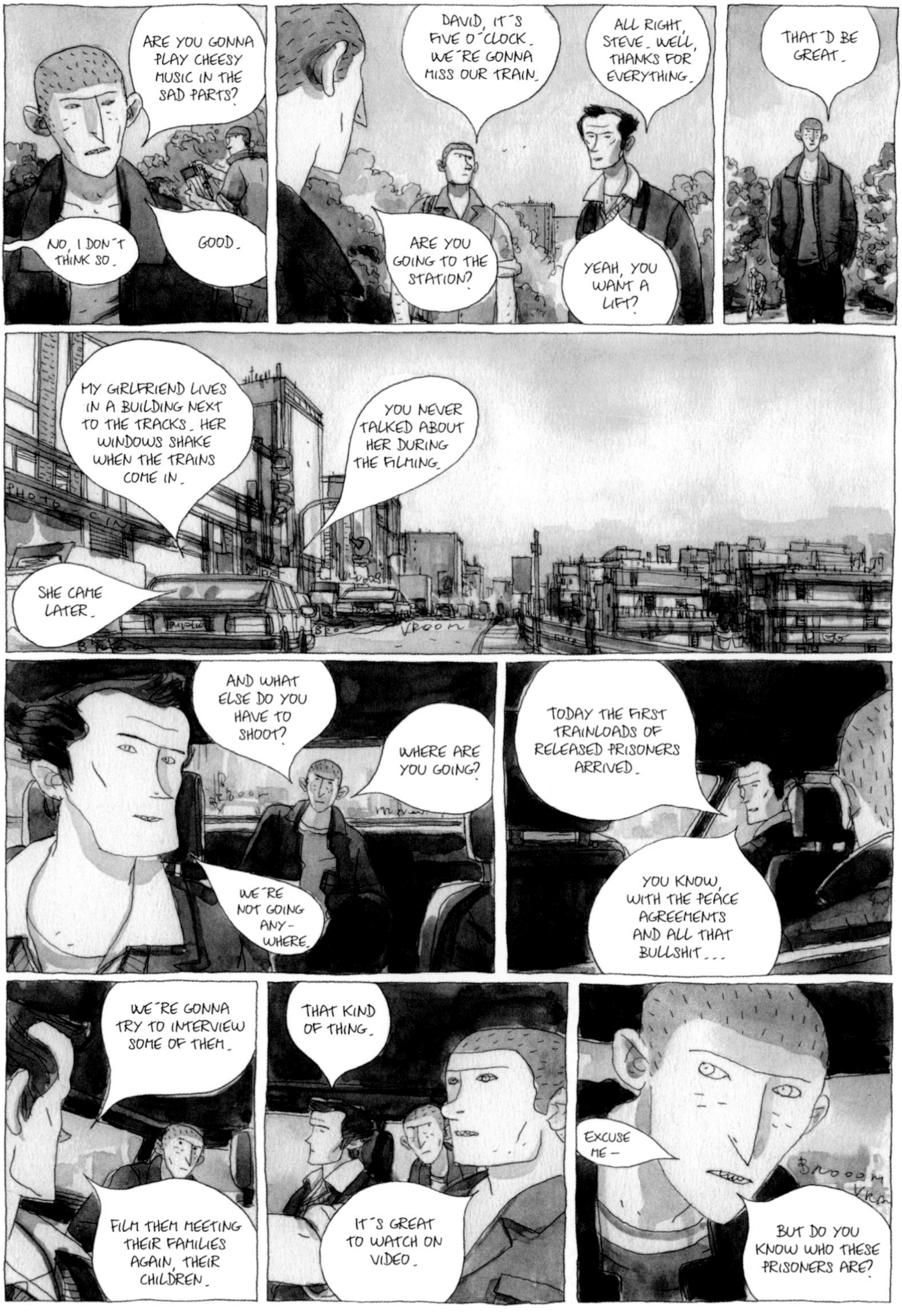
ARE YOU GONNA PLAY CHEESY MUSIC IN THE SAD PARTS?
NO, I DON'T THINK SO.
GOOD.
DAVID, IT'S FIVE O'CLOCK. WE'RE GONNA MISS OUR TRAIN.
ALL RIGHT, STEVE. WELL, THANKS FOR EVERYTHING.
ARE YOU GOING TO THE STATION?
YEAH, YOU WANT A LIFT?
THAT'D BE GREAT.
MY GIRLFRIEND LIVES IN A BUILDING NEXT TO THE TRACKS. HER WINDOWS SHAKE WHEN THE TRAINS COME IN.
YOU NEVER TALKED ABOUT HER DURING THE FILMING.
SHE CAME LATER.
VROOM
AND WHAT ELSE DO YOU HAVE TO SHOOT?
WHERE ARE YOU GOING?
WE'RE NOT GOING ANYWHERE.
TODAY THE FIRST TRAINLOADS OF RELEASED PRISONERS ARRIVED.
YOU KNOW, WITH THE PEACE AGREEMENTS AND ALL THAT BULLSHIT...
WE'RE GONNA TRY TO INTERVIEW SOME OF THEM.
FILM THEM MEETING THEIR FAMILIES AGAIN, THEIR CHILDREN.
THAT KIND OF THING.
IT'S GREAT TO WATCH ON VIDEO.
EXCUSE ME —
BROOOM
BUT DO YOU KNOW WHO THESE PRISONERS ARE?

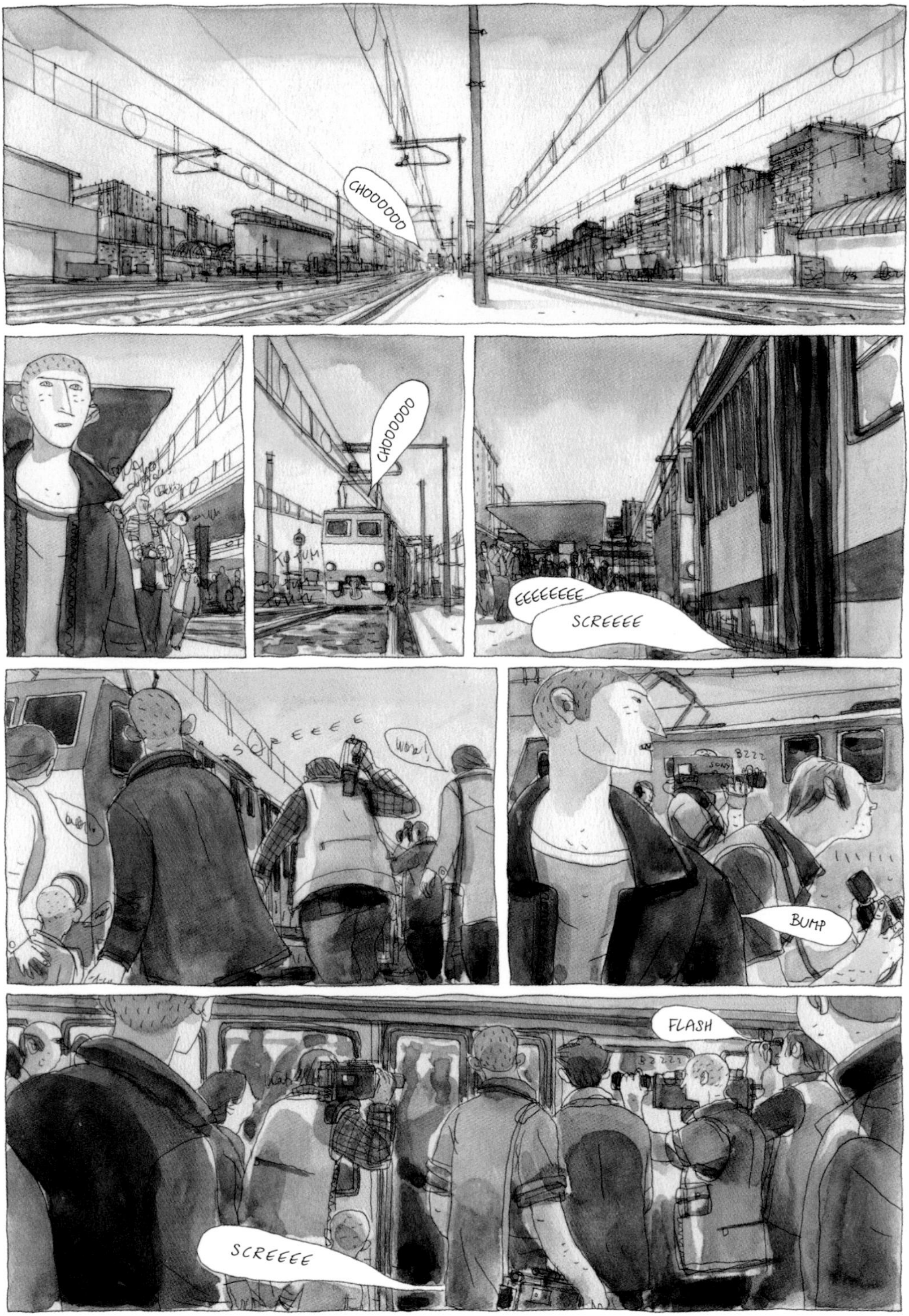
CHOOOOOO
CHOOOOOO
EEEEEEEE
SCREEEE
Wow!
BUMP
FLASH
SCREEEE

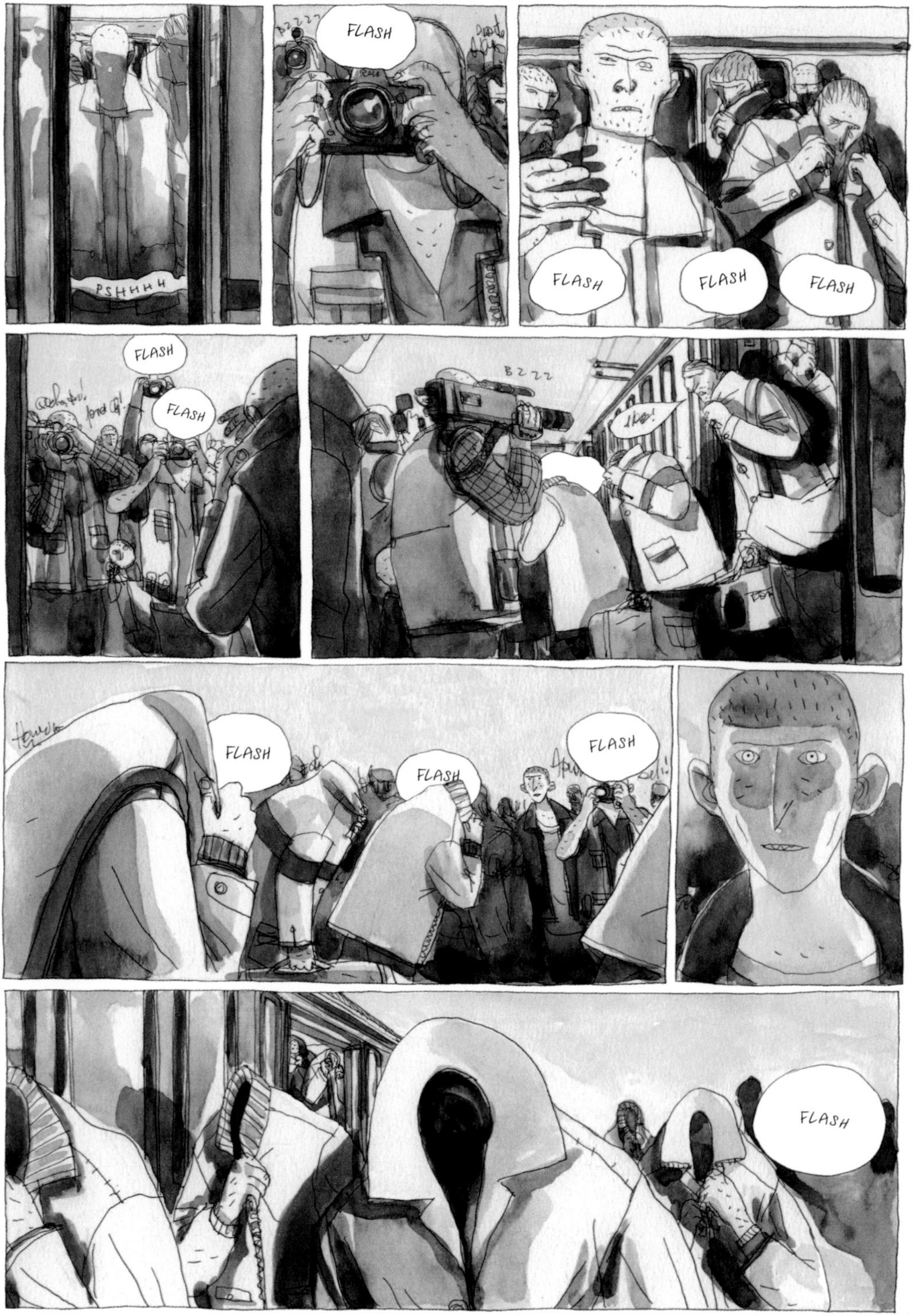
PSHHHH
BZZZZ
FLASH
FLASH
FLASH
FLASH
FLASH
FLASH
BZZZ
FLASH
FLASH
FLASH
FLASH

Notes for a War Story

Afterword

Of Boys and Guns

REFLECTIONS ON GIPI'S *NOTES FOR A WAR STORY*

We are at the margins of a war zone, at the frayed edge of the fabric of society, and it's a harsh environment defined only by relationships among males. The boys "lose points"—whatever those points mean—when they are not strong enough in front of their friends. Stefano wants above all else to be recognized and respected by Felix and his battle-hardened men. We see practically no female characters: a go-go dancer in the background at the bar, the woman who briefly speaks to the Chemist—that's about it. Otherwise, we hear about girls that the boys used to flirt with (not very successfully, by the sound of it), and the militiamen boast of rapes in the war zone, but the presence of a feminine element is even more muffled than the rumblings of war in the distance.

Gipi's book was clearly influenced by the protracted wars of the early 1990s in Bosnia and other areas of the former Yugoslavia, next door to the author's Italy. But it is far more than a "this could happen here" exploration of civil war, even though Gipi does slip in some references to the political turmoil and violence that Italy experienced in the recent past. For example, he names one of the militiamen in the opening scene Pelosi, after the man convicted of (but possibly framed for) the 1975 murder of left-wing filmmaker and writer Pier Paolo Pasolini.

We never see the war itself, so, like the documentary crew at the end of the book, we attempt to piece together these *Notes* to make sense of the war story they refer to. Gipi explains in an essay that, in the three years he spent grappling with this book, he did try to show the war zone directly, but simply couldn't produce the truth of the matter: he lacked the experience to translate his ideas about it into artistically honest story form.

His knowledge of these boys, though, is unmistakably deep and authentic. As the characters gradually appeared on the page—Gipi felt compelled to work in oils, without preliminary sketches, even though that involved "intolerable" drying times—he kept asking himself, "Who are these kids? Where do they come from?" Though Gipi's descriptions of his own childhood make him sound similar to the narrator Giuliano, who is blessed with "other options" and caring parents, the characters of Stefano the Little Killer and Christian are equally believable. They are the far less fortunate kids on the block, irresistibly drawn into a spiral of violence—and Giuliano finds them fascinating.

From the beginning, violence is part of the boys' brutal upbringing. The lessons of growing up are that softness is something to shun and that survival, respect, and self-worth go hand in hand with being as tough as you possibly can be. When civil war erupts, society goes to pieces, and traits that were latent in many kids like Stefano and Christian come to the fore.

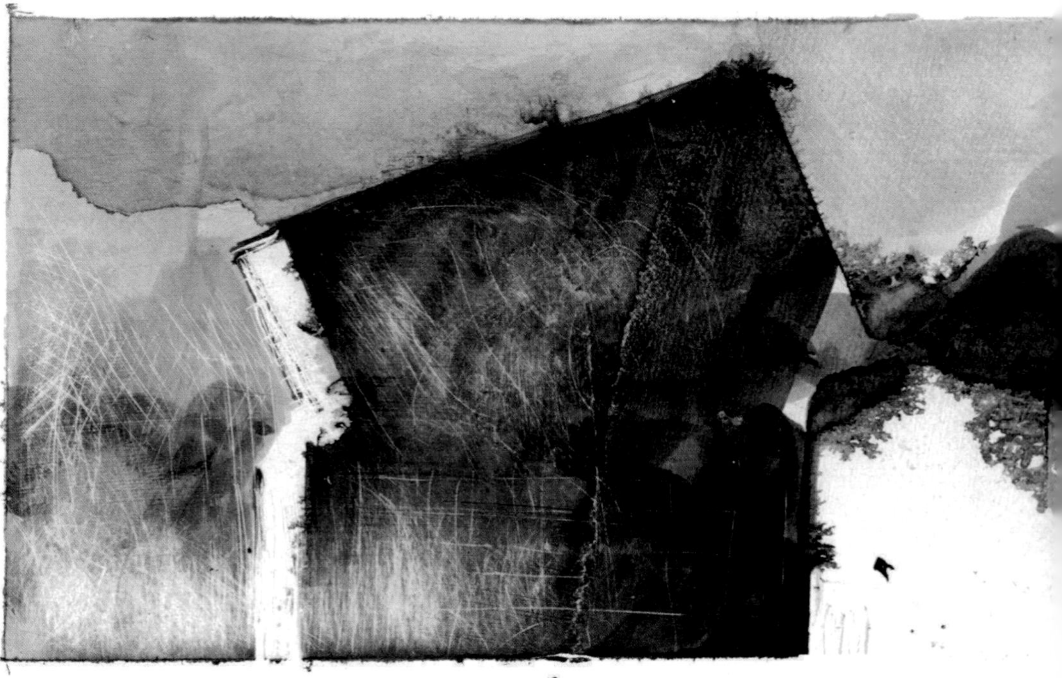

Gipi's book is in fact a contemporary story of unraveling social norms that bears comparison to William Golding's *Lord of the Flies*, which took a group of British schoolboys washed up on a desert island and watched them "go native" —not in the sense of the Noble Savage, but in line with Hobbes's description

of life in the state of nature as "nasty, brutish, and short." Philosophers have long argued over whether we are born with destructive tendencies, or whether society corrupts our innate goodness; in a war zone, that debate seems pretty abstract. None of us will ever experience life in the pre-social condition, if such a thing ever existed, but the lawlessness of a failed State has become a tragically common experience in our world.

The scene in which Felix upbraids Christian for fawningly thanking him and calling him "Mr. Felix" is revealing. The conventions of polite society seem absurdly out of place in a civil war, and Felix himself is characteristic of the people who thrive when society breaks down. He offers leadership to impressionable boys, and he has a charisma that derives from his certainty about how to go on. He knows how to stay at the top of the food chain, how to be predator rather than prey. A street-smart thug, he quotes a famous aphorism of Samuel Johnson's: "Patriotism is the last refuge of a scoundrel." His is the way of the cynic, for whom the cause, any cause, is simply a means to self-serving ends. But even if he had been a fervent fanatic, he would have

had the same effect on the boys, including drawing them into the racketeering operations that groom them for battle among the militias and add years to their youthful faces.

The three boys' experience illustrates accurately the nexus between organized crime and civil war factions. In the Balkans, the circles of nationalist extremism and those of various organized criminal activities overlapped completely. Diamond trafficking sustained the horribly destructive civil wars in Liberia and Sierra Leone. In Colombia, both left-wing guerrillas and right-wing paramilitaries rely heavily on the drug trade, kidnappings, and extortion as their sources of cash for purchasing weapons and recruiting fighters.

Another famous phrase of Samuel Johnson's also sheds light on what motivates the protagonists of these *Notes:* "All boys love liberty, till experience convinces them that they are not so fit to govern themselves as they imagined." Adolescent boys need leaders, and they need role models to help them find, harness, and elevate their masculine power—which is basically their ability to do. Societies work when they give boys a sense of direction and safe activities in which they can aspire to excel, earn merit, and obtain more power. That can mean jobs, art, sports, music (another of Gipi's much-loved books, *Garage Band*, shows teenagers starting a rock group), community life, or just about anything else. In this sense, education can be described as a gradual refinement of our paths to power.

Trouble begins when the older generation fails the younger one in its duty to provide leadership. The three boys in *Notes for a War Story* illustrate different ways in which this can happen. In Giuliano's case, it seems his parents resigned themselves to a life of conformity that offered material comfort but little else, causing him to seek the thrill and excitement of running with the bad boys. For Christian, an abandoned child raised in orphanages, emotional and educational neglect produced a yearning for anything that could pass for a family. And as far as Stefano is concerned, the crass brutality of his family caused him to clench his fists and convince himself that he'd be tougher than anyone out there, that he was not Stefano at all but Il Killerino, the Little Killer, who didn't even feel a thing when he saw "a man"—his own father, in fact—throw himself out of the window.

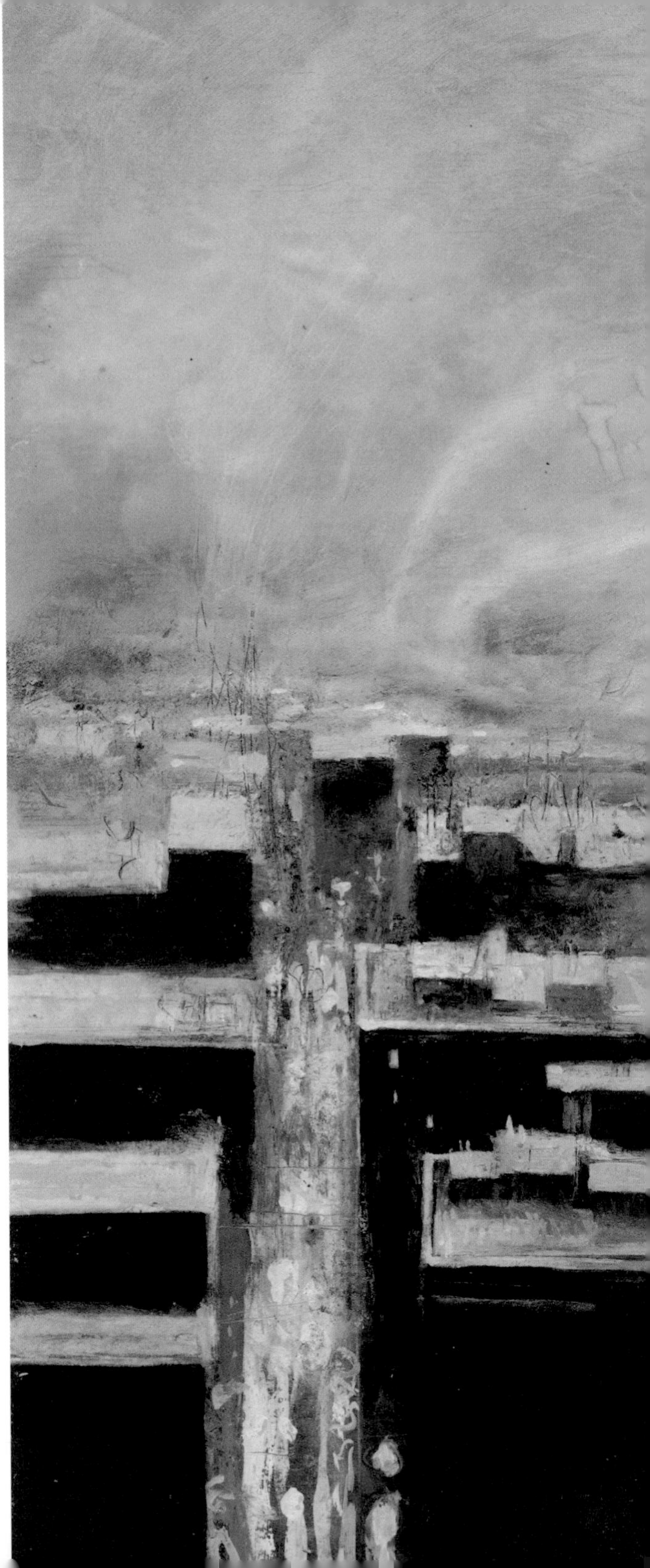

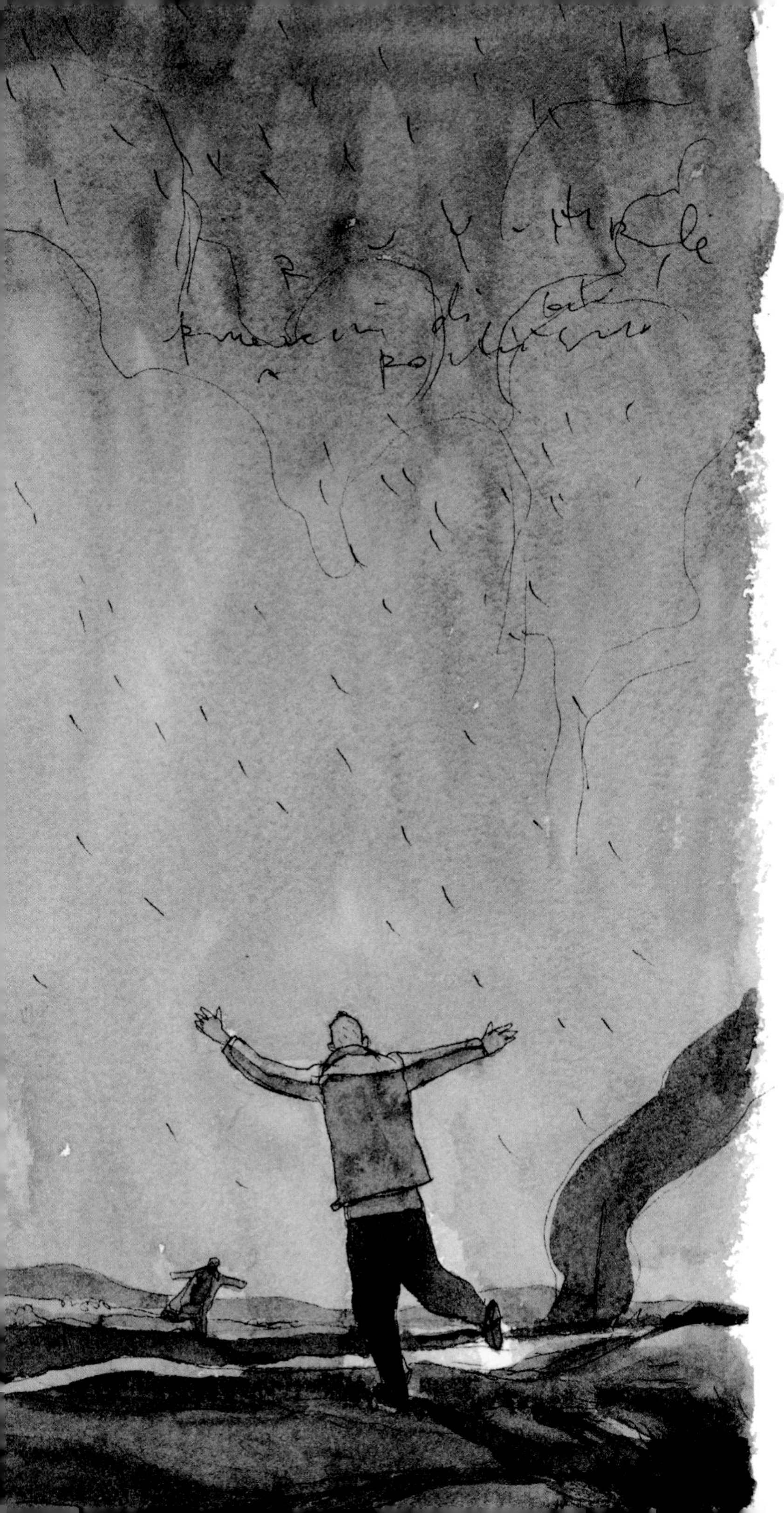

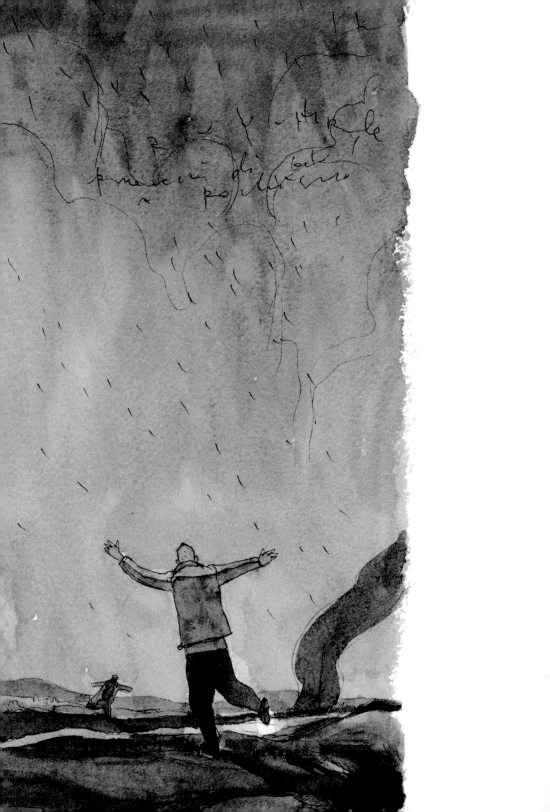

As Giuliano's dream foreshadows and the course of the story bears out, he is different from his two buddies, precisely because he has family ties that give him a way out. The memorable visual metaphor of Giuliano seeing his friends as headless operates at many levels. On the one hand, Giuliano never stops thinking for himself, even daring to challenge Felix's glowing description of war by pointing out that Felix did lose an eye in the process—and getting a beating for it. On the other, having a head also symbolizes having an inner life: while Giuliano tries to work out his feelings about the situation he finds himself in, Stefano can only quash his own and adopt Felix's attitudes and mannerisms, down to the dog-like barking at the people he racketeers at gunpoint.

Guns in fact provide the substitute for having a head of one's own. The sign that Stefano is accepted and respected by Felix comes when he is given a gun, and Christian is delighted when he is able to pick up a gun for himself too. At the time of their induction into the militia, these two boys share none of Giuliano's misgivings about handling an AK-47 assault rifle, and Little Killer wants grenades too. Of course, in the attempts of the powerless to gain some kind of power, guns provide an essential shortcut. For those who lack the opportunity or know-how to change the course of their lives, the ability to destroy provides a thrilling feeling of control. Significantly, the final chapter of the 2006 Small Arms Survey, an independent research report, deals with "Angry Young Men" and is entitled "Few Options but the Gun."*

The story's deliberately inconclusive ending leaves us feeling that Giuliano has a future, even if he is racked by guilt at having abandoned his buddies to save himself. But can those young men hiding their heads in their jackets as they return from the war zone be redeemed? We understand that some sort of amnesty deal has been reached with the militiamen, but will they be able to become members of society?

That agonizing question hangs over most of the post-conflict deals signed in the world today, deals that include disarmament, demobilization, and reintegration programs for the fighters. In many cases, those agreements

---

* See http://www.smallarmssurvey.org

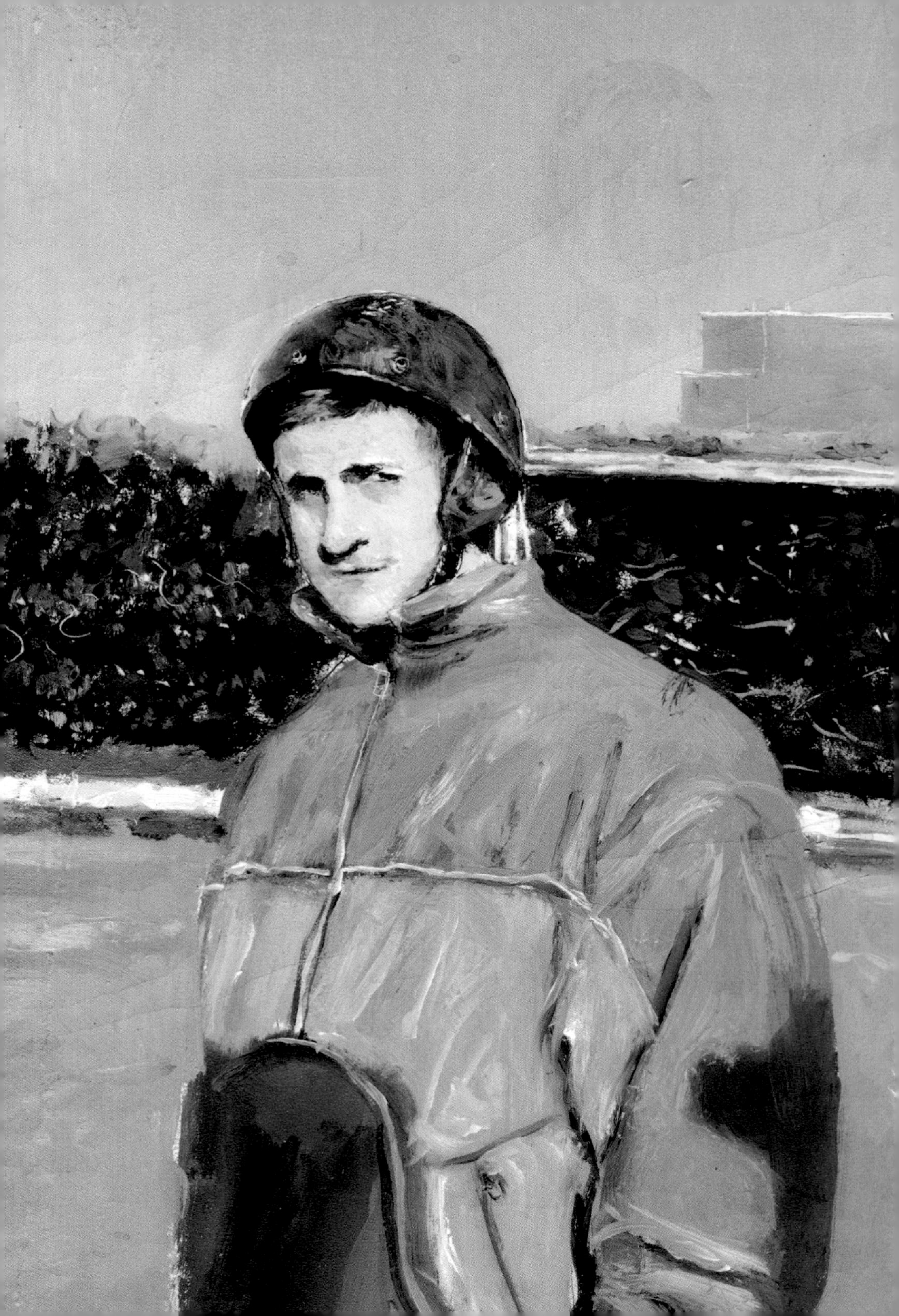

mean letting atrocities go unpunished, in the name of pragmatism—as just one example, trying to give a future to those young boys in the armed groups who fought in Sierra Leone's civil war, even though they savagely terrorized innocent civilians.

The question for young men emerging from civil war or criminal activity within gangs is whether they will be able to find better leadership than the disastrous kind that led them astray in the first place. There are few successful examples in world politics to draw inspiration from—Nelson Mandela in South Africa stands out as a towering, isolated case. His moral integrity (on display in his autobiography, *Long Walk to Freedom*) probably saved his country from a descent into the chaos of a failed State. Closer to home, Gipi's book doesn't offer any easy answers, but it does leave us with a deeper appreciation of the value of the social ties in our lives that, for all their flaws, do help us keep a head of our own with which to build a future.

Alexis Siegel
2006

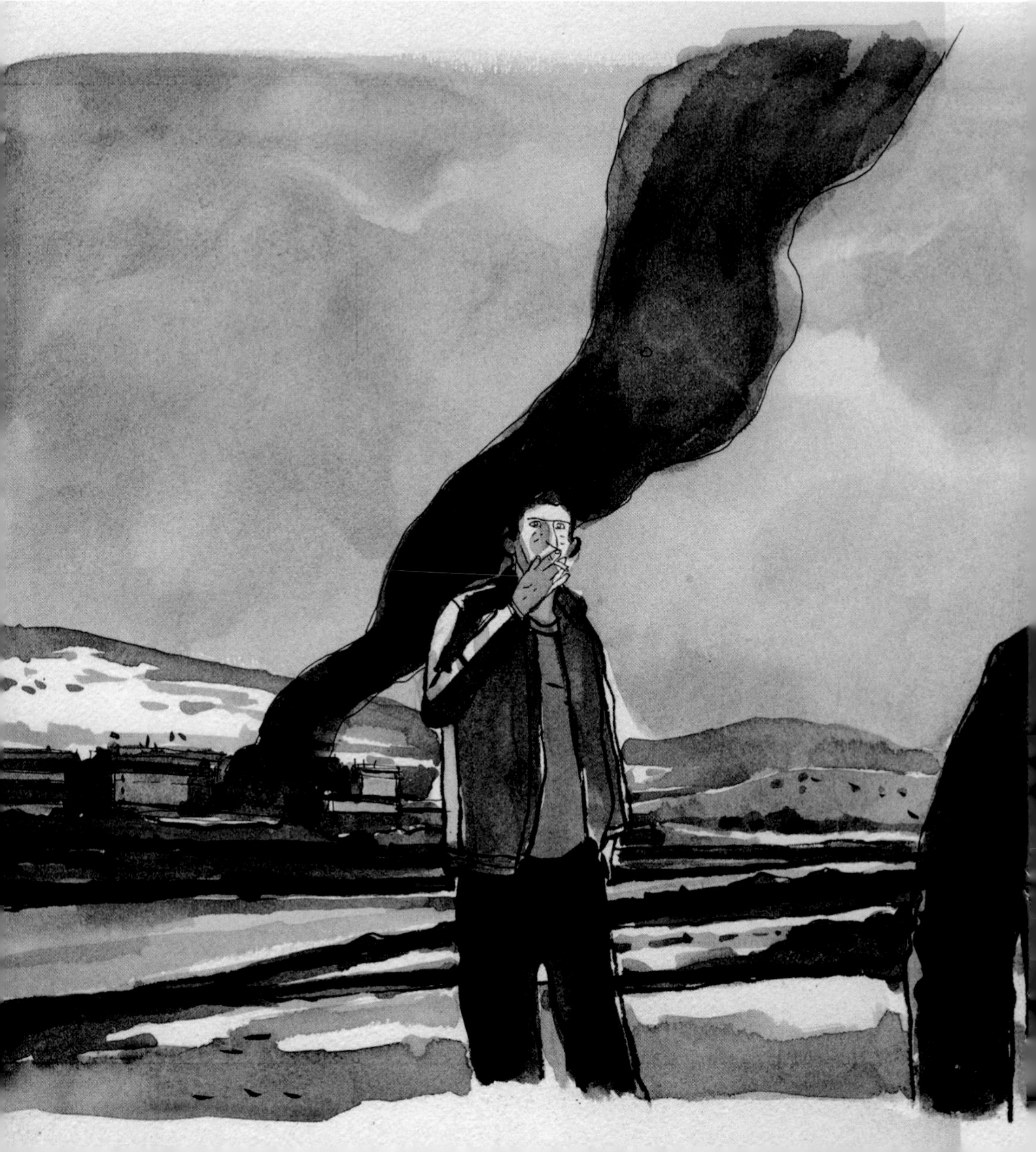

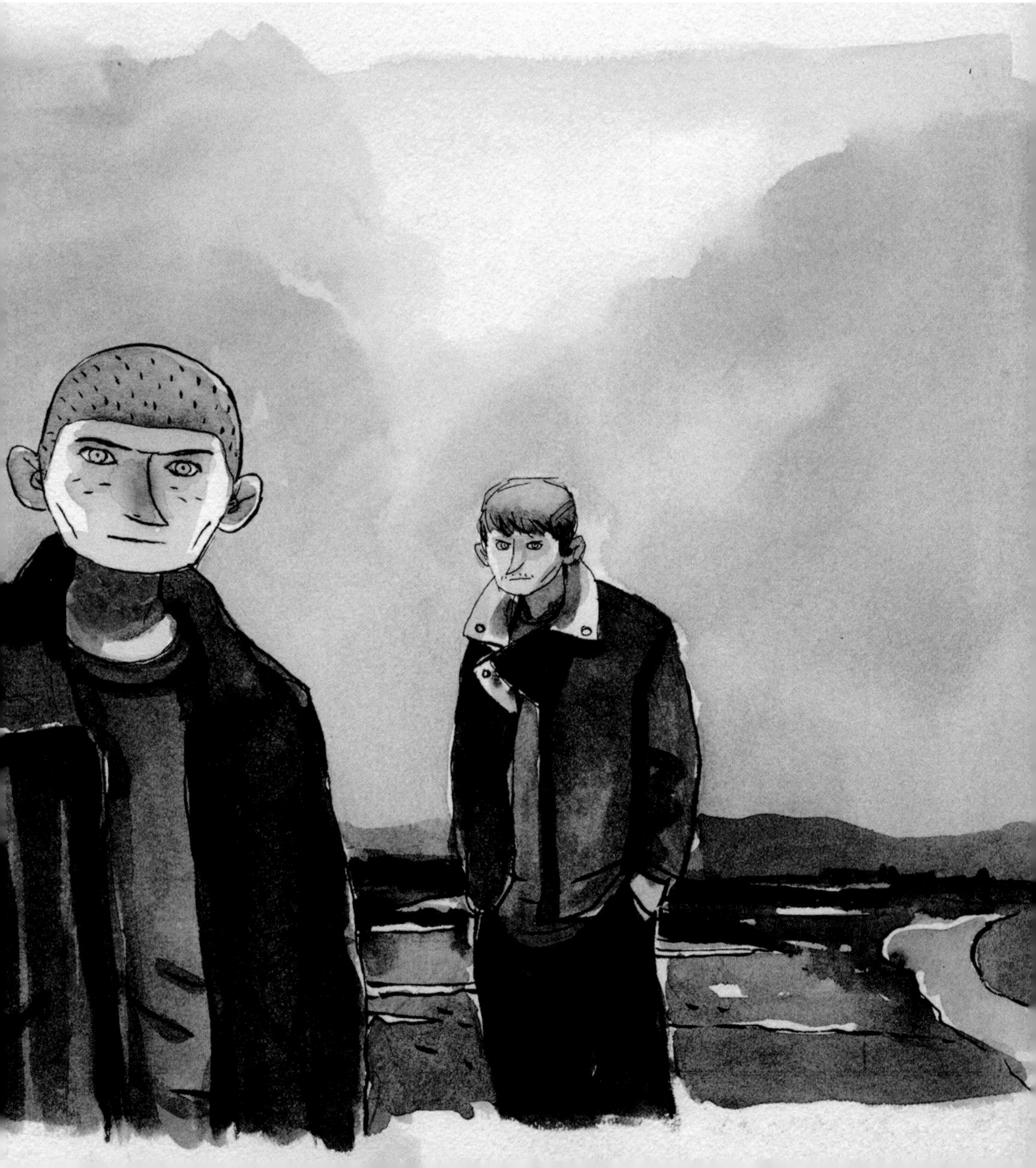

First Second

New York & London

Copyright © 2004 by Gipi

Published by First Second
First Second is an imprint of Roaring Brook Press, a division of
Holtzbrinck Publishing Holdings Limited Partnership
175 Fifth Avenue, New York, NY 10010

Distributed in Canada by H. B. Fenn and Company Ltd.
Distributed in the United Kingdom by Macmillan Children's Books,
a division of Pan Macmillan.

Originally published in Italy in 2004 under the title *Appunti per una storia di guerra*
by Coconino Press, Bologna.

Design by Danica Novgorodoff.

Cataloging-in-Publication Data is on file at the Library of Congress.

ISBN-13: 978-1-59643-261-1
ISBN-10: 1-59643-261-6

COLLECTOR'S EDITION
ISBN-13: 978-1-59643-303-8
ISBN-10: 1-59643-303-5

First Second books are available for special promotions and premiums.
For details, contact: Director of Special Markets, Holtzbrinck Publishers.

First American Edition August 2007

Printed in China

1 3 5 7 9 10 8 6 4 2